Hearts and Minds Without Fear: Unmasking the Sacred in Teacher Preparation

The Inaugural Volume in:
The Center for PAInT Series on Arts-integrated Education

Series Editors
Terry A. Osborn
Brianne L. Reck

The Center for PAInT Series on Arts-integrated Education

Series Editors

Terry A. Osborn
University of South Florida Sarasota-Manatee

Brianne Reck
University of South Florida Sarasota-Manatee

Hearts and Minds Without Fear: Unmasking the Sacred in Teacher Preparation (2014)
By Barbara A. Clark and James Joss French

Hearts and Minds Without Fear: Unmasking the Sacred in Teacher Preparation

Barbara A. Clark
James Joss French

INFORMATION AGE PUBLISHING, INC.
Charlotte, NC • www.infoagepub.com

Library of Congress Cataloging-in-Publication Data

The CIP data for this book can be found on the Library of Congress website (loc.gov).

Paperback: 978-1-62396-726-0
Hardcover: 978-1-62396-727-7
eBook: 978-1-62396-728-4

CONTENTS

DEDICATION AND ACKNOWLEDGEMENTS

We would like to dedicate our book to our parents Lillian T. Clark and Alfred B. Clark, Lelia M. Hay and Thomas D. French, and our loving family reviewers Clare Torre, Pat Smith, and Karen French. Their constant love, support, and insight made the journey a beautiful one to complete this book. A special thanks to our future teachers and the children we have had the honor to meet, create possibility with, and learn from.

ACKNOWLEDGEMENTS

Laura Longo was a research assistant in the Department of Teacher Education at Central Connecticut State University and a graduate student in school counseling. She worked with Drs. Barbara Clark and Joss French to transform their research into a digital reality by building www.compassionateteaching.com. Ms. Longo's research interests include the influence of poverty, school counseling–based interventions, and body image among female athletes. She plans to further explore these topics as a doctoral student at the University at Albany.

Kristen Phoenix is currently working as a graduate assistant in the Teacher Education Department, where she had the opportunity to help with our book. Ms. Phoenix is interested in postsecondary planning with at-risk youth in order to lower dropout rates as well as school counseling interventions to ensure the success of every student. Ms. Phoenix is presently pursuing a master's degree in school counseling and professional licensure.

Shane E. Heckstall, MEd, contributed to our book working as a graduate assistant in teacher education. With an educational background experience in sociology, race, education, administration, and curriculum, Mr. Heckstall is concerned about educational inequalities, Blackness, and educational leadership surrounding minority group success in educational pursuits. His future vision involves teaching, leading, and pursuit of a doctoral degree.

PREFACE

Hearts and Minds Without Fear: Unmasking the Sacred in Teacher Preparation is the first book of its kind that focuses on the critical urgency of integrating creativity, mindfulness, and compassion in which social and ecological justice are at the forefront of teacher preparation. This is especially significant at a time of cultural turmoil, educational reform, and inequities in public education. The book serves as a vehicle to unmask fear within current educational ethical deficiencies and revitalize hope for community members, teacher educators, preservice and in-service teachers, and families in school communities. The recipients of these strategies are explicitly presented in order to build understanding of a compassionate paradigm shift in schools that envisions possibility and social imagination on behalf of our children and our communities. The authors unabashedly place the arts and aesthetics at the core of the educational paradigm solution. The book lives its own message. Within each seed chapter, the authors practice authentically what they preach, offering a refreshing perspective to bring our schools back to life and instill hope in children's and educators' hearts and minds.

SERIES FORWARD

THE CENTER FOR PAINT SERIES ON ARTS-INTEGRATED EDUCATION

The Center for Partnerships in Arts-Integrated Teaching (PAInT) was established at the University of South Florida Sarasota-Manatee in 2012 to support the College of Education's commitment to the development of critical and imaginative literacies in the educators it prepares, and to facilitate their ability to do so in their classrooms, in their schools, and in their communities. In its efforts to learn, lead, inspire, and transform educator preparation and practice, the Center has chosen to focus its efforts on building sustainable partnerships with artists, arts organizations, educational practitioners, and scholars who help us examine the power and the possibilities of arts integration as a way to develop these literacies.

The role of educational endeavors in our society is varied and complex. We are called upon at various times to produce, facilitate, transmit, and/or interrogate what is known and how we learn. To do so we must grapple with deep epistemological questions such as the nature of knowledge, its basis, and its scope. At the core of the Center's mission and conceptual framework are this fundamental exploration, and the notion that education can

Hearts and Minds Without Fear: Unmasking the Sacred in Teacher Preparation,
pages xi–xiii.

be a force for the transformation of community, and that work is tied to daily activity in schools (Darling-Hammond, 2010; Friere, 1995; Jackson, 1968). We embrace arts-integration as an approach that has the power to fuel transformation that creates equitable, inclusive learning opportunities for all children, and recognize the centrality of this advocacy as part of our role as educators.

The Center for PAInT Series on Arts-integrated Education invites scholars to contribute to the broader and deeper understanding of approaches to and models of arts integration that reflect a multi-faceted definition of practice. Our focus is on several critical areas of educational theory and practice. We wish to consider from multiple perspectives on how creative and critical literacies are developed; the roles of the imaginative process and the created product in teaching and learning; how such experiences and products might be measured and assessed for effectiveness; and how partnerships between educators, artists and arts organizations, and the broader community might transform educator preparation and practice. We look for authors who explore how content and process are learned through educational activity. We highlight works that examine how education is experienced by learners and facilitated by instructors. And, we encourage scholars to consider the ways and the extent to which the educational process impacts society.

Hearts and Minds Without Fear: Unmasking the Sacred in Teacher Preparation is the first volume in *The Center for PAInT Series on Arts-integrated Education*. With this groundbreaking work, Barbara Clark and Joss French sound the clarion call for integrating creativity, mindfulness, and compassion into teacher preparation. Acknowledging the climate of uncertainty and fear that create barriers to the return of the aesthetic to a place of centrality in public education, they embrace the arts and aesthetics as keys to the paradigm shift needed to reclaim and rebuild schools as affirming places for all children. The power of this work is in the authenticity of the authors' lived experience as teacher educators. Their metaphor of KIVA (**K**indness, **I**nnovation, **V**oice, and **A**ction), describing a sacred space of learning, and aesthetic studio environment designed by the teacher, elevates our notion of what is possible in practice when we remember that, in the words of the authors: "our hearts and minds are in need of play, hope, voice, change, unmasking, inner-awareness, freedom and love." May the seeds that they introduce become seeds of change.

—Brianne L. Reck
Executive Director, Center for PAInT

REFERENCES

Darling-Hammond, L. (2010). *The flat world and education: How America's commitment to equity will determine our future.* New York: Teachers College Press.

Freire, P. (1995). *Pedagogy of Hope: Reliving pedagogy of the oppressed.* New York: Continuum.

Jackson, P. W. (1968). *Life in classrooms.* New York: Rinehart& Winston.

PROLOGUE

LOVE OF CHILDREN LOST AND FOUND FOR TEACHER EDUCATORS

For the authors of those great poems which we admire, do not attain to excellence through the rules of any art; but they utter their beautiful melodies of verse in a state of inspiration, and, as it were, possessed by a spirit not their own.
—Albert Rijksbaron, 2007

In our own life journeys, we have found great hope in the aesthetic. When we are in this space, practicing the art of creating courage among family, friends, colleagues, and our students, the power potential is quite real. Never before do we feel so energized and excited about possibilities of what we can do with ourselves and those around us than when we are within this realm of the imagination. Like Michelangelo (1513), who stated that his *vision* for sculpture was "liberating the figure imprisoned in the marble," we believe that children and teacher candidates' imaginations (as a result of conventional "schooling") have been imprisoned. Knowing from our previous experiences that there is always another path that we can take out of

Hearts and Minds Without Fear: Unmasking the Sacred in Teacher Preparation,
pages xv–xxxvi.

any issue or artificially constructed obstacle, corner or dead end, allows for endless assurance, confidence, and resiliency.

We are resurrecting, for the education of the child, the arts and the aesthetics of truth, beauty, and goodness from the ancient world. The 21st century has exiled the aesthetic from public schooling and at best has marginalized the arts into a 40-minute time slot once a week for children. How our ancient ancestors would be shocked. Academia has required the arts to be given a label, to therefore be placed in a pocket or a box, and are perceived by many to be only for those few who are entering into specific art fields. Luckily, we the authors, were raised by parents who embraced the arts and aesthetics as a way of life. Storytelling and singing was at every meal, art and music books on every shelf, dance at every family celebration. Field trips to museums, galleries, concerts, and plays were gifts from our parents. We learned to love the arts and could not imagine a world wherein the aesthetic was not an integral part of our development.

Throughout both of our lives collectively, we have had countless opportunities for multiple venues and expressions amid this paradigm, where we have been continually reinforced and reminded of the subtle power potential the aesthetic holds. While we interacted within neighborhood social cultural events, particularly music and visual arts, our families also took us deep into the natural world: oceans, mountains, deserts, farms, and forests. In these spaces we vividly remember playing with our parents, brothers, and sisters, dreaming up and then manifesting the most exciting way to do something, inherently driven to involve each other with something great. We watched our parents write stories and poems, create songs, and paint on canvas mounted on easels with arms outstretched to create a better world. Into the endless night our parents shared ideas on the use of color to create light and texture, melody to create rhythm and shape. They exhibited their work in galleries, played musical instruments in concerts, and published poetry and music in magazines and songbooks.

When we look back at our parents' way of living while raising us with our brothers and sisters, we see their lives through the arts as a sign of their gratefulness to the divine—to God—and a celebration of the creative as sacred. The arts lifted us up during hard times. Storytelling around the kitchen table at the farm or campfire circle made us laugh and created memories we now hold dear in our hearts. Our parents' paintings are displayed in our homes, their songs sung throughout the day, yet sadly, we have admitted that our world has drastically changed. The way of life we grew up in no longer exists for many families as technology has replaced painting, music-making, and storytelling with various forms of social media (i.e., Twitter, Pinterest, SnapChick, and Instagram). Instead of sitting before an easel in a room smelling of paint and turpentine, dancing to a playing fiddle or listening to voices telling a story with laughter; unfortunately, some present-day mothers and fathers sit before flashing blue screens that deaden their creative capacities and connections to their children.

Within formal schooling, and when we decided to pursue becoming certified public school teachers, it was drawing upon our family memories of playing and creating that inspired us through these relatively mediocre institutional experiences. In this way, we continually challenged the rules of our assignments, finding optimism through both our families and the occasional mentors who were fearless in modeling and encouraged us to try out anything.

Then, as classroom elementary teachers, we had a real-time opportunity to formally create curriculum. Our fundamental basis of which was the inspiration and recollection from continued childhood play. While we never told our administrators these playful tales, we do tell our own students of how we would dream and concoct larger-than-life ideas in classes that would break all the dreary rules going on around us, often to the chagrin of some who would shake their heads and some who tried to suppress our whirlwind of spontaneity. But the kids loved us and loved coming to school, and in our adult world we always were able to find the partners for creative institutional change who perceived the arts as the lighthouse of hope sitting between the two oceans in education: the technicist and the humanistic experiential.

They joyfully joined the ride upon a light beam (Isaacson, 2007, p. 3; see also Chapter 6, "Seed of Inner Awareness") of creative activity with us, and co-conspired new ways of creative maladjustment (Kohl, 1994) to keep doing what we did best for children. Ironically, many of these creative endeavors were honored by various districts with teacher awards, grant awards, and even collectively supporting a larger hope for children's education. Dr. Barbara Clark was a finalist in 1986 for the Connecticut Teaching Award. Both Drs. Clark and French have been recognized at a variety of levels in the CCSU Excellence in teaching program for the past 7 consecutive years. This program is notable as the first nominations come from the CCSU students.

And now as two teacher educators writing this book, the same is happening. As possibly fate would have it, we discovered in one another an embodiment of the many kindred spirits we've known along the way through our various life experiences and institutions. In these dark days of overtly corporal educational reform and cognitive testing extremes wherein children are viewed as test scores to teacher education, we are still driven to involve our teacher candidates, as we did with our families and currently still do in public schools with elementary children: with vision, faith, love, and hope—to the power of two. Now it is our future teachers who get to alight with our spirits. "Here we go, time to get excited, it's coming your way. Get ready to reimagine everything you've ever known: here's what we're going to do."

Of course, being "at the top" of the academic ivory tower of hubris, the subtle attacks that we've gotten throughout our lives now are a bit more Machiavellian, but still maintain their basic drive to reject lightness, hope, and possibility. And despite the many obstacles placed in our path that we manage to duck under, around, over, or sometimes through, we continue on for children, for our future, for hope, believing in our sacred core that a life without creativity is a life wasted.

Speaking from experience, it's easy to see why the teacher educators, who hit their drum in a different way, even when they are doing well by their students and generations of future children, can become demoralized to give up and leave the circle. Time and time again we empathize. If you go against the grain—getting kicked out of the drum circle (see Chapter 2, "Seed of Hope") or forced exclusion is omnipresent at all levels of the educational spiral. The shellac (see Chapter 5, "Seed of Unmasking") of the status quo comes from the least mundane subtle glance to the most shocking edicts and in many times originates from those "closest" to us, our fellow teacher educators.

But we understand (and it's part of the reason we are writing this book) and offer an explanation and perhaps demystify the process. People who reject the aesthetic as a means to learn can do so for a number of reasons, or a perhaps collective of them all. That person may never have had a childhood where they were given an opportunity to be immersed in a paradigm of possibility (see Chapter 1, "Seed of Play"), as we had ample occasion within our own lives. They may have been forced or gotten stuck in a rut of seeing that things were done in certain ways and so took refuge or comfort within a particular myopic bandwidth: learning, teaching and ultimately doling it out within their role as a teacher educator.

Not practicing teaching with a "consciousness of possibility" (Greene, 2001, p. 47), and laden with a charge of imparting their self-perceived "wisdom" to future teachers, teacher educators can become the most resolute, taciturn, and reticent naysayers, rutting their foundation of beliefs into granite tablets of teacher education program policy and mission. Whenever someone of this demeanor sees us teaching in multiple directions through the aesthetic, to them it looks too f-u-n, or messy, or it just plain doesn't make sense, it "d.o.e.s.n.o.t.c.o.m.p.u.t.e." When put on top of this is an overblown ego and dynasty dominion that academe culture attracts and deposits, a masked emotional professional outrage may ensue. A large part of their fury lies in not wanting or being able to come to terms with the unknown—fear, essentially. Unfortunately, to quell their lack of confidence or a perceived false sense of superiority, attacks are made against the aesthetic, which is the experiential and divergent way of thinking wherein one answer does not exist.

Often, any aggression against the arts are framed in a "professional" manner, buttressing statements against certain assumptions that are readily accepted as material truth by the status quo, but which may run in apparent contradiction to an aesthetic approach. Most of these "micro-aggressions" are subtle yet reveal a deeper stab of exclusion of the arts from teacher preparation (Solorzano, 2001, p. 60). Is the PowerPoint lecture down the hall really the actual "worthwhile" teaching and learning for the 21st century? Teacher candidates, overhearing such subtle comments against the arts and aesthetics, are receiving conflicting messages. However innocuous or blatant, placing aesthetic methods (such as practicing play) on the margins may inhibit teacher candidates from taking risks and trying the aesthetic out.

Still other aggressions, with great portent and academic qualm, may come from more of a philosophical or intellectual origin. These usually come from critical educators who are so caught up in the depths of despair that they cannot permit themselves to see the hope that the aesthetic holds. Alongside a self-induced barrier of their academic cognitive intellectual abstractionism, perhaps reinforced from an early age and professional teaching experience, they cannot permit themselves to see beyond or believe, as Matisse declared, that "creativity takes courage" (Brown, 1998, p. 62). Compared to the strength of their robust critical intellectual deconstruction of the human social sphere, mere "art" simply does not measure up.

Thus, aesthetic educational practitioners may be attacked not only by conservative nut-and-bolt bean counters—"We are not teaching the material basics"—but by also so-called self-touted progressive critical intellectuals—"We are weak-minded liberals." The reaction from both of these lopsided zones of technicist-body and cognitive-mind are framed by their mutual lack of experience within the spiritual domain of imagination the aesthetic provides. They both too easily fall into the ill-informed adage that art is "weak." And both fail to understand the subtle, powerfully profound impact aesthetics can have for the teacher-artist (see Chapter 5, "Seed of Unmasking") perhaps because they were never permitted the experience themselves or have somehow isolated these experiences apart from who they are as teacher educators.

Amid this paradox, the arts are undervalued in a double blow for artists. For one, they are not seen as "practical," "robust," or "strong" by "upright" (or uptight) society. While there may certainly be a fear of creativity by people who praise the persona by thinking of themselves as analytical robots, as Robert Pirsig (1974) brings to understanding the cultural divide between creativity and analytic: Our "train" of quantitative progress is powered by the quality of the aesthetic (p. 360). Yet such wisdom is sheepishly ignored, and barbs and insults from behind tightly bound masks are easily and regularly thrown upon the backs of art and artists, that being creative is somehow "less than" because such manifestations are not "rigorous" or "serious" enough.

The second blow is that art and artists are tethered to the material world. And unfortunately money, that by which the artist/artisan puts food on the table, really is not commensurate with Art. Art is on the spiritual plain, not the material, and was at one time viewed as sacred in the Western culture (Highwater, 1982). It is disgraceful, an insult to our higher faculties, to offer material-based appreciation for such lofty immaterial expressions of divine imagination. To illustrate this unfortunate paradox, we have seen this play out all too often, where potential true artists have "sold out" to instead create works that satisfy theirs and others' material-world obsessions while neglecting the spiritual. Taking an even further "purist" stance, for instance, as soon as Art is made, copied, and sold, it ceases to be Art. But with nothing sold, how does the artist live to create another day?

This double blow, each with a different psychological impact, one an artificially constructed judgment and the other a Catch-22 (Heller, 1994) emanating from an aesthetic epistemological base, combine to create a perfect storm that puts art and artists out in the cold as far as funding, institutional longevity, and societal change. As a society, we want the aesthetic, but only to a point: as evidenced by the daily celebration of kitsch in pop culture that is mass produced and gaudy. Yet, out of this despair, great works of expression are created. Ironically, Art is how we have our impetus and hope to imagine ways out of these social constructs that create the very formidable lashings that artists experience daily. In a very real way, if Art were genuinely "valued" by mainstream, status quo society, it would cease to be "Art."

And so we find that true artists must creatively maladjust to come into such an unrelenting secular material world. Sitting upon our, what is perceived as being "in the clouds" imaginings, we are invited into educational communities to inspire children and teachers and are instantly received, ironically, by the status quo: "How did you do that?" we are continuously asked. We appeal to people's innate sense of self and beliefs of best practices for children, which is at first dimly seen through their masks but then brought to fuller fruition by multiple aesthetic "miraculous" events (see www.compassionateteaching.com). Creatively maladjusted, we satisfy the seemingly omnipresent secular world vying for our attention.

Of course, creative maladjustment through aesthetics (see Chapter 2, "Seed of Hope") helps people to understand how to *unmask* years of standardization as being the "way." The community of the aesthetic places the child at the top of the agenda, often to the chagrin and surprise of those around us who may lambaste us with jealousy and old school "we've always done it this way." Some power-players still don't want to open their minds with their hearts and acknowledge that a child's imagination is sacred and at the core of the development of human decency. They just want to continue "doing school" the same way because the system rewards them (French, 2005; Gatto, 2002). In a larger society that relegates art as "less than," it's tempting to be a mindless puppet pretending we are doing a good job for our children and then look the other way when they can't read or write or think for themselves. → or *differently?*

On the job, as most professors are lecturing about standardized testing, we creatively maladjusted like experienced artists, and radically symbolized the forces of educational reform; after all, the very nature of making art is political. We shaped and juxtaposed these forces as an aesthetic metaphor of good vs. evil. Indeed, educational reform is really now a "play" wherein two character archetypes investigate the sacred, from within our hearts to be made manifest within our schools (see birth of Mr. Rat & Ms. Honey in Chapters 1, "Play" and 5, "Unmasking"). This is our first step in unmasking teacher preparation: to startle our teacher candidates and awaken the realities of what educational reform is doing to children.

We continue to surmount various systemic obstacles. A rich repertoire of strategies and solutions have been accumulated via our research and practiced by teaching together. We have learned from the children we have been blessed to work with, and our teacher candidates that seize the moment who take risks even against great odds. Together as a community, we continue to expand outward with our colleagues who are open to trying. When encountering the aesthetic, experience is belief. Unfortunately, with constant pressure, like many of our preservice teachers we describe in this book, teachers of teachers who may approach their craft in alternate ways are often marginalized within the system. Thus, this book is also a piece of resilient hope for them.

Not only do teacher candidates need to understand mixed methods using the aesthetics, but also on a more urgent level; so do in-service teachers and teacher educators. As the pendulum swings, common core standards enacted in schools and teacher preparation programs by "design" are "promoting higher order thinking skills"; however, how can this be achieved when the system is consistently teaching to the test? By contrast, the examples presented in this book pushed our teacher candidates to begin to understand just what "analysis," "synthesis," and "creation" actually looks and feels like through the aesthetic.

The Cave of Fear and the Kiva of Love in Teacher Preparation

Our book title, *Hearts and Minds Without Fear: Unmasking the Sacred in Teacher Preparation,* symbolizes the core of our beliefs for teacher preparation programs. It is our greatest hope that this book may impact teacher preparation programs so that future teachers will hold dearly in their hearts and minds the belief that nurturing a child's imagination is of utmost importance and must be protected.

The teacher candidates we work with have (for many reasons) buried their own imaginations and creative potential in order to accept the technicist status-quo sermons and meritocratic promises of good grades and job obtainment. In order to develop our teacher candidates' beliefs and imaginative and innovative dispositions, an aesthetic process of unmasking their fears was of primary importance. It was through the arts and aesthetic pedagogy within a compassionate community that these teacher candidates revealed brilliant creative potential as is presented in the following eight seed chapters of *play, hope, voice, change, unmasking, inner awareness, freedom,* and *love.*

Before adventuring into the light of the space we call the KIVA[1], where kindness, innovation, voice, and action embrace the eight sacred seeds of compassion, we ask you to enter first the *Cave of Fear,* a dark political labyrinth composed of twisting programmatic pathways. It is important to note that as you finish reading this section, it is a relief to exit the cave of fear. The first chapter is the "Seed of Play" and will lift you up with possibility and fill you with hope for our children's future in public education.

In order to unmask and peel back the onion to honestly reveal the weight of the technicist regime present in teacher preparation for American public schools in the past 20 years, we present a dark critique of teacher preparation that we have witnessed firsthand. Simultaneously, it is important to note that our book was not designed to be a rant about of the inequities in teacher preparation. We did however feel compelled to flush out the reality of what we have been fighting against since entering into teacher preparation many years ago. With this said, we are almost abashed to write such words of gloom here for fear the reader may sulk in despair. But alas, to reach a true understanding and action we must unearth the skeletons of ignorance and in so doing, perhaps crack some deep foundations. Sometimes to see the highest summits we must go into the deepest valleys. Unlike an endless track of critical systemic de(con)struction, we *can* promise a resilient foundation of hope. So we shall fight the good fight and at the end of the book you will see that we finish the race.

The "Seed of Play," our first chapter, presents a studio paradigm wherein our teacher candidates practiced divergent thinking through play and the use of mixed methodologies in the arts. The "Seed of Play" juxtaposes the technical fear in teacher preparation today with the current educational reform movement. The *Cave of Fear* (unfortunately) takes you into the fierce reality we face in schools and currently, in teacher education.

Continuing from "Play," the "Seeds of Hope and Voice" (see Chapters 2 and 3) explore the studio paradigm with an emphasis on the arts and

---

[1] See Seed of Play for Anasazi cultural origins of "Kiva" and our metaphorical application of this sacred space within the context of teacher preparation

experiential learning placed in the local community schools. These seeds collectively provide evidence for the aesthetic enacted in real time that is addressing, with teacher candidates and children as partners, the social and ecological justice issues our communities face. Through this, united beliefs are revealed, symbolic messages created, and actions for justice are materialized and enacted within the school communities.

The "Seed of Change" (see Chapter 4) explores the power of social imagination as a result of the aesthetic and possibility in a community when artistic and symbolic messages are co-created and shared. The community is transformed, if only for that moment, when the whole body joined with other bodies are swept up in the aesthetic idea proposed by Greene (1978, 1988, 2001) that perhaps the world we live in can be fairer and better (Ayers & Miller, 1998, p. 157). In-service teachers who experienced this sacred KIVA paradigm are currently transferring these artistic experiences into their public school curriculum and learning activities.

How can our communities flourish and develop an understanding of diversity unless universal messages such as the mask, music, and movement are explored in addressing issues of justice? Through the process of unmasking that is explored in the "Seed of Unmasking" (see Chapter 5), multicultural concerns in education are authentically revealed in the KIVA, whereby collectively divergent thinking is a belief and goal for all teacher candidates and children.

The final three chapters, 6, "The Seed of Inner Awareness"; 7, "The Seed of Freedom"; and 8, "The Seed of Love" reveal the sacred in teacher preparation. These chapters celebrate the child's sacred core, the imaginative realm wherein their soul is lifted toward the light of the KIVA. As explained below, in teacher preparation we must be careful to not indoctrinate our obsession with the critical wherein we are left with a blankness of hope. Throughout history, artists are by nature critical, yet for a greater good. The critical, through artistic methods however, promotes infinite challenges so that the artists can continue inventing new possibilities. In our paradigm of the aesthetic learning environment (KIVA), multiple realities are explored, unmasked, and re-created into new ideas and realities of a multiverse of possibility. Teacher candidates begin to perceive the sacred aspect of teaching when working with the hearts and imaginations of children.

To exit upon such a spiritual plain, we must first know where we are now. Entering the *Cave of Fear*, just below, we answer the question of why the *technicist, multicultural,* and *critical* masks may prevent the sacred in teacher preparation to reveal the "real" in human community.

Unmasking the Cave of Fear

Whereas some teacher educators may call for new strategies of pedagogic engagement to develop transformative educators, there exists an overwhelming tension to overcompensate or reject attempted alternatives with the status quo (Bartolomé, 2004; Giroux & McLaren, 1986; Kincheloe, 2004). Such is the drive of a *technicist* approach to teacher education. Mr. Albert Cullum (1940–2003), veteran elementary aesthetic practitioner and author of *The Geranium on the Window Sill Just Died, but Teacher you Went Right On* (1971), remarked after his experience working within a teacher education program, "Teacher education on the national level is a cancer of mediocrity. It is. And that sounds very negative, but it's true" (Gund & Sullivan, 2004). Unfortunately Cullum's words ring true on all sides of the particular aesthetic island of hope that we intend to provide our teacher candidates; we see their spirits attacked by an infested deficit-technical mode of teacher education.

While this may seem overstated, perhaps by our very perspective and vision of what is possible from our engagement within an aesthetic place-based paradigm, we have observed our teacher candidates being consumed with endless jargon-laden lesson-plan templates, blanket management strategies, isolated methodology techniques, multicultural caveats, exceptionality protocols, decontextualized individual concepts, and items that a teacher "should" know and learn—"or else." Mandated by national Common Core standards (originating from the private business sector) (McGroarty & Robbins, 2012, p. 1), state curriculum and teacher evaluations are increasingly controlled by these invisible privatized agents.

As a result of these national mandates, in order for states to receive money, we may be losing, at the most sacred core, what a true child pedagogue is and does. As districts within states adopt guidelines for teacher evaluations and align Common Core standards to the curriculum, the pressure on teacher preparation to also accept these national mandates impacts our curriculum and teacher candidates' program experiences adversely. Our students, who specifically embrace the creative, critical, and community approach that we present, are deterred the following semester and in some cases lose interest and possibly withdraw from the program under the pressure of mandated assignments.

Oppressing students is nothing new and has been a lasting and pervasive control mechanism by both teachers and peers in educational institutions (Gatto, 2006; Kohl, 1994; McLaren, 2007). If students who have a better "game" aren't willing to play by particular system rules, they are often pushed or pulled from their school or program—"misunderstood" rather than accommodated and "weeded out." Teacher candidates who offer alternative thinking that may disrupt a mainstreamed status quo system are often encouraged to drop out, through sometimes subtle, sometimes overt, discrimination practices (Haberman & Post, 1998). In fact, many of these students who fit this description ask to be included in our particular courses for this very reason. Once they experience an alternative with us, they are often are reluctant to leave our protective KIVA space.

As in the case of our teacher candidate below: While she stayed in the technical tangle after leaving us, she was almost effectively silenced, along with her teaching career; saddled with an unfair grade from student teaching. Despite this institutionalized weight put upon her record, she did manage to secure a teaching position in an urban district and is very successful. Prior to her student teaching experience, she confided during an interview the downhill slope she was experiencing within her current mode of learning in contrast to her aesthetic experience with us.

> I learned so much more the past couple of semesters than I have this semester, because the focus is on something completely different: on finishing the work. You are not so much focused on doing it correctly, but just *doing* it. . . . to finish it, because there is so much more you have to go and do. . . . I feel *exhausted* as a learner—drained, stressed. It is not as fun. I mean, when you are learning through the arts and you are able to learn through your style of learning they allow you to be yourself, then you are learning, putting in the same amount of work, but it's fun and you like it and you enjoy it, whereas if you don't get to learn that way, it's stressful, and you are, like, "I don't get it." You don't absorb it.

Going through the hollow motions of just "doing" schoolwork to get it done is a waste. Ultimately, in the technicist laundry-list rush, many of our teacher candidates are not being given opportunities to consider the life-learning themes of how people feel, think, and learn (French, 2005). Given class after class of content, methods, decontextualized concepts, and teaching lists to memorize, any larger visions are often abandoned in the process.

While technicist bomb words may be disguised as a preparation for the superficial (and failing) infrastructure "realities" of Scientific Research-Based Intervention (SRBI), No Child Left Behind (NCLB), Race to the Top (RTT), Connecticut Mastery Test (CMT), newly furbished Common Core Standards (CCS) and Smarter Balanced Assessment (SBA), our teacher candidates are losing opportunities to truly learn how to teach to the whole child, where they can freely express who he/she is in multiple forms. Ironically, in 1945, the Association for Childhood Education in Washington, DC, published a journal titled *The Arts and Children's Living*, emphasizing the arts in child development and teacher preparation. Hopkins (1945), one key author of this publication, pronounces the inherent importance of the arts, stating,

> When art is considered as qualitative living every child in every school is a potential artist. Under the right conditions he is capable of contributing to the improvement of living of every group in which he has active membership. Every child can feel the thrill of creativeness if the surrounding field

encourages and appreciates such effort. To fail to cultivate it in any child is to discriminate unfairly against him. Every child has or is capable of developing something which enriches the lives of others whether it be an encouraging word, a sympathetic smile, the telling of a story. (p. 6)

Banishing the arts and aesthetics to promote "schooling" is the technicist way of pressuring the teacher candidate to constantly accumulate knowledge without considering any larger themes and systems. This results in a litany of lesson plans with lost opportunities to hope and envision.

Some of the students enrolled in our courses may perceive the aesthetic as an "island resort," a nice "getaway" vacation, only to jump back onto the technicist barge afterward, leaving only faint memories and the pain of what could be. And while they may for a time protect themselves with an aesthetic ardor, they still may be vulnerable. The technical approach in isolation is a disservice to these valuable students' particular strengths and an insult to the potential and possibility of teacher education's role in reversing these trends.

While those in our classes may be provided the opportunity to develop awareness and rethink status quo technicist modes of learning, the vast majority of teacher candidates within our larger program nationally accept it as the norm. They *expect* nothing more. The automatic stimulus response student appetite for instant rewards—"Just tell me what you want so I can get my points for an A"—is the behaviorist mindset from many of our students at the beginning of each semester. As aesthetic practitioners, while we invariably cull and sustain a critical mass of students who will carry along those who are beginning to awaken from this programmed behaviorist stupor, we have always lamented the massive uphill learning curve we experience with the majority of our students who have been indoctrinated through years of public schooling. This indoctrination includes their current rote learning from college coursework amid some faculty who may have content knowledge but little practiced skill in how to teach.

Ironically, the exclusionary *de facto* recruitment and retention techniques (as further discussed in Chapter 2, "Seed of Hope") for most teacher education programs are "perfect" for securing the very applicants who will succeed and graduate by their technicist-honed systems. Garnered by years of practice from similar schooling and the dominant *cultural capital* (Bourdieau & Passeron, 1977) to excel, candidates who are given access to fly through their teacher programs are predisposed to a debilitating deficient "banking" orientation modes to learning (Friere, 2005, p. 72). The status quo of teacher education curriculum and pedagogy attracts and retains particular students who further propagate program mediocrity (Haberman, 1993) while rejecting and marginalizing those who could potentially be our saving grace.

With our students' traditional format of teaching and learning unquestioned by their programs, ultimately our candidates may continue their views of teaching in how they had been taught: uncritically, nontransformative, and with just enough effort to understand and regurgitate the itemized mile-long list and get the "A." But while their GPA's may excel from well-honed hollow motions, as revealed by the literature, they are ill prepared and both vulnerable and toxic to the real world of children (French, 2005, pp. 6–7), especially those who are marginalized, tramatized, and devoid of voice (Clark, 2005, p. 219).

Certainly, even at its "best," a technicist school-based learning-model program completely avoids showing our teacher candidates how to promote social justice and student empowerment and simultaneously fails to motivate our candidates to pose a more self-critical approach in both their practice and reflection. Such candidates' are certainly not being prepared to cultivate a garden of imagination for our children. Children in poverty areas who have the most need and the most untapped talent and skill to transform our collective impudence will especially be treated unkindly in this manner. Perceived as a threat to status quo, like our marginalized teacher candidates, they are often the ones increasingly estranged from the aesthetic (Clark & French, 2012): squeezed out to other barren spaces and flattened with inferiority (Boyle-Baise, 2002; Ladson-Billings, 1994).

Beyond creating larger potential ripple effects through teacher education recruitment strategies, another factor for resilient hope is to do something about *how* we teach new teachers. In this regard, the *multicultural* education movement in teacher education is the closest institutionalized manner in which we've come to systematically addressing these issues. Even so, the literature has found that teachers graduating from additive multicultural programs felt unprepared to work with a diverse range of students (Cochran-Smith, 2004; Davis, 1995; Gollnick, 1992; O'Grady, 1998; Sleeter, 2001). The majority of teacher candidates who "made it" through their multicultural teacher education program circles went on into schools and larger society either lacking confidence or having a false sense of superiority that was soon met with resistance and burnout. Teachers who are not prepared to be culturally responsive are more likely to experience frustration when confronted with diversity and are ineffective and fall back on their own preconcieved stereotypes (French, 2005; Goodlad, 1990; Haberman, 1988; Nieto, 1999; Terrill & Mark, 2000).

It appears that multicultural education intervention, when applied in modicum of amounts of marginalized course and fieldwork experiences within an overwhelming backdrop of a passive technicist mode of learning, can backfire with disastrous psychological results. Such findings should really not come as any surprise. Being told what you need to think or believe from isolated coursework or seminar attempts, alongside other learning experiences that permit passive learning, can easily be seen as contrary, annoying, or even a threatening obstruction. Insisting that students acknowledge or even denounce racism, for example, even through the best multicultural education course, may not be enough and can actually play into the honed technicist "doing school" system quite well. As two critical teacher educators describe the range of responses teacher candidates do to avoid taking their multicultural "medicine,"

> There is a range of ways that students appear to respond. . . . For instance, they can resist engaging in critique; they can reassert their existing understanding of the now as also the most desirable possibility; they can assert a romanticized version of a possible future which is not grounded in the reality of the now; they can play the academic student game of "reading" what the lecturer wants as a "right' answer that would show as engagement or critique or imagination; they can go along with the tutorial process because their friends are conforming, and like their friends, they can forget about the content as soon as they walk out the door of the classroom. (Cartwright & Noone, 2006, p. 14)

Honestly, to sympathize with students, for just 3 months of their lives, why bother to transform when it's easier to circumnavigate? It's too much, because through their entire schooling career they haven't been given the practice. Not until this moment, within the twilight of their formal education, have they been asked to perform critical self-analysis and act upon their thoughts. While it may not be so for their university professor, social justice awareness may be furthest from their minds. Instead, what is paramount is what has always been: completing schoolwork, getting grade credit, and getting through the program to a job. Becoming a teacher is the career end rather than a means for using their learning experience toward a calling of identifying, acknowledging, and taking action on injustice. If there is nothing truly and genuinely authentically inspiring for them to learn or teach in another paradigm, why start now?

As evidenced from our students and within the literature, when students are told to think in a certain way, beyond "bending the rules" to get through critical or multicultural course hurdles with no learning, the best-laid multicultural plans can be completely rejected. With paltry "multicultural" requirement blips, often to the chagrin and despair of instructors teaching these courses, teacher candidates' belief systems are not adequately prepared for dealing with the conflicting realities of the urban school systems they will enter or seek to avoid. Influencing real hope in preservice teachers may be impossible without first changing the learning approach at the institutional programmatic level.

At the very least, it may be argued that teacher educators, while they still have some charge of their programs amid privatization interests, must reevaluate how they teach. They must go to the epistemological beginnings and question the sacrosanct beliefs that they may have been taught their entire lives (French, 2005; Palmer, 1993; Zajonc, 2006). In this regard of critically rethinking learning and teaching, recommendations for a more *critical* teacher education approach are 10-fold. Among sage advice based on abstract and empirical observation as well as clinical trials of programs and individuals, critical pedagogy researchers offer compelling directions to decipher paths between the conflicting realities of mainstream teachers and marginalized student populations (Apple, 1995; Bartolomé, 2004; Batchelder & Root, 1994; Cochran-Smith, 2004; Darder, Torres, & Baltodano, 2002; Delpit, 1995; Delpit & Dowdy 2002; Freire, 1970; hooks, 1994; King, 1991; Leonardo, 2003; Sleeter, 2001; Vadeboncoeur, Rahm, Aguilera, & LeCompte, 1996).

In most recommendations, a metacognitive approach (which the aesthetic embraces) is dominant, turning the relentless deficiency drive of more technical or ineffective multicultural approaches on their heads. However, as Ellsworth (1989) points out, there are psychological repressive factors for the learners immersed in the critical process that may prevent them from embracing possibility and hope. Even the bastion of critical theory, while it seeks solution to empower, can stop aspiring teachers dead in their tracks from reaching an acclaimed advent space of mindfulness. A critical pedagogy approach to teacher education, while it provides stunning illuminations of world and teacher education power atrocities, may be by its very overwhelming nature, undermining its own intentions. As teacher educator Elizabeth Ellsworth acknowledges

> Key assumptions, goals, and pedagogical practices fundamental to the literature on critical pedagogy—namely, "empowerment," "student voice," "dialogue," and even the term "critical"—are repressive myths that perpetuate relations of domination. By this I mean that when participants in our class attempted to put into practice prescriptions offered in the literature concerning empowerment, student voice, and dialogue, we produced results that were not only unhelpful, but actually exacerbated the very conditions we were trying to work against . . . to the extent that our efforts to put discourses of critical pedagogy into practice led us to reproduce relations of domination in our classroom, these discourses were "working through" us in repressive ways, and had themselves become vehicles of repression. (p. 298)

Beyond teacher candidates' adverse reaction to critical pedagogy, C. A. Bowers (2007), similar to Ellsworth's critique, has also called attention to Paulo Freire (2005) placing "transformed consciousness" as the highest form of understanding, thereby inadvertently devaluing all other cultural forms of understanding, including known practices that have been the most sustainable and resilient to date (see Chapter 4, "Seed of Change") (p. 47). From the microcosm of our teacher education classrooms to the macro of entire cultures' foundations, a critical approach, while it may be asking us to rethink cultural identity, appears to be simultaneously insulting our personal core to the point of paralysis. A critical approach to teacher education in these manners, despite their "promise" of personal transformation and empowerment, at its starting block may be a race into darkness and condescension—an endless track of critical deconstruction that never reaches a haven of reconciliation.

While critical pedagogues may be comfortable with living in dissonance as an occupational hazard, they may lose most of their audience along the way, which ultimately places children at risk. Other pathways are needed. For instance, Ellsworth (1989) embraces the aesthetic paradigm when she describes her strategies for teacher candidates. Within "context specific" school classroom and community event spaces like "planning, producing and 'making sense' of a day-long film and video event against oppressive knowledges," she and her students engaged "with one another to find a commonality in the experience of difference without compromising its distinctive realities and effects" (pp. 299, 324).

When teacher candidates have not been invited into the process of creation (like Ellsworth describes above) and have been chained to the negative aspects of the technical, multicultural, and/or critical approaches, their learning has been predetermined; there is nothing to sink their imaginations into and no space for their spirits to shine. Speaking to the drum circle analogy opening the "Seed of Hope" chapter, we cannot force the means of a particular way of learning, because when teacher candidates, or children "do not see their ways in the world valued, they will reject what is being taught, or worse, reject themselves as being less than" (see Chapter 2, "Seed of Hope"). In this regard, critical pedagogy may be similar to its own noncritical nemesis of technicism: Both stay outside the mystery—only what you can see is what you can believe.

Unmasking the Kiva of Love

What teacher education needs is a way out. Yet, the *way out* is what we cannot see; it is unquantifiable and immaterial. It exists in the imaginative realm where it must be unmasked by the eight seeds of compassion to come to fruition. Without spiritual and creative guidance, empathy, and a provision of contextual opportunity to truly see our selves with others in the larger universe of possibility, without the deeper core connection that the aesthetic provides, technicist, multicultural, and critical approaches to teacher education will always fall short of the *sacred*. As Highwater (1996) stated, "All our ancestors understood when they looked up into the endless sky and realized how desperately small they were and yet how unspeakably immense is the human imagination."

Regardless of whether our students are metacognitively aware of the effects, with the overwhelming fatigue of pre/current/postindustrial trauma of society upon our future teachers, a larger-than-life curriculum has been at work upon their hearts and minds (see Chapter 5, "Seed of Unmasking"). To counter all of this, there must be something of great substance, hope, and vision. As we attempt to illustrate vibrantly within these pages, our approach to aesthetic teacher education fast-forwards the psychology, instantly undoes layers of the seemingly impossible programmatic exacerbations and individual baggage for our teacher candidates to allow hope to reappear with resilient personal and cultural transformative return.

Yet, if we do acquiesce to our current educational climate, we might ask ourselves if we or other facilitators belong as teachers of teachers. Why are artists, activists, spiritual practitioners, and community educators, with their ideas and experiences, being excluded from participating in the preparation of our future teachers? How willing are we as academics and teachers to change the system and renounce our privileged positions to let in those from a larger or different community who could hit the drum of education in ways we never will (French, 2005)?

The aesthetic is both the remedy and the salvation for self and societal analytical obsession. Aesthetics and the arts simultaneously provide awareness *and* hope and do so innovatively and meaningfully in the person's own unique way (see also Chapter 6, "Seed of Inner Awareness"). The mind and the heart unite through the aesthetic experience, resulting in synergistic relationships. Educators can instantly perceive their ability to become empathic toward one another within the creative process largely due to the capacity of our emotional imaginations (Csikszentmihalyi, 1996; Greene, 2001).

Thomas Merton (1995) observed that when distracted by that which is "exterior, objective and quantitative" our imbalanced "one-sided" culture creates a selfish meritocracy based in fear and competition (p. 48). So too, collectively as a postindustrial mass of "superior" adult beings, we may feel that we have thus determined the "best" way to deal with the world around us. We do the things we do in what we believe to be an efficient, rational way to procure the most pleasure or progress using a predetermined process. Among our elite enclaves, we develop the false sense of security that we have somehow evolved and obtained through our "superior" means, the "ultimate" understanding. Granting ourselves dominion over all, we then may replicate such systems of hubris among our future teachers (Bowers, 2007).

In this way, as teacher educators within a postindustrial culture and society, we tend to be sleepwalkers anesthetized visually and emotionally (Clark & French, 2012; Coles, 1993), as social and ecological devastation continues to grow at rapid rates (see Chapter 4, "Seed of Change").

Rather than rejoicing in diversity in thought, critical questioning, and active community engagement rooted in ecological and social sustainability, we

[may] instead pleasure ourselves to suffer in the shadow of hard, cold, fear-laden facts of measurement, data-driven instruction, and individual accountability thereby hampering the creation of a new educational reality. (French & Clark, 2012, p. 94)

In our collective nonpossibilizing means and mindset, as Tagore (1913) suggests in his poem, *Where the Mind is Without Fear*, reason has "lost its way into the dreary desert sand of dead habit" (p. 35). The masks on our susceptible hearts and souls may thicken, with ultimately, our egos stealing from children and the earth.

The system of teacher education must be changed, and we hope our book may be part of a beginning to change the system of teacher preparation. The following work presented rests on the shoulders of past and present change-makers throughout history who have researched the human experience and championed a world of human decency for children. We hope to resurrect the brilliant progressive researchers from the 20th century who celebrated the child's imagination, like Rudolph Steiner, Maria Montessori, John Dewey, Anna Freud, Robert Coles, and Maxine Greene; and the sacred practitioners like Thomas Merton, Henri Nouwen, Dalai Lama, Mahatma Gandhi, Mother Theresa; and artists like Vincent van Gogh, Martha Graham, Langston Hughes, Romare Bearden, Pablo Picasso, and Jackson Pollack. These are but a few of the inspirational change-makers who unmasked their creative potential and unleashed a view of life as sacred—a gift to be used for others. Their hearts and minds were free from fear and, although marginalized by critics, continued on making their mark on our hearts and our world.

The literature presented here offers an integrative paradigm that is eclectic, inclusive, for teachers and children, a harmonious celebration of human experience that embraces educational, spiritual, philosophical, and aesthetic research domains that proclaim, "We are human and responsible for one another!" We hold deeply in our hearts and minds all the children we taught and meet on a daily basis, because they are our greatest teachers, our greatest gifts, and we dedicate this book to them. May all future teachers unmask their fears in order to plant harmonic seeds of *play, hope, voice, change, unmasking, inner awareness, freedom,* and *love* to celebrate the creative and sacred in all children.

As further detailed in this book, we designed a cutting edge metaphor of the KIVA, describing a sacred place of learning where empathic light, when revealed, fills the KIVA with (K)indness, (I)nnovation, (V)oice, and (A)ction. The KIVA represents the sacred space of learning designed by the teacher, a place-based aesthetic studio environment (as presented in Figure 1 in a visual map), whereby we enter through an aesthetic portal to fully actualize our understanding of the sacred within us: our potential to create, love, and grow in human decency toward one another and our world.

FIGURE 1. The "Kiva": Symbolic Representation of the KIVA as Metaphor For Kindness, Innovation, Voice, and Action and Space To Reveal The Composite Eight Seeds Of Compassion.

Each chapter will present a seed painting symbolizing each concept that is explored in this book. The seed paintings provide a process for meditation to visually reflect on what is perhaps invisible to our daily eye. We forget that our hearts and minds are in need of *play, hope, voice, change, unmasking, inner awareness, freedom,* and *love.* The seeds introduced may be the most important qualities of life.

So here now, just as we promised, is the inviting glimmer of light as you exit the dark cave. This light will envelop you further as you step into the KIVA and into the seed chapter pages of "Play" to continue among the natural outcomes of learning and sharing experiences through the eight seeds of compassion, where we find LOVE as the ultimate expression of human wholeness.

> *I do not simply teach the mind I reach the heart and—When I reach the heart I touch the soul.*
>
> —Rabbi Zev Schostak

REFERENCES

Apple, M. (1995). *Education and power.* London, UK: Routledge.

Ayers, W., & Miller, J. (Eds.). (1998). *A light in dark times: Maxine Greene and the unfinished conversation.* New York, NY; London, UK: Teachers College Press.

Bartolomé, L. I. (2004). Critical pedagogy and teacher education: Radicalizing prospective teachers. *Teacher Education Quarterly, 31*(1), 97–122.

Batchelder, T. H., & Root, S. (1994). Effects of an undergraduate program to integrate academic learning and service: Cognitive, prosocial cognitive, and identity outcomes. *Journal of Adolescence, 17*(4), 341–355.

Bourdieau, P., & Passeron, J. (1977). *Reproduction in education, society, and culture.* London, UK: Sage.

Bowers, C. A. (2007). *Critical essays on the enclosure of the cultural commons: The conceptual foundations of today's mis-education.* Retrieved from http://cabowers.net/pdf/Title-critical essays.pdf

Boyle-Baise, M. (2002). *Multicultural service learning: Educating teachers in diverse communities.* New York, NY: Teachers College Press.

Brown, C. (1998). *Artist to artist: Inspiration and advice from artists past & present.* Corvallis, OR: Jackson Creek.

Cartwright, P., & Noone, L. (2006). Critical imagination: A pedagogy for engaging pre-service teachers in the university classroom. *College Quarterly, 9*(4) Retrieved from http://www.senecac.on.ca/quarterly/2006-vol09-num04-fall/cartwright_noone.html

Clark, B. (2005). *Moral imagination and art: Echoes from a child's soul* (Doctoral dissertation). University of Hartford, Connecticut. Retrieved May 10, 2012, from Dissertations & Theses: Full Text. (Publication No. AAT 315 7797).

Clark, B., & French, J. (2012). ZEAL: A revolution for education, unmasking teacher identity through aesthetic education, imagination and transformational practice. *Critical Questions in Education, 3*(1), 12–22.

Cochran-Smith, M. (2004). *Walking the road: Race, diversity, and social justice in teacher education.* New York, NY: Teachers College Press.

Coles, R. (1993). *The call to service.* New York, NY: Houghton Mifflin.

Csikszentmihalyi, M. (1996). *Creativity: Flow and the psychology of discovery and invention.* New York, NY: HarperCollins.

Cullum, A. (1971). *The geranium on the window sill just died, but teacher you went right on.* Brussels, Belgium: Harlin Quist.

Darder, A., Torres, R., & Baltodano, M. (2002). Introduction. In A. Darder, R. Torres, & M. Baltodano (Eds.), *The critical pedagogy reader.* New York, NY: Routledge/Falmer.

Davis, K. A. (1995). Multicultural classrooms and cultural communities of teachers. *Teaching and Teacher Education, 11*(6), 553–563.

Delpit, L. (1995). *Others people's children: Cultural conflict in the classroom.* New York, NY: New Press.

Delpit, L., & Dowdy, J. (Eds.). (2002). *The skin that we speak: Thoughts on language and culture in the classroom.* New York, NY: New Press.

Ellsworth, E. (1989). Why doesn't this feel empowering? Working through the repressive myths of critical pedagogy. *Harvard Educational Review, 59*(3), 297–325.

Freire, P. (2005). *Pedagogy of the oppressed.* New York, NY: Continuum. (Original work published 1970)

French, J. (2005). *Culturally responsive pre-service teacher development: A case study of the impact of community and school fieldwork* (Doctoral dissertation). University of

Connecticut, Connecticut. Retrieved from Dissertations and Theses: Full Text database. (Publication No. AAI3167589).

French, J., & Clark, B. (2012). Revitalizing a spiritual compassionate commons in educational culture. *Religion and Education, 39*(1), 93–108.

Gatto, J. T. (2002). *Dumbing us down: The hidden curriculum of compulsory schooling.* Gabriola Island, Canada: New Society.

Gatto, J. T. (2006). *The underground history of American education: An intimate investigation into the prison of modern schooling.* New York, NY: Oxford Village.

Giroux, H. A., & McLaren, P. (1986). Teacher education and the politics of engagement: The case for democratic schooling. *Harvard Educational Review, 56*(3), 213–238.

Gollnick, D. (1992). Multicultural education: Policies and practices in teacher education. In C. Grant (Ed.), *Research in multicultural education: From the margins to the mainstream.* (pp. 218–239). London, UK: Falmer.

Goodlad, J. I. (1990). *Teachers for our nation's schools.* San Francisco, CA: Jossey-Bass.

Greene, M. (1978). *Landscapes of learning.* New York, NY: Teacher College Press.

Greene, M. (1988). *The dialectic of freedom.* New York, NY: Teacher College Press.

Greene, M. (2001). *Variations on a blue guitar: The Lincoln Center Institute lectures on aesthetic education.* New York, NY: Teachers College Press.

Gund, C. (Producer), & Sullivan, L. (Director). (2004). *A touch of greatness* [Motion picture]. First Run Features.

Haberman, M. (1988). *Preparing teachers for urban schools.* Bloomington, IN: Phi Delta Kappa Educational Foundation.

Haberman, M. (1993). Teaching in multicultural schools: Implications for teacher selection and training. In L. Kremer-Hayon, H. Vonk, & R. Fessler (Eds.), *Teacher professional development* (pp. 267–294). Amsterdam, The Netherlands: Swets and Zietlinger B.V.

Haberman, M., & Post, L. (1998). Teachers for multicultural schools: The power of selection. *Theory into Practice, 37*(2), 96–104.

Heller, J. (1994). *Catch-22.* London, UK: Vintage. (Original work published 1961)

Highwater, J. (1982). *The primal mind: Vision and reality in Indian America.* New York, NY: Harper & Row.

Highwater, J. (Writer), Perlmutter, A. (Producer), & Lenzer, D. (Director). (1996). Primal mind: Alternative perspectives on self, environment and the development of culture [Documentary]. The Primal Mind Foundation.

hooks, b. (1994). *Teaching to transgress: Education as the practice of freedom.* New York, NY: Routledge.

Hopkins, T. (1945). A philosophy of art. In *The arts and children's living* (pp. 5–8). Washington, DC: Association for Childhood Education.

Isaacson, W. (2007). *Einstein: His life and universe.* New York, NY: Simon & Schuster.

Kincheloe, J. L. (2004). *Critical pedagogy primer.* New York, NY: Peter Lang.

King, J. E. (1991). Dysconscious racism: Ideology, identity, and the miseducation of teachers. *Journal of Negro Education, 60*(2), 133–146.

Kohl, H. (1994). *"I won't learn from you" and other thoughts on creative maladjustment.* New York, NY: New Press.

Ladson-Billings, G. (1994). *The dreamkeepers: Successful teachers for African-American children.* San Francisco, CA: Jossey-Bass.

Leonardo, Z. (2003). Discourse and critique: Outlines of a post-structural theory of ideology. *Journal of Education Policy, 18*(2), 203–214.

McGroarty, E., & Robbins, J. (2012). Controlling education from the top: Why common core is bad for America. *Pioneer Institute and American Principles Project White Paper, 87*. Retrieved from http://blogs.edweek.org/edweek/state_edwatch/Controlling-Education-From-the-Top%5B1%5D.pdf

McLaren, P. (2007). *Life in schools: An introduction to critical pedagogy in the foundations of education.* New York, NY: Allyn & Bacon.

Merton, T. (1995). *Thoughts on the east.* New York, NY: New Directions.

Michelangelo (1513). Retrieved from www.artchive.com/artchive/M/michelangelo.html

Nieto, S. (1999). *The light in their eyes: Creating multicultural learning communities.* New York, NY: Teachers College Press.

O'Grady, C. R. (1998). Moving off center: Engaging White education students in multicultural field experiences. In R. Chávez & J. O'Donnel (Eds.), *Speaking the unpleasant: The politics of (non) engagement in the multicultural education terrain* (pp. 221–228). Albany, NY: State University of New York Press.

Palmer, P. (1993). *The violence of our knowledge: Toward a spirituality of higher education.* Paper presented at the the Michael Keenan Memorial Lecture, the 7th lecture, Berea College, KY. Retrieved from http://www.kairos2.com/palmer_1999.htm

Pirsig, R. M. (1974). *Zen and the art of motorcycle maintenance: An inquiry into values.* New York, NY: William Morrow.

Rijksbaron, A. (2007). *Plato. Ion. or: On the Iliad.* Leiden, The Netherlands: Brill.

Sleeter, C. E. (2001). Preparing teachers for culturally diverse schools: Research and the overwhelming presence of Whiteness. *Journal of Teacher Education, 52*(2), 94–106.

Solórzano, D. (2001). Critical race theory, racial microaggressions, and campus racial climate: The experiences of African American college students. *Journal of Negro Education, 69*(1/2), 60–73.

Tagore, R. (1913). *Gitanjali (song offerings): A collection of prose translations made by the author from the original Bengali.* London, UK: Macmillan.

Terrill, M., & Mark, D. L. H. (2000). Preservice teachers' expectations for schools with children of color and second-language learners. *Journal of Teacher Education, 51*(2), 149–155.

Vadeboncoeur, J. A., Rahm, J., Aguilera, D., & LeCompte, M. (1996). Building democratic character through community experiences in teacher education. *Education and Urban Society, 28*(2), 189–207.

Zajonc, A. (2006). Cognitive-affective connections in teaching and learning: The relationship between love and knowledge. *Journal of Cognitive Affective Learning, 3*(1), 1–9. Retrieved from https://www.garrisoninstitute.org/contemplation-and-education/article-database/details/18/70

CHAPTER 1

THE SEED OF PLAY

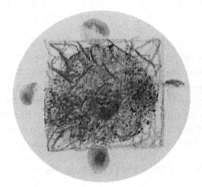

Seed of Play Painting
(Clark, 2009b)

He called a child, who he put among them, and said, "Truly I tell you, unless you change and become like children, you will never enter the kingdom of heaven. Whoever becomes humble like this child is the greatest in the kingdom of heaven. Whoever welcomes one such child in my name welcomes me."
—(Matthew, 18:2–5)

Children live in a world of constant wonder and amazement of the world around them. "Children, when they are allowed to be children, connect

Hearts and Minds Without Fear: Unmasking the Sacred in Teacher Preparation,
pages 1–35.

their fantasies and connect to the powers of the universe . . . and with many forces" (Fox, 2004, p. 178). Fox believes that "play is a kind of meditation, for it takes us back to the Source of all things, including joy and beauty" (p. 179). Teachers must reconnect with their own inner child and relearn how to play, and to celebrate play, in order to release their inner source of creative potential. As Chesterton (1908) stated,

> It is not only possible to say a great deal in praise of play; it is really possible to say the highest things in praise of it. It might reasonably be maintained that the true object of all human life is play. Earth is a task garden; heaven is a play-ground. To be at last in such secure innocence that one can juggle with the universe and the stars, to be so good that one can treat everything as a joke—that may be, perhaps, the real end and final holiday of human souls. (p. 96)

Through play, the sacred well of beauty and joy within every one of us fills, opening creative paths toward innovation and enlightenment. Spiritual leader Eckhart Tolle (1999) explains manifestation intention and how our universe (playfully) creates diverse life forms. Tolle (2013) states,

> Your own life is a microcosm of the macrocosm. If you look at the Universe, the first thing you will see is that it likes to create, and it likes to manifest. On this planet alone, the Universe is continuously creating and manifesting countless life forms. And in outer space, we can only assume—we don't know what exactly is there—but there is a vastness of life out there, and probably many more life forms than we have on this planet. The life forms, both in the sea, and on land, including humans, they seem to enjoy a dance of coming into being and destruction. It's a transformational process.

Both Tolle (1999) and Fox (2004) place an emphasis on the time adults waste with activity that causes fear, judgment, and suffering. Tolle states, "This incessant mental noise prevents you from finding that realm of inner stillness that is inseparable from Being. It also creates a false mind-made self that casts a shadow of fear and suffering" (p. 15). Fox, however, says that "Play takes us to realms that are preconscious and prejudgmental. . . In play, our imaginations not only get refreshed they also get set up to connect with new and untried possibilities" (Fox, 2004, pp. 180–181). Through play, we are enlightened, we are natural, we are in the moment, we break down boundaries and borders, stereotypes, illusions, bias, and seemingly manifest to a higher sense of connectedness with the universe.

To celebrate play and understand the importance of play for a child's healthy development, the teacher must unmask the exterior shell of adult-hood and deeply reflect upon their childhood. The mask of adulthood is perhaps the thickest layer on the faces, hearts, and minds of our teacher candidates. They come to us with preconceived notions of what it means to be a teacher. At our initial meetings, it is obvious that most of our teacher candidates do not understand that play is critical to developing creativity; as "the true artist plays with his or her tools, inspiration, intuition, forms, colors, musical instruments, even mind" (Fox, 2004, p. 180).

Our teacher candidates were the test babies of the NCLB (No Child Left Behind) reform, in 2001. They were between the ages of 8 and 10 when the NCLB testing started, and based on their public schooling experience, they believe that testing is teaching. Our preservice teacher candidates who were students in public schools through the NCLB reign have shared with us that they did not experience place-based learning and discovery learning in their elementary classrooms. Instead their teacher models were mandated to use scripted lessons and teach to the test. And so, from their own schooling experience, many of our future teachers perceive direct instruction and the use of worksheets as "real" teaching. Their experience of the teacher's role becomes one of controlling children through fear and power. Freire (1998) explains the damage of methods by teachers who dominate the child's natural world, stating, "The person who is filled by another with 'contents' whose meaning s/he is not aware of, which contradict his or her way of being in the world, cannot learn because s/he is not challenged" (p. 88).

Inspired by Thich Nhat Hanh (1991), world-renowned Zen master, we wanted to develop an "ecology of mind" regarding play, possibility, and peace. Thich Nhat Hanh believed that we must be present and mindful in all that we do to ignite "a deep ecology" of mindfulness within our course experiences. The arts and aesthetics are to promote "not only deep but universal [awareness and mindfulness], because [as Hanh warned] there is pollution in our consciousness" (p. 114). We knew we had to have the courage to go against the grain through creative maladjustment to pioneer a new type of "ecology of mind" for teacher preparation: an aesthetic learning environment.

We first decided to utilize the arts and experiment with play during course workshops. We provided the freedom and mentorship for our teacher candidates to explore social and ecological issues, thereby taking the first step to *unmask* their mediocrity, fear, and stereotypes about becoming a teacher and thus examine the purpose of education in a democratic society. We began each semester with a series of playful experiences. We felt that only through playful experiences would our teacher candidates dare to remove their adult masks—the masks of fear, rejection, and judgment—and begin to understand the concept of the teacher as an artist, a guide, a "shape shifter" of realities.

The artist teacher employs the *Seed of Play*, both consciously and unconsciously, to manifest a duality of spontaneous actions in the learning environment. We perceive the artist teacher to be in essence very much like a painter who sees the blank canvas of possibility in learning and guides the child's hand, heart, and mind to paint an original piece; or like a maestro who composes a unique song with varying degrees of tonal consonance and dissonance to achieve harmony or wholeness. According to Gardner (1994), play "involves a continual interplay between creation and criticism, manifested in the painter's alternation of working on the canvas and stepping back to observe the effect" (p. 134). It is only through the reciprocal interplay of ideas that play provides that we truly experience possibility. As you read further throughout the seed chapters, a variety of artists will be used as examples of critical and creative processes.

Adults by nature bury their inner child and retreat from spontaneous play as a daily activity. For the teacher, play must be an integral part of their repertoire to trigger possibility and creativity. Gardner (1994) perceives "play as a necessary antecedent of participation in the aesthetic process" (p. 166). Gardner states,

> The play impulse becomes the art impulse (supposing it is strong enough to survive the play years) when it is illumined by a growing participation in the social consciousness and a sense of the common worth of things, when in other words it becomes conscious of itself as a power of shaping semblance which shall give value for other eyes or ears and shall bring recognition and renown. (p. 166)

Barnes and Lyons (1986) describe the Steiner method (1919) that also places the child at the heart of learning. There is great respect and love of the child from the playful teacher. The playful teacher dignifies the child's response to the "harmony of the world she creates and with which he so actively identifies. Life speaks to the preschooler as gesture: he answers in creative play" (p. 4).

The focal point of this chapter is the presentation of aesthetic education methods to be utilized within play-based curriculum emphasizing that preservice teachers must understand the critical importance of play for the development of a child. Play is celebrated through the arts as a symbol of social imagination, as teacher candidates explore concepts of social and ecological justice to realize civic agency (see Figure 1.1). They begin to identify and recognize that their interests, unique perspectives, and talent can in fact contribute to the world. Our goal is to guide our teacher candidates to understand that the "little child longs to enjoy spontaneous freedom [through creative play]—but within the clearly defined security of order and form" (Barnes & Lyons, 1986, p. 4).

One of the most critical aspects in the KIVA is the sense of play between teacher candidates—making the invisible visible. Professors created a studio paradigm for teacher candidates to explore infinite possibilities, developing an "ecology of ideas" (Bateson, 1987, p. 467), fostering mindfulness and awareness of one another. Play promotes community sharing that leads to a greater imagination for social change (Greene, 2001). As you meditate

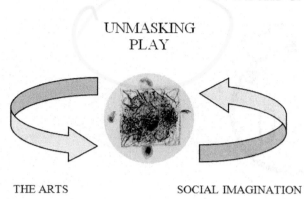

UNMASKING
PLAY

THE ARTS   SOCIAL IMAGINATION

FIGURE 1.1.   Unmasking Play concept map.

on the *Seed of Play* painting (Clark, 2009b) within the concept map above, focus on the shadows, dancing and moving around a thread-like center. Play does not allow for stagnation or judgment but instead provides endless scenarios and interpretations. When you experience play, do you perceive others in new ways?

The arts and aesthetics promote play and expand and shift realities of what the community may become. Clark (2009a) stated,

> According to Maxine Greene (2001), aesthetic education is "integral to the development of persons—to their cognitive, perceptual, emotional, and imaginative development" (p. 7). Gardner (1973) like Greene presents the arts as a cognitive tool necessary to fuel the human developmental systems including how we see, feel and make new ideas within our imaginative core. When confronted with a painting, or piece of music we open "ourselves as perceivers to the work, entering into it kinaesthetically, we free ourselves to grasp it in its vital fullness and complexity" (Greene, 2001, p. 13). Greene (2001) asserts that aesthetic experiences provide us with a window to encounter the arts conscious that "we are in the present as living, perceiving beings becoming aware that there is always, always more." (p. 9)

Within the studio paradigm (we call the KIVA; see Figure 1.2), teacher candidates experiment with play to solve problems, to develop cognitive capacity, practice reflective dispositions, mindfulness, a new sense of tolerance, and respect for diverse expressions and cultural identities.

KIVA for Play

The chart titled, *Seed Outcomes* (see Table 1) presents the effects on teacher candidates after their participation in the arts and aesthetics to create diverse performances with children that focus on issues in their local and

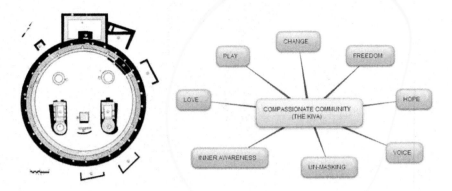

FIGURE 1.2. Great Kiva (Chetro Ketl) and Our Compassionate Community; KIVA, 2013.

global communities that are related to social and ecological justice themes. Compassionate Community presentations with teacher candidates and local children in urban schools include *A Compassionate Community to End Homelessness* (Spring, 2009); *Creating a Compassionate World Community* (Fall, 2009); *Make a Wave* (Spring, 2010); *Echoes from a Child's Soul: Children of Incarcerated Parents Release their Voices through Art, Music, Dance, Mask Making, Movement and Creative Writing* (Fall, 2011); *Stepping Out of a Painting: Releasing a Child's Voice* (Spring, 2012); and *Storybook Characters Promote Compassion and Love of Reading* (Fall, 2012).

As evidenced by Table 1.1, the outcomes of diverse aesthetic experiences (*Seeds*) enacted within the KIVA paradigm impacted the development of the teacher candidate's sense of self over time. Throughout this book, many examples of play are presented that were enacted within a compassionate and creative community we are calling the KIVA, as described in the introduction. KIVA is a metaphor for a learning environment (playfully derived from the ancient Anasazi) where (K)indness, (I)nnovation, (V)oice, and (A)ction by compassionate teachers are paramount in the success of developing potential within each child. In Figure 1.2, space is designed within a circular form in the *Great Kiva* (on the left) and in a rectangular form (on the right) in our *Compassionate Community KIVA*. However, in our schools, the 21st century classrooms are rectangular. The juxtaposition of these two spaces in Figure 1.2 represents the loss of the sacred in our everyday life.

Metaphorically speaking, the KIVA paradigm we present in our book to explore critical issues and the sacred in all of us, parallels the Anasazi Kiva that archeologists called a "ceremonial room." Our compassionate community projects (described throughout the book) modeled an ideal of the ancient Kiva whereby each individual fully participated, contributing their

TABLE 1.1.   Seeds' Outcomes Chart (2013): Arts and Aesthetics Project Effects on Teacher Candidates

| SEEDS | OUTCOMES | | | | | | | |
Diverse Aesthetic Experiences	Social Imagination	Self Knowledge	Empowerment	Creative Capacity	Agency	Exploration	Belief	Learning
Play	✓			✓		✓		✓
Change	✓	✓	✓			✓		✓
Freedom	✓	✓	✓	✓	✓	✓	✓	✓
Hope	✓	✓	✓	✓			✓	✓
Voice	✓	✓	✓	✓	✓	✓	✓	✓
Unmasking	✓	✓	✓	✓	✓	✓	✓	✓
Inner Awareness	✓	✓	✓	✓	✓	✓	✓	✓
Love	✓	✓	✓	✓	✓	✓	✓	✓

unique expressions while spontaneously experimenting with the arts and each other.

> Each kiva had its own group of participants and it was the job of each member of that kiva to participate fully in their own parts of the ceremony so that the entire ritual could be completed properly. . . the place where the family or families gathered for (some kinds of) work, play, and ritual. (Brockway, 2013)

One of the most critical aspects in our creative KIVA is the sense of play between teacher candidates. The aesthetic-based community projects highlight forms of play that lift up teacher candidates to rejoice and share in spontaneous celebrations of discovery (Bowers, 2006). Playful aesthetic discoveries that utilize the arts are later translated into compassionate strategies to be enacted in local school and community venues in forms of place-based learning (as illustrated below in Michelle's case study). Research has shown that children are learning while playing and inventing (Barnes & Lyons, 1986; Brown, 2011; Dewey, 1980; Elkind, 2007). Play is a critical pillar of the KIVA's architectural framework, wherein creative learning may flourish, resulting in a multitude of inspirational outcomes.

J. Brown (2011) uses the analogy of play to tinkering, wherein the learner has an epiphany. This tinkering—felt in the mind—"brings thoughts and action together in powerful and magical ways" (see http://www.instituteofplay.org/press/). But unfortunately, the power and importance of play has been neglected in the 21st century. Within strict state certification programs, teacher candidates must become practitioners of test-taking rather than magicians of aesthetic, dramatic and pretend play (Vygotsky, 1986). Play is not only devalued in education, it is discouraged as not real learning. This absence of play in our school and teacher education classrooms reinforces mediocrity, breeds racism and stereotyping, and protects the status quo wherein possibility is not present or even allowed.

Ironically, the beginning of the 20th century was titled the "Century of the Child" by Montessori (Standing, 1962), a theorist and highly regarded child educator who placed the act of play high among teachers' strategies for children's learning. In fact, Montessori believed that allowing children to develop an inner life through play would in essence lead to world peace. Montessori believed that the imagination was celebrated through play, making room for the child to fully and peacefully develop. Cognition was developed through play. Creative ideas were created through play. Innovation was stimulated through play.

Some 100 years later, play is now perceived as an evil in education. Now it is the "lazy" teacher who allows play. And the child who plays is perceived as a "distracted" learner. A child who plays at their desk is a "daydreamer." A child who plays and invents at "inappropriate" times must be medicated in order to focus. In our rigid structures of schooling, we have seemingly forgotten that the truest form of "play is not to be directed by someone else, but by their own will" (Hino, 2003, p. 20). Children are naturally curious, and ask "why" all the time. That is, until they begin public school education and are told not to ask "why" and not to take things apart or experience ideas.

Beyond the classroom, teacher preparation programs simultaneously do not utilize play as a critical theory to promote the understanding of a child's world. Fox says that "without keeping play alive, adults become ill at ease with goalless activity and tend to play very little" (Fox, 2004, p. 180). Due to the politically charged climate on educational reform, Elkind (2007) warns that we have completely gone afar from the concept of the child. The basic love of a child and the openness necessary to nurture a child's imagination is not part of the educational reform agenda in teacher education. This systemic masking of critical needs for a child's well-being is the reason why bringing back the importance of play for children into teacher training is so critical. We are at risk if we ignore the importance of understanding play for children in teacher preparation. As Elkind (2007) admonishes,

> With the rapid expansion and acceptance of early childhood programs, the basic principle of early childhood education, supported by an overwhelming amount of contemporary research and classroom experience, is dismissed as irrelevant. Instead, we have had a politically and commercially driven effort to make early childhood education "the new first grade". . . a play-based curriculum is best suited to meet the emerging needs, abilities and interests of

young children. We have come too far from where early education began: with the child. (p. 5)

Like Elkind (2007) and many other advocates for play (Erikson, 1950; Montessori, 1912; Piaget, 1951; Vygotsky, 1986), we must bring the child's needs into the light for the 21st century, cast off the darkness of adult-world testing for profit and place the curriculum at the center of the child's life. In so doing, we resurrect our greatest 20th century theorists on the importance of play in child development. As pioneers in teacher preparation, they believed that the cornerstone of all the truth, beauty, and goodness lies within the child. One such prominent researcher, Dr. Stuart Brown (2009), has pursued research on play since 1989 after leaving his practice in medicine. He designed a scientific investigation to explain how and why human play is critical to our healthy development. Brown illustrated through a series of experiments that it is by our very nature as humans to participate in play not only during childhood but also throughout our entire lives. Resounding with Brown and researchers before us, our KIVA supports the aesthetic methodology and creative community commons approach for teacher preparation to emphasize the critical nature of play for children and teachers.

Play is unique in unmasking the sacred; it is a purely human and spiritual act, as there is a natural purging of toxic biases. We want to unmask the bias against play and the imagination. Bias may cause a teacher in the classroom to react negatively against children who are indeed creative and innovative. On the other hand, preservice teachers who are creative at once finally feel, when engaged in aesthetic play within the educational community KIVA environment, that they belong. This is the paradigm that we want our preservice teachers to intrinsically hope to become—self-identifying as a "creative" who as an educator is driven to nurture a child's imagination (S. Brown, 2009). Once the *Seed of Play* is planted and experienced, preservice teachers can step into the sacred imaginative realm, the mystery of the sacred, what is possible and what is hopeful, thus releasing their "child's" inner imagination.

As one example of opening the KIVA play space for a group of prospective teacher candidates, the CCSU Make Your Mark Project was designed for our incoming freshman to experience play. The freshman aspiring to become teachers were asked to be playful, spontaneous, and to make their unique mark on a community mural. The mural was a spiral, a labyrinth of sorts (see Figure 1.3), and the future teacher candidates were asked to make their mark within the swirling forms and textures. Freshman gathered and selected assorted found objects and discussed how the objects might symbolize their journey when placed in the mural labyrinth.

Many students were playful and naturally quick to express their journey through spontaneous action and use of materials. The *Seed of Play* in this

FIGURE 1.3.   Make Your Mark Project: Inspired by Dag Hammarskjöld Welcoming incoming CCSU Freshman, 2010.

context was felt among the participants, laughing and moving their driftwood or sea glass many times on the expansive mural (8' x 10') as if playing a game. Dag Hammarskjöld (1964), author of *Markings*, was the inspiration for this activity as his love for nature was depicted in many haikus he composed. It was known to many that Hammarskjöld was deeply spiritual, and his work in the United Nations exemplified his aesthetic philosophic nature and commitment to social justice. "The more faithfully you listen to the voices within you, the better you will hear what is sounding outside" (Hammarskjöld, 1964, as cited by Blank, 2001, p. 34). The following haiku exemplifies Hammarskjöld's belief for all to pursue the aesthetic in search of self-evolution and the pursuit of truth (2012).

> Still far from the beach
> the sea's freshness played
> in bronze-shining leaves

The preservice teachers presented throughout this book were exposed to a *studio environment*, which placed an emphasis on playful tasks and invention to authentically replicate an environment wherein the child's need for play is considered foremost. Preservice teachers acquire a sense for adapting play for individual children in the field, to appropriately provide the freedom that celebrates each child's unique perspective, culture, and interests. Like food, water, and love, play is critical to the development of a child's imagination and fundamental to a child's language development (Vygotsky, 1986).

As illustration, one of our community school performances to end homelessness utilized arts-based methods in the aesthetics, inspired children labeled autistic by the school to spontaneously jump upon the stage to join in singing and dancing with our teacher candidates. The school's classroom teachers were in shock, as these children never willingly participated, let alone in a community forum. What triggered the desire to come to the stage to dance and sing? As the children viewed the 30-minute performance, their imaginations were sparked, their hearts were full of hope and the natural desire to be connected, and to celebrate with others ensued. But why are the arts and celebrations of this caliber such a misunderstood need for children to learn, autistic or not? Both Dewey (1980) and Montessori (1912) agreed that a child's play is a child's work—after all, this is how they make sense of the world (as cited by Standing, 1962). As Dewey (1980) describes,

> Education takes the individual while he is relatively plastic, before he has become so indurated [abnormally hardened] by isolated experiences as to be rendered hopelessly empirical in his habit of mind. The attitude of childhood is naïve, wondering, experimental; the world of man and nature is new. Right methods of education preserve and perfect this attitude and thereby short-circuit for the individual the slow progress of the race, eliminating the waste that comes from inert routine. (p. 156)

So too, aspects of the critical nature of Freire's research celebrates the hopeful yearning for education to be renewed for children in a way that celebrates each child's uniqueness: "The great difficulty (or the great adventure) is how to make education something which in being serious, rigorous, methodical, and having a process also creates happiness and joy" (Horton & Freire, 1990, pp. 168–172). At the root is the spiritual fiber that is sacred to a child's heart and mind, and essential in their healthy development as a human. When children play, their imaginations grow and they begin to make sense of their discoveries. After involvement in KIVA playing community experiences, our teacher candidates began to understand the need children have to feel loved by a teacher and that the first way they feel loved is to be allowed to be.

Play and Thinking: Sailing to the Lost Island of the Imagination

Various educational advocates for children point to the fact that schools are failing to inspire children to be innovative. According to Stuart Brown (2009), play alters our perception and allows us to see the possible together. As we play, we explore and enter into new realms of possibility and create new worlds that did not exist before. In fact, a recent poll by the National

Association of Music Merchants (NAMM) reveals that the current educational practice, due to the reform movements, critically impairs a child's imagination from developing:

> "These are surprising results that indicate a strong set of shared public values are not being detected by public leaders," said Celinda Lake, president of Lake Research Partners. "A significant number of voters believe that today's educational approaches are outdated, impair critical capacities of the imagination, and stifle teachers and students alike, blocking potential for innovation. These data show a large population we call the 'imagine nation' are hungry for imagination in education and are going to take action accordingly—both in their local schools and at the voting booth, so that children are prepared for the world in which they will live." (NAMM, 2013)

As professors, we plan for spontaneous play. While that may sound like a contradiction, however slight the idea or the actual process, it is not spelled out to the letter. For instance, opening one of our courses, we decided to tell a tale of a search on the "high seas" for a "far distant" island.

The island was a symbol of our imaginations lying dormant, uninhabited. We devised a type of pirate ship in which we could fit. We were able to navigate the pirate ship in the middle of the room with the preservice teachers' tables around the sides of the room. As the ship swayed in simulation, fighting the mighty storms, we finally ran ashore upon the island, symbolizing the universal need throughout the ages of the "human search for meaning" (Frankel, 1984). Frankel recalls an act of kindness and the impact that kindness has on his imagination and search for meaning amid great human suffering. Frankel states,

> I remember how one day a foreman secretly gave me a piece of bread which I knew he must have saved from his breakfast ration. It was far more than the small piece of bread which moved me to tears at that time. It was the human "something" which this man also gave to me—the word and look which accompanied the gift.

> From all this we may learn that there are two races of men in this world, but only these two—the "race" of the decent man and the "race" of the indecent man. Both are found everywhere; they penetrate into all groups of society. (p. 108)

If it were not for Frankel's imaginative capacity to see beauty amid cruelty, the day-to-day horror he faced would have enveloped him into despair. Like Frankel, we wanted our teacher candidates to liberate their imaginations to develop their moral imagination capacity as teachers and to place the importance of the imaginative realm at the center of their work. We knew in our hearts, as we said aloud to one another and our listening audience, that perhaps we would find our treasure, another symbol for the imagination. And we did indeed find the treasure that contained a type of playbook for our students. These booklets, called the *Mustard Seed Playbook* (see Figure 1.5, Fortune Teller, for an excerpt example), were lovingly made full of visuals to stimulate thinking, values, and beliefs on teaching and learning.

Our students watched our stormy play upon the made-up waves and listened to our dialogue. Some had smiles on their faces; others expressed shock that their professors would act so playfully. And yet others were expressionless. Honestly, we had the most fun with our play upon the imagination ship and realized that our students, beyond this initial experience, needed to be immersed in spontaneous play and not just be passive observers. If they had any chance to find their playful spirit and joy, they had to risk "losing face," "looking silly," and feeling uncomfortable with their peers. As told somewhere in their life experience, identity formation, or teacher training, play was stigmatized, labeled a waste of time and not a vehicle of cognition or the way academics are supposed to behave. At least 80% of our students struggle, for the first time, when stepping out of their comfort zone. The more play is practiced, cognitive capacity and creativity grow, making their playful actions more natural and spontaneous.

Another example of play as a sociodramatic concept involved dressing up as a mermaid to first shock and then inspire. Teacher candidates were asked to examine play by becoming a character and enacting a story for children. By invitation, Dr. Barbara Clark entered a colleague's class of secondary teacher candidates. She was dressed as Abigail the mermaid (see "Michelle's Story"). The secondary professor was surprised to see her education majors make fun and bully Abigail based on the outer shell, hair, and overall demeanor. The secondary professor reminded the students that they had just finished a class discussion on racism, prejudice, and stereotyping. It was quite evident that even though the teacher candidates were engaged in academic discussion and "critical" thinking, they could not however intrinsically apply concepts to this moment in real time. In their hearts and minds they instantly wanted to terrorize and reject Abigail's playful nature, and her differences they found absolutely irritating. This one example of play unmasked the latent racism of the room in all its purity.

It also illustrates how teachers must be prepared to understand, and not dismiss, the complex relationships that play can reveal. According to Miller & Almon (2009) "The play-based approach calls for teachers to know each child well and to differentiate the teaching methods to meet individual needs. It is the antithesis of the one-size-fits-all model of education" (p. 5). The seed of play is continuously nurtured within the teacher candidate's mind: a labyrinth of experiences, prejudices, and judgment. At first, they do not understand how play impacts all learners' backgrounds. Play is a universal human necessity for children. Teacher candidates explore puppets, improvisations, paintings, dance, masks, and movement, realizing that when they enter into play they are being spontaneous and reactive without judgment.

Teacher candidates observe each other engaged in playful possibilities as a starting point in order to learn how to design creative play for children. If we engage in playful scenarios and see how these types of experiences impact our thinking, we learn to value play as teachers. Play is a form of constructivism whereby our immediate lived experiences are at the forefront as we role-play, manipulate materials, and invent possibilities. In teacher preparation, play-mediums and mixed methods act as an entry point into first meeting and then learning about others' interests and strengths.

For example, in one instance, our preservice teachers were given manipulatives (a variety of drums) to create soundscapes that evoked their beliefs on teaching and learning. In order to create the soundscape, the preservice teachers had to playfully incorporate a cacophony of invented sounds using found objects to tell a story. Emotional imagination emerged as sound and movement were evoked to tell a story. The soundscapes told a once-hidden story and prompted instant access to a new type of dialogue and reality. "Education is communication and dialogue. It is not the transference of knowledge, but the encounter of Subjects in dialogue in search of the significance of the object of knowing and thinking" (Freire, 1998, p. 139). The playful soundscapes incorporate role-play and masks to further symbolize teacher candidates' beliefs on teaching and learning. They became characters in stories and interacted with other characters, problem-solving compassionate action, myths, and moral messages.

As seen in Figure 1.4, the teacher candidates were alive with excitement. Their playfulness was further heightened as they found a *Mustard Seed Fortune Teller* at each of their seats to experiment with.

Look closely within (see Figure 1.5). Inside, discover a sacred spiral design, representing how we manifest our personal journey inward and outward. The constant interplay of the seeds represents a spiritual reflection of self and others. The intra- and interpersonal worlds are revealed, toward further making the abstract concrete; and the invisible (the sacred) visible.

As a child, they all knew what fortune-tellers were and instantly their memories and emotional imagination conjured up wonderful ideas. Treasure packs also included sound-makers and scrap materials. Teacher candidates began to playfully experiment and instantly shed fear, as sounds were exchanged like a conversation between a child and teacher. A multitude of ideas bubbled up by manipulating the fortune teller, revealing the metaphysical spiral within as they navigated and lifted layers of research celebrating play and the imagination. The chorus of ideas from the teacher candidates ultimately paved a pathway to their inner most sanctum—their soul force—the thread to their imaginative realm, simultaneously unmask-

FIGURE 1.4. Pre-service teachers drum and musical soundscape: 2009 "The greatest gift is to give people your enlightenment, to share it" (Buddha).

ing fear and celebrating play, divergent thinking, creativity, and compassion.

The arts provide instant access (Arnheim, 1969, 1989; Eisner, 1994; Perkins, 1994) and multiple methods to manipulate divergent thinking in practice. The aesthetic medium may include a dance, drum, mask, or rap integrated to create a symbolic message that is then presented and choreo-

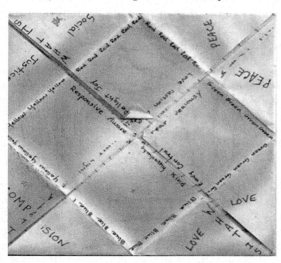

FIGURE 1.5. Fortune Teller Sample.

graphed for children to promote peace and a compassionate community message. Whatever the form, by experiencing the aesthetic paradigm in action, preservice teachers are consistently surprised with the diversity of thinking that is revealed from their peers. Likewise, preservice teachers are surprised at their own creativity revealed. As one student said, "I never thought I was creative until this semester. Even my mother was surprised. She said I never brought home any evidence that I was creative from my public school experience. Now I know I will be a creative teacher."

Being in the moment with myriad ideas to "play" with reveals a multiverse of realities that are necessary for a thriving compassionate learning community. Teacher candidates from a variety of backgrounds realized that aesthetic pedagogy uses mixed methodology to create "cognitive symbolic product" or messages. According to Clark (2005a),

> The cognitive symbolic product [is] the result of two unique mediums, art and poetry . . . Eisner (1989) stated that the medium counts and. . . is "one of the best ways to know just how much to compare and contrast the messages that are conveyed through the use of media. The emerging evolution in cognitive science is only beginning to discover the significance of Arnheim's (1989) insights into the process of cognition"(p. 7). The cognitive symbolic product was a result of combining art and poetry within a visual thinking process, and as Eisner (1989) stated, "these two mediums performed as an epistemological function—they help us know . . . what children can convey . . . and how they experience the unique features of the world they inhabit" (p. 6). (p. 440)

Beyond teacher candidates playing out ideas to promote the value and practice of immersion in the arts, the critical nature of play also enhances their creative intelligence (Csikszentmihalyi, 1996; Dewey, 1980; Eisner, 2002; Gardner, 1994; Sternberg & Lubart, 1993).

> Creativity is an expression of our unique perspective to a situation or problem. It transcends our desire to be part of the group. Abraham Maslow referred to self-actualization as the need to express our individual talents and become the best that we can. It is a drive to fulfill our potential. Maslow identified fifteen traits of a self-actualized person. These included highly valued traits such as self-acceptance, spontaneity, independence, tolerance, altruism, ethics, and capable of loving others. (Walonick, 1993, p. 24)

According to Clark (2009a), "An intimate sense of empathy evolved as pre-service teachers listened to each other's stories" (p. 41). Creativity comes from the practice of playful experiences wherein possibilities develop and the player has many ideas to choose from. The player (learner) thus becomes a reflective practitioner by knowing how to see. Seeing is enlightenment, especially when one perceives self-knowledge and knowledge of others in new ways. As interpersonal relationships deepen through experiences in the art and aesthetics, likewise in a reciprocal fashion, the individual's intrapersonal intelligence deepens, as a greater awareness develops of one's unique individual, empathic voice (Clark, 2005b). One teacher candidate expressed her cognitive symbolic message after reflecting on her mask.

> When you look at me I hope you see more than just a layer of skin.
> I hope that you catch a glimpse of my beauty that glistens from within. My heart and my mind are ready with open arms.
> Ready to see what this wild world has in store for me whatever those surprises may be.
> Whether I dance, jump, skip, or hop my journey will never, ever stop.
> I will continue to shuffle my excited feet to the beat of my own unpredictable drum.
> Along with passion, the passion that drives my singing heart.
> What you see is not always what you get. I'm not just a brunette.
> I am much more than that.
> My new journey has just begun.

Play and Magic: The Playful Birth of Rat and Honey

Playfulness when enacted promotes startling surprises as the precedent to great thinking. Like artists before us, talking endlessly about ideas in local hangouts, we too found a corner booth at a local establishment near our campus where we created an archetype to symbolize educational reform. How could we aesthetically portray NCLB and Race to the Top reform initiatives to our students through the eyes of children facing the horror of mandated testing? We decided to first portray the "rats" in education. Mr. Rat became a symbol for darkness and oppression. Second, we developed the opposing icon depicting creativity and light in learning. Thus, Miss Honey was born. Miss Honey fights the evil violence of testing on children and banishes Mr. Rat and his influence on the hearts and minds of children and teachers.

Once the archetypes of good and evil were born, we instantly started to play with our character development. The voice and dialogue of Rat and Honey emerged, as did the costumes, mannerisms, and choreography. Sketches were drawn and skits played with for the design of videos. The initial video of the all-empowering puppet master, the emperor of educational reform (played by a puppet ironically) was filmed in our offices with a backdrop and chains rattling in a distant soundscape (see Figure 1.6; see in action at http://www.compassionateteaching.com/).[1]

---

[1] To view *Rat and Honey* in action, visit www.compassionateteaching.com and click on book tab on home page, then click on *Play* tab.

FIGURE 1.6. The Birth of Miss Honey: Archetype of Imagination—The Birth of Rat: Archetype of NCLB, 2009.

Rat and Honey's debut was during a methods class in front of teacher candidates dressed as children from storybooks (see also Chapter 5, "Seed of Unmasking"). The teacher candidates viewed the video where the master puppet emperor ordered Mr. Rat to chain the hearts and imaginations of children. Instantly, when the emperor vanished, Rat appeared and proceeded to chain the teacher candidates with a wicked hypnotic laughter. Simultaneously, Miss Honey appeared and challenged the wickedness of Rat and chased the weakling away. The children (teacher candidates) chained by Rat (NCLB Darkness) are set free by Honey (Truth, Beauty, Goodness, Light).

The teacher candidates feared the Emperor of Educational Reform (see Figure 1.7), the master puppet behind Mr. Rat. The puppet emperor spoke to our students with chains clanging in the background. The Emperor's eyes bulging with depression and despair touched our teacher candidates' hearts and minds causing an emotional reaction. However, the most shocking for them was the unmasking of Rat as he ran away from Honey, ultimately to reveal a bungling abusive administrator being controlled by the testing bureaucracy of NCLB (see more on Rat and Honey performances in Chapter 5, "Seed of Unmasking"). Teacher candidates' imaginations were emotionally triggered. They instantly felt the depth and devastating impact of NCLB on children in divergent forms. Ultimately, this playful and aesthetic experience prompted our preservice teachers to critically discuss the pros and cons of educational reform.

Playful methods and strategies designed and implemented with our teacher candidates such as the Rat vs. Honey archetypes do in fact reveal hope within our teacher candidates. They have a sense that perhaps they can make an impact on children's hearts and minds using aesthetic pedagogy in their lesson design rather than teaching to a test. Ultimately, teacher

FIGURE 1.7.   Puppet Master: Emperor of Educational Reform: Created by Dr. Joss French, 2005/2009.

candidates found that immersion in play deepens the awareness of oneself and others as Desaulniers (2009) explains:

> Deep players are not externally motivated or even goal-directed; they are motivated by internal growth, the actualization of themselves and their potential. Transcendence is the process of growing to one's potential, ultimately moving beyond the ego towards a connection larger than the self. This connection often takes the form of service—helping others move towards *their* potential. Self-transcendence brings with it an acceptance of all that exists and a deep resonance with whatever life brings in all its manifestation. (2009)

Play Creates a Compassionate Community

Teachers in our teacher preparation program are renewed to the importance of play for self-discovery in themselves in relation to the importance of play for a child's cognitive, social, emotional, and psychomotor development (Piaget, 1951; Vygotsky, 1986). In order to discover how to inspire children beyond the above mediums mentioned, teacher candidates also explore possibility and invention with humor, role-playing, shaping materials, gestures, funny faces, dance, using their body, playing, leaping, jumping, wearing a mask, or holding a puppet.

Our aesthetic community environment supports teacher candidates to feel safe playing together and utilizing this variety of mediums for expression.

Play through aesthetic pedagogy allows teacher candidates to socially interact and provide instant feedback to one another. Playful actions and problem-solving promote spontaneous thinking and the urgency to embrace diverse perspectives and possibilities in the moment. Critical thinking through playful actions transfers into the development of curriculum for children.

Placing an emphasis on the concept of "playful thinking," aesthetic pedagogy for teacher candidates allows for an in-depth investigation of various generative topics and aesthetic curriculum design. Through the medium of role-taking as a generative exercise, teacher candidates develop new solutions for problem-based learning. Generative topics such as *power* are critically unwrapped and investigated. For example, beginning one semester, the causes and authentic faces of homelessness were introduced through a variety of perspectives for teacher candidates to address and apply in a real sense and through critical thinking. Our teacher candidates began to play with masks, voice, sounds, and movement, or no voices and movement, to portray the reciprocal nature of teaching and learning. Afterwards, they continued to explore onstage diverse ways to create a new face of homelessness for children to understand. Onstage, each teacher candidate designed and performed in groups, skits that utilized puppets or a mask artifact representing rejection, isolation, and poverty. This culminated in a school community performance for children.

Following their compassionate community-shared experience of playing with one another and with and for children, many of our teacher candidates realized how play has been rejected in schools. From their contrast of experience, compared to their other schooling experiences, they began to unmask the sacred discovery of their hidden potential within themselves and in children. Realizations led to the conclusion that there had ultimately been a split in education between the sacred natural world, our soul force, and the secular material world (French & Clark, 2012; Highwater, 1982; O'Donohue, 1997).

Teacher candidates shared why "wearing their masks" influenced how people perceived them. As one student admitted,

> I was afraid to look foolish playing, because I was trained that art and play is a foolish waste of time and that in the western society mindset you will not be successful wasting your time creating, playing, singing, dancing or sharing in a community setting.

That which does not make money or create power or status, the industrialized culture rejects. "Third world" primal cultures revere art and play as part of their daily communal life (Graham, 1991; Highwater, 1982; Picasso, 1907; Pollack, 1948). Experiencing *Play* within our compassionate KIVA unmasked the secular world of deception for our teacher candidates where they began to "see" what they had been missing.

Play, Possibility, and Innovation

Discovery learning that is place-based (see also Chapter 2, "Seed of Hope") provides the conceptual scaffolding that infuses playful tasks and cooperative problem solving within our curriculum methods and assignments. Themes that address social and ecological issues are identified and explored through the lens of aesthetic education methods; developing skills to be a change-maker. In another example (see Figure 1.8), teacher candidates utilized found object materials in a *studio environment* to create dolphins and scenery to address the dolphin slaughter for profit in Taiji, Japan. Students discussed how a variety of mediums could be used to "play" with and to become the dolphin.

In order to problem-solve, to "step into the skin of a dolphin," teacher candidates were forced to become playful—to dance and move with their cardboard dolphins, to make dolphin sounds and dolphin movements. How else can you become like a dolphin unless you approach the problem in a playful state of mind? A playful state of mind is one that is not afraid to look silly or be embarrassed. A compassionate community that utilizes the aesthetics is a safe environment wherein risk-taking and playful actions by teacher candidates are accepted and rejoiced. Teacher candidates begin to discover through the play-nurtured classroom environment that they have talents and skills that have been hidden for years.

As one can see in Figure 1.8, the teacher candidates are in action—busy and motivated yet relaxed and moving—they are self-regulated and enjoying the experience of a *studio environment* that celebrates play. Behind the teacher candidates, drums are waiting to be used to accentuate the spontaneous movement of the dolphins. This was in preparation of *Make a Wave*, a com-

FIGURE 1.8. Yesenia (Left) and Katya creating dolphins for Make a Wave Community Performance, 2010.

munity performance wherein teacher candidates taught 4th- and 5th-grade children about ecological justice through the arts in order to acquire empathy for the dolphins and to take civic action to stop the dolphin slaughter for profit in Taiji Japan.

As you examine the above photograph of teacher candidates at play in the studio environment, one can see the intense concentration on their faces as they make critical decisions and choices to design the dolphin they will become. Wardle (2003) states that,

> Open-ended play materials are those that offer children many ways to engage with them. For example, children can play with sand, water, or clay in a variety of ways. In creative play, children use objects and toys to create stories, build constructions, and engage in a fantasy world. The use of materials in flexible and creative ways teaches children to be flexible and creative thinkers with abstract ideas and concepts. (p. 20)

Lewis (2009) states that,

> Perhaps it is part of the genius of childhood to integrate play and imagining into one seamless activity. A way in which the life of our minds and our bodies are in dialogue with each other. Or, as one child, Maggi, said to me: "*When I play it feels like you can't fall down. And it feels like the stars are carrying me.*" (p. 8) (emphasis added)

In Figures 1.9 and 1.10, teacher candidates exhibit innovative problem-solving through collaborative playful design of costumes and dance. As de-

FIGURE 1.9.   Teacher Candidates perform, "I Promise" Community Performance to End Homelessness, 2009.

FIGURE 1.10. Teacher Candidates perform Dance of Possibility, Community Performance to End Homelessness, 2009.

picted in the images, the teacher candidates are illuminated with "creative confidence" (Kelley & Kelley, 2012). The symbolic messages artfully captured the elementary school audience's hearts and minds. Aesthetic symbolism raised awareness of homelessness in the local community.

Picasso often expressed that his greatest creative achievements were the result of playful action when working with parts of the whole and experimenting with various mediums. Picasso stated,

> Every child is an artist. The problem is how to remain an artist once he grows up. . . The artist is a receptacle for the emotions that come from all over the place: from the sky, from the earth, from a scrap of paper, from a passing shape, from a spider's web . . . The purpose of art is washing the dust of daily life off our souls. (as cited in Bergland, 2007, p. 318)

Picasso was one of the most playful artists of the 20th century. His constant exploration and creative play revealed and shaped new forms of art and ways of perceiving the world. One of Picasso's most famous murals, *Guernica* (1937; see Figure 1.11), was studied by teacher candidates as an entry point to dissecting NCLB and the testing mandates (see also Chapter 5, "Seed of Unmasking").

Doyle (2013) explains how Arnheim's (2006) study of Guernica impacted her creative vision. Doyle explained,

> Arnheim's [study] on "Guernica" led us through Picasso's visual thinking from the initial sketch through all the working drawings to the final mural. We saw very concretely how changes in form, often the same element in a

FIGURE 1.11. *Guernica* by Pablo Picasso (1937).

new configuration, created new meanings. In an early compositional study, a large bull jumps across the center of the sketch surveying the desolation of a doubled over horse and a prone warrior below. The bull is alone, above the fray. Later, Picasso gives the central place to a wounded, agonized but defiantly rearing horse. The bull has been moved to the side, an observer. The characters in the mural are no longer prone, but tend to the vertical, actively appealing to the bull. And the bull himself is no longer alone, but part of a configuration with a horror-stricken mother and her dead baby. "Formal considerations," Arnheim (1962) wrote, "lead to solutions that are always more than formal. When an object had to be moved, the formal change entailed a change in meaning. (p. 133)

This playful nature of artists is an innovative process that play promotes. Like Picasso, researchers have suggested the profound effects of play and the significant contributions of playful actions on our cognitive, physical, social, and emotional well-being. From the earliest of human stages, we are drawn to play in search of meaning to life's many mysteries. Through a visual thinking process (Arnheim, 2006), teacher candidates became the tortured figures in the mural and spontaneously portrayed the child's emotional imagination under attack when facing 3 weeks of testing. The bomb that fell on Guernica was used as a metaphor for the bomb of testing that falls on the hearts and minds of children and teachers every school year.

Play and the Development of Pre-service Teachers Sense of Self

Golinkoff, Hirsh-Pasek, and Singer (2006) assert that, "playful pedagogy supports social, emotional and academic strengths while instilling a love of learning" (p. 4). If we want our teacher leaders to be collaborative, innovative, critical, culturally responsive, and communicative then play must be at the epicenter of our preservice teachers' community experience. According to Hirsh-Pasek, Golinkoff, Berk, and Singer (2009),

> Based on classroom research, we argue that free play and playful learning, as exemplified in developmentally appropriate pedagogy, improves children's school readiness in two broad domains: cognitive skills (literacy, math, problem solving, imagination, and creativity) and social and emotional skills. (p. 18)

Professors in teacher preparation may, without hesitation, identify the importance of implementing playful tasks and problem solving in teacher preparation methods courses. One teacher candidate, Travis, stated,

> Coming together as a class is not always easy. We all have different personalities and different beliefs on education, but as we learn about becoming effective teachers I remember John Dewey and how children learn through doing. I was lucky enough to work with two other classmates acting out homelessness in America. We role-played a social worker, a teacher, and a homeless child. By playing the teaching and constructively learning about the child who is without a home and being able to take something they hold dear, like a toy or we used a stick, and bring it into the learning development of a child is exactly what I take from my teacher preparation course. It is not all about teaching to the test, it is about engaging children so that they want to learn and learning by play is one of the great ways children can learn and become impacted by your teaching.

How will teachers understand the importance of play for children if they have not experienced the play paradigm themselves and its impact on their own creative and innovative skills and sense of self as a teacher? Will they know how to unmask the playful child within? "When students actively participate in a constructive learning environment, they play with concepts in a deeper, more meaningful context" (Ortlieb, 2010, p. 243). Ortlieb goes on to assert the importance of play, stating,

> If this spirit to play is so prevalent among most children, it should be harnessed within all classroom environments. . . How can teachers create such an environment where students can play, learn, and build knowledge on subject content all at the same time? The method is rather simple in form, but its implementation takes practice to reach its potential. In science class, children act as scientists—observing, formulating, testing, and making surprising discoveries. "This is what stimulates mental neural development, and without it you don't get that development" (The National Institute for Play, 2000). Through reflective play, the mind becomes expanded, enriched, and experienced. (pp. 243–244)

Teachers need to be trained to implement play into their curriculum activities. Hewes (2007) asserts that

> Creating environments where children can learn through play is not a simple thing to do consistently and well . . . The role of the adult is critical . . . The adult designs an environment with hands-on, concrete materials that encourage exploration, discovery, manipulation and active engagement of children. (as cited in Ferrara, Hirsh-Pasek, & Golinkoff, 2009, p. 14)

Reflecting Hewes' suggestion of crafting a playful space, Rudolph Steiner's (1919) Waldorf School environment methods (Barnes & Lyons, 1986) revealed that education is in fact an art wherein teachers are very creative and thoughtful in designing the learning environment. By contrast, our students have been in environments in local suburbs surrounding our university where an increasing percentage of parents have felt the need to hold their children hostage inside in front of video games and television or enrolled in organized sports and such due to the fear of predators. Thus, our teacher candidates that were born in 1990 have not had the experience of running free, playing outside, or even building tree forts in the woods like previous generations (Louve, 2005). It is our responsibility to teach our teacher candidates what play is, as seen in Figure 1.12. They need to first know how it feels to play, to experience how this impacts divergent thinking, and understand the ways to implement play into strategies within their lessons. Once this occurs, teacher candidates can understand how to utilize play as a strategy to promote cognition and a deeper epistemological approach to what one knows, one has experienced.

FIGURE 1.12.   Pre-service teachers engaged in aesthetic play, 2009.

*Transfer of Aesthetic Play Into the Classroom by a Preservice
Teacher*

Michelle, a former teacher candidate, describes her personal experience
with play in an elementary methods class. As a final tribute to the potential
and power within our KIVA of play, this case study focused on how implementing play into a methods course impacted her skills and beliefs as a
future teacher. She explains in detail what it was like for her to walk into her
undergraduate methods course and find her professor dressed as a mermaid. In addition, Michelle describes how she transferred her experience
to her student teaching by inviting the principal and curriculum specialists.
They were so impressed with Michelle's innovative skills to impact literacy
for English language learners that they offered her a job before her student
teaching was completed.

MICHELLE'S STORY

It was 2005, fall semester. I was running a little late to class. I thought that I
would just sneak in without being noticed and without interrupting the lecture that would have already started. As I walked in the room I found the
desks in a large circle and my classmates peering down at something on the
floor. To my surprise I found a mermaid lying there. She had beautiful green
fins and her whole body seemed to sparkle. Her voice was soft and kind. I was
completely overwhelmed with feelings of curiosity, excitement, fear and wonder as I found my way to an empty desk. This was the first time I met Abigail.
This was the moment that changed my teaching career forever. This was the
beginning of my thrilling adventure.

After this moment, my life in my ED322 class changed. We no longer an-
ticipated long, boring lectures about what would make a great teacher, but
began to live and learn how our strengths and weaknesses would make each
one of us the best teachers we could be. We became characters from our
favorite storybooks and created poetry by using our senses. As a class and as
individuals we took the risks that a teacher should take and we also took the
risks that we would soon expect from our students. We were able to feel, make
connections, and think on higher levels. We had the opportunity to put our
hearts, our souls, our fears, and our excitement out in the open without fear
of rejection or judgment. This was the environment that Dr. Clark/Abigail
created for us and inspired us with.

A year later I began my student teaching in Hartford. I was pleasantly surprised to find out that the professor who had inspired me the most was now
my supervisor. I knew that Dr. Clark would give me the support and understanding that I needed. Soon into the semester, Dr. Clark and I began to plan
a writing unit I had in mind using fairytales. She was wonderful to plan with.
She allowed me to voice my ideas and never thought anything was too big

or too over the top. She added her input and gave me constructive criticism when needed. By the end of our planning session we were both very excited and could not wait to get started. However, at this time, I could never have imagined what this unit would have in store for everyone involved.

I began my planning by choosing six fairytale stories that I wanted to focus on. These included *Little Red Riding Hood, Goldilocks and the Three Bears, Cinderella, Snow White and the Seven Dwarfs, The Three Little Pigs,* and *Jack and the Beanstalk.* These six books and their characters were the basis for the entire unit. The goal of the unit was for the students to create books that would include six letters. The letters would be a correspondence between two fairytale characters. I knew this was not going to be an easy task and would demand the highest level of thinking and organization. To help me with this process I spoke to the school librarian and asked if she would read some of these stories during their library time. By doing this she would be exposing the students to the stories that they may not have heard or could not remember. She was thrilled to be involved in the unit. Then, I spoke to the art teacher and asked if she would be willing to help the students with their illustrations that would be included in the book. She designed a unit on character drawing and used the books/characters that I had already picked out. This was only the beginning of the countless hours of planning that I had to do to make this unit successful.

To kick off the unit, I wrote a letter to the entire class from the fairytale characters. (See letter for details.) This letter asked the students to help the characters who were in need of advice. They were to write a letter back if they were willing to help. If they did a "magic mailbox" would appear in their classroom. After hearing the letter and who it was from the students were bubbling with excitement. They demanded that we write a letter right away. During this lesson we spoke about the format in which a letter is written and made a poster of this. We also agreed to help. The next day a "magic mailbox" appeared in the room along with individual "magic mailboxes" for each student. There was also another letter addressed to the whole class that explained what was going to happen next. (See letter for details.)

The next day letters appeared in each of the student's individual "magic mailboxes." These letters were specifically addressed to a student from one of the characters. That day the students responded to the letters and this began a correspondence between the two. From then on the students became very involved in the lives of the characters. They felt that they were friends and they would give them advice.

Now that the class felt that they had a connection with the characters I began to introduce the book. We began with a story map that would layout their six letters. I realize now that I may have moved too quickly with this process. Since I had them thinking about all six letters at once I noticed that they, and I, became overwhelmed and frustrated with the project easily. However, with modifications and individual help we were able to work through it.

During the next few weeks we worked on the books while writing the personal letters as morning work. I would begin each writer's workshop with a "mini-lesson" that focused on perspective and point-of-view. I would read stories such as *The True Story of the Three Little Pigs* (which is from the wolf's perspective) and *The Beanstalk Incident* (which is from the giant's perspective). During the writing portion students would write their letters as I conferenced with individual students. I also had the help of my cooperating teacher who focused on editing with students and my paraprofessional who worked with our special education students. As students finished their writing they were able to add their illustrations and then type their letters on the computers in the classroom.

To keep the characters alive I had some of the characters show up in the classroom from time to time. I had Goldilocks come in at night to check their desks to see if they were "too messy" or "just right." She left a letter to the class and a note on each student's desk to let them know what she thought. (See letter for details.) I also had the seven dwarfs appear around the classroom to see how the class was doing. This was followed by another letter to the whole class. (See letter for details.) This kept the students excited, interested and thinking.

As exciting as this may all have been the best was still to come. While planning with Dr. Clark we had decided to involve her new [elementary education methods class of preservice teachers]. I wrote them a letter asking them to become the characters that the students were writing to and writing as. Fortunately, they agreed and I gave them specific instructions of what I needed and expected from them. On the big day it seemed like any Wednesday afternoon and I was bringing the students to art class. Little did they know the surprises that were in store. As they entered the art room the lights had been turned off so all they could see were a dozen figures sitting around the tables with their backs turned. They all began to whisper in excitement. When the lights were flicked on they began to realize what was happening. As they inched forward, in a mass of anticipation and fear, the characters turned around to show their true faces. The realization and excitement sparkled in their wandering eyes. As a whole, they could not figure out what to do next.

Everyone was there to witness this amazing spectacle: other teachers, the principal, the vice principal, special education teachers, and even one of the pre school classes. My students were so proud because they knew this was all for them no matter who came in. First, I had the characters introduce themselves. Then I handed out the student's books (that magically appeared in the art room) and sent them off to a table of characters. After the students shared their books I had them rotate to another table of characters. They rotated about four times to meet with the different characters.

The most exhilarating part of this whole experience was the conversations the students were having with the characters. They spoke to them as if they were long time friends. They gave the characters advice and asked them questions about their lives. Some of them even stood up to the Big Bad Wolf in defense of The Three Little Pigs and Little Red Riding Hood. In the end, we set up a panel so the students could ask the characters any questions they had and, as asked, the ED322 students stayed in perfect character. Everyone involved left that day with a feeling of inspiration, wonder and success.

As I look back now at the entire experience it still feels overwhelming. I sometimes cannot believe that it all happened. It all came full circle from when I was in ED322, to teaching this unit, to involving the new ED322 and now becoming a fifth grade teacher. In every aspect there were risks, fears, curiosity and excitement. My students, my co-workers, my classmates, the new ED322 class; we all had to think on every level from low to high for this, and for us, to be successful. I hope that not only did I inspire my students to become better writers but that I also inspired the ED322 students to become better teachers. I know that I could have administered this unit more effectively but as a teacher I can learn from my mistakes. I wonder now if it is possible to go above and beyond what I have already done with this class. However, the point that remains is if you believe in yourself and what you can do anything is possible.

Michelle
5th Grade Teacher
March 2007

With thanks to all those who helped, supported, and were involved in this magical adventure!

Storybook Character Project Letters

Letter #1:

November 7, 2006

Dear Mrs. H's and Ms. J's Third Grade Class,

Greetings from Fairytale Land! We are writing you this urgent letter because some of us need your help. We are having some troubles and could really use advice.

We do not like to be seen in human form so we will communicate only through letters. However, always keep an eye out for us around your school because we may be checking up on you.

If you decide to help us, a magic mailbox will appear in your classroom. Please send us a letter with your decision as soon as possible.

Sincerely,

Cinderella   Prince Charming

Fairy Godmother   Evil Step-Mother and Step-Sisters

Little Red Riding Hood   Big Bad Wolf

The Three Little Pigs   Jack

The Giant   Snow White

     The Seven Dwarfs   Goldilocks

The Three Bears   Wicked Queen

Letter #2:

November 8, 2006

Dear Ms. J., Mrs. H. and students,

Thank you so very much for replying to our letter so quickly. We are so grateful that you are all willing to help us. All of us are eager to hear from you.

Your magic mailbox is all set up in your classroom. You should use this mailbox to send your letters to us. You will only receive mail in the mailbox if it is addressed to the whole class. We have also included mini magic mailboxes for each of you. This is where you will receive your personal mail from us. Please, put your name on it, decorate it and leave it on top of your desk.

Since we are so excited to begin writing to you we held a meeting last night to brainstorm how we should begin this exciting adventure. We decided it would be best if we got to know you first. We came up with a few questions that we would like to ask. These questions are written in your own personal letter from one of us. We hope you can respond quickly.

Thank you again for starting this exciting adventure with us.

Sincerely,

Cinderella   Prince Charming

Fairy Godmother   Evil Step-Mother and Step-Sisters

     Little Red Riding Hood   Big Bad Wolf

The Three Little Pigs   Jack

The Giant   Snow White

     The Seven Dwarfs   Goldilocks

The Three Bears   Wicked Queen

Letter #3:

November 13, 2006

Dear Mrs. H's and Ms. J's Class,

Over the weekend I was having dinner with the desk fairy and she told me she checks your desks to see if they are messy. She is going on vacation for a few weeks and was worried that your desks would be a disaster by the time she got back. So, I volunteered to check your desks for her. I have left notes on each of your desks. If they are not just right you must clean them out during free time.

Thank you,

Goldilocks

The Power of Play in Practice for Future Teachers

Michelle is one of many teacher candidates that went on to become a successful innovative teacher. The *Seed of Play* was planted in her heart when she was a teacher candidate, and she was inspired to continue methods of play with her children. That day in 2005, when Michelle met Abigail the mermaid, will forever be etched on part of Michelle's memory, as it inspired a teaching repertoire in which play is critical for children. The sacred spiral of the mustard seed of play, from preservice to in-service teachers continues to grow. Michelle is currently director of math curriculum in a local urban magnet school.

As portrayed in Michelle's case study, she quickly discovered as a teacher utilizing aesthetic methods that "In every aspect there were risks, fears, curiosity and excitement." She also witnessed the joy that comes into the learning environment, the KIVA, when imagination becomes personal and communal at the same time through play. As Michelle stated, "The students were bubbling with excitement." She concluded that as the Fairytale event unfolded for the third graders and teacher candidates, "everyone involved left that day with a feeling of inspiration, wonder and success." Who could ask for a more intrinsic experience with literature than through aesthetic play methodology? Michelle looked back after the day ended and reflected, "I could never have imagined what this unit would have in store for everyone involved." This is a beautiful and exemplary example of the power of play as aesthetic pedagogy is enacted with children and teacher candidates.

Through the *Seed of Play*, a wellspring of hope in the child and teacher gushes forth as their relationship builds in trust. The *Seed of Play* leads to the development of all the other seeds as hope inspires the child's voice to be released, building on inner awareness, intrapersonal intelligence, change, and unmasking fears in both the teacher and child. Play inspired hope is critical in a child's learning. Teachers must become ambassadors of play and hope. A greater spirituality of knowing develops through play as "learning becomes personal . . . , communal . . . , reciprocal . . . and transformative" (Palmer, 1993, pp. 1–2).

In the next seed chapter, the concept of hope in action is unmasked within the KIVA (Kindness, Innovation, Voice, and Action). Emotional imagination when revealed by a child seeks a place of trust in the sacred learning space (KIVA) in which a teacher, through wisdom, has sown like a carefully treasured garden.

REFERENCES

Arnheim, R. (1969). *Visual thinking*. Berkeley: University of California Press.

Arnheim, R. (1989). *Thoughts on art education*. Los Angeles, CA: Getty Center for Education in the Arts.

Arnheim, R. (2006). *The genesis of a painting: Picasso's Guernica*. Los Angeles, CA: University of California Press. (Original work published 1962)

Barnes, H., & Lyons, N. (1986). *Education as an art: The Rudolf Steiner Method*. Great Barrington, MA.: Association of Waldorf Schools of North America.

Bateson, G. (1987). *Steps to an ecology of mind: Collected essays in anthropology, psychiatry, evolution, and epistolomology*. Northvale, NJ; London, UK: Jason Aronson. (Original work published 1972)

Bergland, C. (2007). *The athlete's way*. New York, NY: St. Martin's Press.

Blank, W. (2001). *The 108 skills of natural leaders*. New York, NY: AMACON.

Bowers, C. A. (2006). *Transforming environmental education: Making the renewal of the cultural and environmental commons the focus of educational reform*. Retrieved from https://scholarsbank.uoregon.edu/jspui/handle/1794/3070

Brockway, A. (2013). *Anasazi Kivas*. Retrieved from http://www.abrock.com/InterimReports/Kivas/Kivas.html

Brown, J. (2011, February 25). Digital media: New learners of the 21st century: PBS. *Institute of Play*. Retrieved from http://www.instituteofplay.org/press

Brown, S. (2009). *Serious play*. Talk presented at the Art Design Conference, Pasadena, CA. Retrieved from *http://www.youtube.com/watch?v=HHwXlcHcTHc*

Chesterton, G. (1908). All things considered: "Oxford from without." *The American Chesterton Society*. Retrieved from http://www.chesterton.org/

Clark, B. (2005a). Moral imagination and art: Echoes from a child's soul. *Forum on Public Policy: Issue Child Psychology, 1*(4), 428–446.

Clark, B. (2005b). *Moral imagination and art: Echoes from a child's soul* (Doctoral dissertation). University of Hartford, Connecticut. Retrieved May 10, 2012, from Dissertations & Theses: Full Text. (Publication No. AAT 315 7797).

Clark, B. (2009a). Aesthetic education and masked emotions: A model for emancipatory teacher preparation. *Critical Questions in Education, 1*(1), 40–50. Retrieved from http://education.missouristate.edu/AcadEd/75534.htm

Clark, B. (2009b). Mustard seeds: A personal search for "Ahimsa" (The truth of non-violence). *Closing the Circle Exhibition*. B. Clark & M. Cipriano (Artists). New Britain, CT: New Britain Commission on the Arts.

Csikszentmihalyi, M. (1996). *Creativity: Flow and the psychology of discovery and invention*. New York, NY: HarperCollins.

Desaulniers, M. (2009). *Deep play and spirituality*. Retrieved from http://suite101. com/article/deep-play-and-spirituality-a100998

Dewey, J. (1980). *Art and experience*. New York, NY: Macmillan.

Doyle, C. (2013). Visions of the creative process: What Rudolf Arnheim taught me. *Sarah Lawrence College Magazine*. Retrieved from http://www.slc.edu/magazine/krl/arnheim.html

Eisner, E. W. (1994). *The educational imagination.* Upper Saddle River, NJ: Prentice Hall.

Eisner, E. W. (2002). *The arts and the creation of mind.* New Haven, CT: Yale University Press.

Elkind, D. (2007). *The power of play: Learning what comes naturally.* Cambridge, MA: Da Capo.

Erikson, E. H. (1950). *Childhood and society.* New York, NY: Norton.

Ferrara, K., Hirsh-Pasek, K., & Golinkoff, R. M. (2009). Building blocks for learning. *The wisdom of play: How children learn to make sense of the world.* Retrieved from http://www.communityplaythings.com/resources/.../WisdomOfPlay.pdf

Fox, M. (2004). *Creativity: Where the divine and human meet.* New York, NY: Penquin.

Frankel, V. (1984). *Man's search for meaning.* New York, NY: Pocket Books.

Freire, P. (1998). *Pedagogy of freedom: Ethics, democracy, and civic courage.* New York, NY: Rowman & Littlefield.

French, J. J., & Clark, B. A. (2012). Revitalizing a spiritual compassionate community commons in educational culture. *Religion and Education, 39*(1), 93–108.

Gardner, H. (1994). *The arts and human development.* New York, N&: Basic. (Original work published 1973)

Golinkoff, R. M., Hirsh-Pasek, K., & Singer, D. G. (2006). Play = learning: A challenge for parents and educators. *Play Equals Learning, 1*(1), 3–12.

Graham, M. (1991). *Blood memory.* New York, NY: Washington Square.

Greene, M. (2001). *Variations on a blue guitar: The Lincoln Center Institute lectures on aesthetic education.* New York, NY: Teachers College Press.

Hammarskjöld, D. (1964). *Markings* (L. Sjöberg & W. H. Auden, Trans.). New York, NY: Knopf.

Hammarskjöld, D. (Artist). (2012). *Haiku poem.* Retrieved from http://haikulines.blogspot.com/2011/03/haiku-of-former-un-general-secretary.html

Hanh, T. N. (1991). *Peace is every stop: The path of mindfulness in everyday life.* New York, NY: Bantam.

Hewes, J. (2007). *Several perspectives on children's play: Scientific reflections for practitioners.* Philadelphia, PA: Garant.

Highwater, J. (1982). *The primal mind: Vision and reality in Indian America.* New York, NY: Meridian

Hino, Y. (2003). Restriction and individual expression in the "Play Activity/Zokei Asobui." *Journal of Aesthetic Education, 37*(4), 19–26. Retrieved from http://www.jstor.org/stabel/3527330

Hirsh-Pasek, K., Golinkoff, R., Berk, L., & Singer, D. (2009). *A mandate for playful learning in preschool: Applying the scientific evidence.* New York, NY: Oxford University Press.

Horton, M., & Freire, P. (1990). *We make the road by walking: Conversations on education and social change.* Philadelphia, PA: Temple University Press.

Kelley, T., & Kelley, D. (2012). Reclaim your creative confidence. *Harvard Business Review, 90*(12), 115.

Lewis, R. (2009). Imagination. The wisdom of play. How children learn to make sense of the world. Retrieved from http://www.communityplaythings.com/resources/.../WisdomOfPlay.pdf

Louve, R. (2005). *Last child in the woods: Saving our children from nature-deficit disorder.* Chapel Hill, NC: Algonquin.

Miller, E., & Almon, J. (2009). Crisis in the kindergarten: Why children need to play in school. *Alliance for Childhood.* Retrieved from http://www.thestrong.org/sites/default/files/play-studies/Crisis_in_Kindergarten.pdf

Montessori, M. (1912). *The Montessori method.* New York, NY: Frederick A. Stokes.

National Association of Music Merchants (NAMM). (2013). New poll reveals stifling imagination in schools underlies innovation and skills deficit. *National Association of Music Merchants.* Retrieved from http://www.namm.org/news/press-releases/new-poll-reveals-stifling-imagination-schools-unde

O'Donohue, J. (1997). *Anam cara: A book of Celtic wisdom.* New York, NY: Harper Collins.

Ortlieb, E. T. (2010). The pursuit of play within the curriculum. *Journal of Instructional Psychology, 37*(3), 241–246.

Palmer, P. (1993). *The violence of our knowledge: Toward a spirituality of higher education.* Paper presented at the Michael Keenan Memorial Lecture, the 7th Lecture, Berea College, KY. Retrieved from http://www.kairos2.com/palmer_1999.htm

Perkins, D. (1994). *The intelligent eye: Learning to think by looking at art.* Santa Monica, CA: Getty Center for Education in the Arts.

Piaget, J. (1951). *Play, dreams, and imitation in childhood.* New York, NY: Norton.

Picasso, P. (1907). *Les demoiselles d'Avignon* [Painting]. New York, NY: Museum of Modern Art.

Picasso, P. (1937). *Guernica* [Painting]. Retrieved from http://upload.wikimedia.org/wikipedia/en/7/74/PicassoGuernica.jpg).

Pollack, J. (1948) *Composition (white, black, blue and red on white)* New Orleans, LA: New Orleans Museum of Art.

Standing, E. M. (1962). *Maria Montessori: Her life and work.* New York, NY: New American Library. (Original work published 1957)

Sternberg, R., & Lubart, T. (1993). Creative giftedness: A multivariate investment approach. *Gifted Child Quarterly, 37*(1), 7–15.

Tolle, E. (1999). *The power of now. A guide to spiritual enlightenment.* Novato, CA: Namaste /New World Library.

Tolle, E. (2013). *Eckhart on manifestation.* Retrieved from http://www.eckharttolle.com/newsletter/Eckhart-Tolle-on-Manifestation

Vygotsky, L. S. (1986). *Thought and language* (rev. ed.). Cambridge, MA: MIT Press.

Walonick, D. (1993). Promoting human creativity. *StatPac Survey Research Library.* Retrieved from http://www.statpac.org/walonick/creativity.htm

Wardle, F. (2003). *Introduction to early childhood education: A multidimensional approach to child-centered care and learning.* Boston, MA: Allyn & Bacon.

CHAPTER 2

THE SEED OF HOPE

Seed of Hope Painting
(Clark, 2009b)

We have to make truth and nonviolence not matters for mere individual practice but for practice by groups and communities and nations. That at any rate is my dream. I shall live and die in trying to realize it. My faith helps me to discover truths every day.

—Gandhi

If a child is to keep alive his inborn sense of wonder, he needs the companionship of at least one adult who can share it, rediscovering with him the joy, excitement, and mystery of the world we live in.

—Rachel Carson

Don't think about making art, just get it done. Let everyone else decide if it's good or bad. Whether they love it or hate it. While they are deciding, make more art.

—Andy Warhol

Hearts and Minds Without Fear: Unmasking the Sacred in Teacher Preparation, pages 37–62.

You are in a circle of strangers. Everyone is given a drum. There is no wrong or right way of creating your sound. If you hit your drum in the circle, you might think, "I've never been in a drum circle before, but perhaps there is something unique that I can offer to it." Everyone is going to be making a different sound for whatever reason, context, or being. There are many different valid ideas and there are many different ways to interpret these ideas. Whatever the medium, each person will view the aesthetic paradigm in a different way. Give everyone a paintbrush, or present an event and voice ideas on the basis of your own perceptions. Watch and listen to one another.

The aesthetic invites a myriad of perceptions and choices when examining social and ecological issues. Within the community circle, social imagination is revealed through the aesthetic by celebrating instantaneous diverse possibility. When we come together in a way wherein our diversity and experience are shared and valued as part of something great, we begin to self-actualize what our potential is, who we are, and what we contribute to the health and compassion within the community. Where and when we feel valued, free, and loved, we feel hope (Glasser, 2010). Hope emerges from having many choices in the learning community: The drums have all the rhythms, the brushes have all the strokes, the rainforest has all the cures. This is not a liberal view; it is a hopeful one—it is seeing the potential of the aesthetic and is critical to our very existence. These choices are found naturally in creation. Because of the power of our imagination, we find hope and feel hope by the very act of creation and through our relationships with nature and with each other (Berry, 1999).

The limitlessness of the aesthetic is fundamental to nature. In children especially there are an infinite set of possibilities, and there are endless ways to view and interact with those possibilities. As was illuminated in Chapter 1, "The Seed of Play," children possibilize everything inherently. Children go forward with their hearts and emotional imaginations triggered to celebrate each drop of the life-giving force that surrounds them. Children are able to possibilize in their actions constantly because they are allowing their hearts to act with minimal interference from their discerning minds. Teacher candidates must learn how to discover the vast creative possibilities that children hold in their hearts in order to address this in their planning and design of learning activities.

Although we often peg children as "irrational," when we watch them we marvel at how they pick up objects (like a drum for instance) and proceed _reads into_

to move and interact with it in ways that an adult may never imagine or try (Wardle, 2003). Through play, children discover a sense of hope and self-actualize their talent, learning to express their ideas to the world. The expression of creative ideas within a spiritual community is a force of action that expresses our love of creation and for one another (Nouwen, 1983). Hope is revealed in the creative act of compassion whereby we can serve one another with humility for a greater good (Nouwen, 1983, pp. 48–49). "Do not model yourselves on the behavior of the world around you, but let your behavior change, modeled by your new mind" (Romans, 12:2, as cited in Nouwen, 1983, p. 49). → _open-ended choices geared towards autonomy_

In order to maintain hope, we must remember how to feel comfortable with dissonance, and with being messy when engaged in the creative process, rather than run to a finite set of answers we've been told are correct. The teacher as artist is a guide who asks children questions to delve deeper into the process while maintaining the disposition to reflect, analyze, synthesize, and evaluate multiple solutions. This allows new ideas to be created that at one time did not exist. To remember, play must be practiced with one another. Helping us to remember a child's mindset, teacher candidates can begin to understand the purity of children at play through the meditative process to prevent thoughts of the secular world from getting in the way of our hearts' intent. The aesthetic medium, nonentrenched on the low-level material pleasure plains, moves with great difficulty through a tough process of evaluation that is inherent within the spiritual, emotional, and visionary domains of an individual.

As described by Csikszentmihalyi (1996), creativity must be perceived as necessary for the future of our world. Csikszentmihalyi would agree that the aesthetic permits a tricky paradox that fools the mind just enough to let the heart shine through and that perhaps may be why the creative process is so misunderstood. Throughout history and timeless cultures, we know the aesthetic holds universal mediums and messages that remind us that we are human first. The creative process is inherent in humans and is characteristic of creative peoples from all walks of life: biologists, physicists, artists, and politicians alike; capturing creative energy defines whether or not we "have lived a full and creative life" (Csikszentmihalyi, 1996, pp. 342, 348, 372). We have a great hunger for hope, love, power, and the freedom to feel, weep, and laugh. The aesthetic portal triggers creativity first through our spirit-hearts before our mind-brains can interfere. And within these multiple aesthetic shapes and forms of expression, we realize how we are all connected to each other in the human experience.

Educators must nurture and create an aesthetic relationship of possibility, so children can feel trust in the teacher who is guiding them through the creative process with compassion and love for their beautiful potential. Together, teacher and children celebrate individual voice. The greatest teachers *believe* in possibility. They see children as mysteries from nature and as incredible symbols of hope for our future because they go into the heart-mindset of the child. They are the gardeners who children love because they are able to step into the common ground of the unknown. They know anything can be possible if it is given the sustenance to grow. Seeing no limit to what they or the children can accomplish, they keep their eyes open for opportunities. They create spaces and experiences in order to observe themselves and children. They have faith in themselves and in children because they are looking beyond, creating questions that will keep the process going (Palmer, 1993; Zajonc, 2006).

But what if you were rejected from the drum circle after you hit your drum, or in a more literal sense, asked to leave the classroom and denied learning because you did not bring in your homework. What happens to hope when a child is homeless, segregated, excluded, or dismissed from the experience? Currently children are often removed from field trips to plays, performing on stage, attending museum exhibits due to falsely penalized behavior at school. The child's ideas are rejected, excluded, locked down, and their choices and possibilities stolen. The aesthetic experience becomes only for the select few. Everything a child might have wanted to do or discover through that particular aesthetic portal of experience would be negated—the heart of the child is placed behind institutional bars. Unvalued and unloved, the child's unique and individual way of access to learning would be denied.

Often in teacher preparation and in schools, some individuals believe that any attempts at integrating the arts will be scrutinized and judged and could possibly fail even before beginning, because we know the *status-quo* will always say that education must be done a certain way. This is significant to our book as we present a methodology that would be impossible to achieve under a technical behaviorist approach. Even those around us who have been allowed to stay in the box because they did it "correctly" have self-limited their choice and may go on to use their false sense of accomplishment-ego to limit others' potential (Glasser, 2010; Merton, 1951). In this, hope is lost.

A child becomes lost within a web of institutional school structures that does not place compassion at the whole. Compassion means to suffer with another, to deeply feel their despondency; to understand and to stay present with and for one another. Compassion is the "creative inspiration" in and through the life experience and is especially critical for teachers in order to understand each child (Bhuchung, 2012). Hope is found in the very act of creativity as creativity is directly linked to compassionate action. According to Bhuchung,

> Through creative imagination within the state of one's meditation, one gives birth to compassion. Compassion may then proliferate in various creative ac-

tivities and art. Compassion can give rise to a way of being and an art of living filled with a desire to innovate ways to make a difference in the world for oneself and others. In modern times, the lives and works of His Holiness [Dalai Lama] and Mother Teresa, among others, come easily to mind when we think of the link between compassion and creativity. (p. 164)

In our teacher preparation methods courses, themes were investigated through the arts and aesthetic. As illustrated and explained throughout the seed chapters in this book, a garden of creative compassion in action was cultivated between the relationships of our teacher candidates and children. The qualities of creative compassionate action need to be a critical aspect of a teacher's beliefs so that the class community fosters hope and well-being for one another. No child is lost and no child should exist in a daily cycle of despair in school.

We have countless examples of teachers and administrators who never developed creative compassion, and they as members of institutions of education attack children's creativity, bullying their spirits. When our children do not see their ways in the world as valued, they will reject what is being taught, or worse, reject themselves as being "less than." Fundamental to this loss is the loss of hope that no one believes in them. It is this constant and consistent rejection and exclusion from the dominant school culture (Cullum, 1971; Delpit, 1995; Kohl, 1994) that over time gradually corrodes and diminishes children's capacity to learn and express themselves. Noncreative behavior is learned: in just 5 years of schooling, a kindergartener's once-vibrant divergent thinking can diminish drastically (Land & Jarman, 1992; Robinson, 2010)[1]. When imagination exercise slows, ideas lie repressed and submerged; the potential solutions to the world's social and ecological ills are laid dormant. When children lose hope in themselves, in a very real way, we have lost our future. As depicted in this chapter's beginning metaphor, the drum is never touched because of fear, and we all collectively lose.

In teacher education programs with our future teachers, as in schools with our children, fear can continue to dampen, stifle, and suppress who and how future teachers come into being, which further jeopardizes the possibility of creative compassion and hope for children and our world.

---

[1] In his presentation on creative learning, Sir Ken Robinson (2010) describes divergent thinking: "Divergent thinking isn't a synonym, but it's an essential capacity for creativity. It's the ability to see lots of possible answers to a question, lots of possible ways of interpreting a question, to think . . . laterally, to think not just in linear or convergent ways, to see multiple answers, not one!" In the related study that Robinson references (Land & Jarman, 1992), of 1,600 kindergarteners tested for divergent thinking abilities, 98% scored at the genius level. For 10-year-old children tested, the percentage at genius level dropped to 32%. And 5 years later, the percentage for 15-year-olds was at 10%. When 200,000 adults were given the same divergent thinking test, only 2% tested at the genius level.

UNMASKING
HOPE

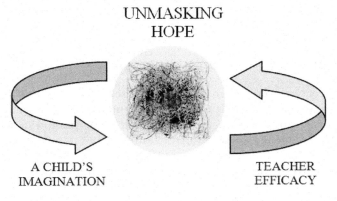

A CHILD'S
IMAGINATION

TEACHER
EFFICACY

FIGURE 2.1.   Unmasking Hope Concept Map.

"We are afraid of being looked at as if we can't become a teacher and we will fail," one teacher candidate confided to us. Limiting ourselves to a finite set, or excluding possible educator identities, many teacher educator program staff and their students have left the mystery, forgotten the imaginative realm, and so have come to believe that there is actually only *one* answer, only *one* way.

By contrast, as illustrated in this seed chapter, the aesthetic education paradigm can restore and revitalize our faith and hope in one another through the teaching belief of creative compassion and the hope that will blossom within the children we teach. Our students and the children we do teach have faith that we are going to support and hold them, that we will not let them fall, and that we will be there with them throughout the aesthetic process. And so, they hit the drum with joy and great expectations.

The above concept map (Figure 2.1) presents the *Seed of Hope*, which unmasks the teacher's ability to spark the imaginative realm within students, as the aesthetic evokes the senses. Before you read any further, meditate on the intricacies and visual threads depicted in the above seed painting (Clark, 2009b) that symbolizes the depth a teacher must explore as they journey beside the complex tapestries of a child's imagination—the source of hope. The multiple possibilities of expression fill the child with hope, as the teacher is not looking for the same answer, but many answers to one problem—many voices equal many realities. The teacher can provide examples of greatness through the arts, and this includes a sense of hope for greatness in children. As students absorb hope, they in turn transfer hope into the world around them. Children will gain a greater empathic awareness for others, which fosters a sense of efficacy in themselves. Hope grows as professors and teacher candidates' work within school communities creating a studio paradigm for and with children.

A Prerequisite Caveat: Recruiting Hope Into Teacher Education

Children get the aesthetic instantly. Although our teacher candidates carry the weight of shellacked layers of control from their own schooling and thus the dominant discourse that has inevitably formed their sense of what a teacher should be. When we first meet the teacher candidates that have been accepted into our program, the unmasking of the layers begins. As any experienced chef knows, before delving into any culinary masterpiece that has any hope of making a lasting impression, ideally the cook must acquire quality, raw, and fresh ingredients. If the only available ingredients are of low quality—making-do—time-tested skills and expertise could cull out the flavors. But imagine the taste if the chef were given opportunity to use their adept skills upon the highest quality food. So too in teacher education: To create greater sustainable hope for children, we must take very seriously the means by which we select the highest quality students; those whose flavors will flow into an alternative approach—in our case, the complexity of the aesthetic (see Chapter 4, "Seed of Change").

In our combined 15 years of experience in teacher preparation, the quality "raw" character content of teacher candidates has often come from students who have also been historically underrepresented as educators. From their unique life experiences, cultural perspectives, and talents, underrepresented college students are often not only the best match for the children they will be teaching in the future, they are also the teacher candidates who have been the ones to most readily embrace the aesthetic paradigm in our courses, as they already enthusiastically embrace the arts as an inherent part of their culture and their families' daily life. From our experience, traditionally marginalized students have been attracted to the aesthetic and actively seek enrollment in our courses because it opens up the hopeful possibility that may have been systematically denied them within their own schooling.

Through the protective compassionate imaginative spaces our KIVA aesthetic paradigm provides, and in seeing these spaces simultaneously come alive with the children we work with in schools, these few teacher candidates from diverse cultural backgrounds and life experiences are often the ones who take leadership opportunities to carry the day with their more mainstream classmates. As one such student proclaimed,

> I would love to be able to create that [aesthetic compassionate community] in my classroom, you know how we feel about each other and how we were so comfortable and how we love each other so much to this day and will con-

tinue down the line to rely on each other and call each other. I want that for my students. I want them to feel like that as well.

In a very real way, underrepresented teacher candidates, like the student above, are our co-teachers, co-creators and a critical component of our aesthetic practitioner dream team, whom we would hire to work with children in a heartbeat.

Unfortunately, at the behest of quality candidates for teacher preparation programs and future graduate practitioners for our children in schools, most of these students never even get the chance. On the basis of GPA, standardized test scores, and other culturally biased factors, schools of education continue to systematically weed out teacher candidates who have strengths and talents that would better enable them to transform themselves, their program, and future teaching practice (French, 2005; Zeichner, 2003). Culturally isolated, marginalized students' experience and identity perspectives often do not match the overwhelmingly showcased definition of who can become a teacher and what a teacher looks like (Delpit, 1995; hooks, 1995). As one our students confided to their classmates and us,

> There is one teacher type, and it's not me. Most of my university education classes are all white students. Most of the schools have all white teachers. Most of the children look just like me and then people in charge don't understand how we feel and why our culture is different and why our behaviors are different and why perhaps a young Latino male may wear a hat in the restaurant and it is seen as a sign of rudeness, when it is part of his cultural identity.

Preparation programs have not attracted or recruited students (Haberman & Post, 1992) who perhaps have not done well by a *status quo* system of learning, but as described above, are the very candidates that kindle hope within an aesthetic teacher education program. With this overwhelming lack of prerequisite quality "raw" character teacher candidate material, it makes it a particularly daunting task for programs to change preservice teachers' beliefs and attitudes that have been developed over a lifetime of school and societal sanction (Haberman, 1993; Sleeter, 2001). The arts provide for a culturally responsive culture in the classroom, and social stigma from mainstream discourse (Zeichner & Hoeft, 1996) is diminished as divergent thinking flourishes (Clark, 2005b, 2013). The aesthetic, through fostering a compassionate learning community, permits *all* our student's resiliency and *retention*, especially for our underrepresented students who may have been silenced within other mainstream education institutional contexts through their public school experiences.

Nevertheless, given *recruitment* disparities and consequences for the quality of teacher education programs and our present population of children in schools, one immediate need for teacher education in order to increase sustainable hope is to actively seek and implement alternative means of recruitment. Recruitment strategies and techniques designed specifically around the parameters of innovative teacher education programs (Smaller, 2007) can only attract and retain those special future educators who ultimately will foster genuine spaces of *hope* among the generations. These teacher candidates, quoted extensively throughout this seed chapter and book, can aptly address the real needs of our children's learning, and, in our program case, bring to life a KIVA studio paradigm in their schools and communities where the planted *Seeds of Hope* in their teacher preparation have a much better chance to be nurtured and to resiliently flourish.

Play Gives Rise to Hope

As already discussed previously in Chapter 1, "The Seed of Play," any individual who practices aesthetics in their lives for survival and/or as a profession knows that play is a necessary pathway to joyfully engage in creating new ideas. Ironically, in U.S. school culture, the withholding of play is used not only as a punishment but is perceived by some educators to be irritating, messy, and nonessential to the learning process. Contrasting with the U.S. perspective, other select world cultures perceive play to be a very powerful experiential pathway to change. For example, the term *cultural disobedience* (Bjørkvold, 1992) is used by Mans (2002) to describe the impact of "pamwe" or play in Nambia, Africa, known for the wealth of music, dance, and performance that is strongly ingrained in the youth for social change. Mans writes,

> Play is a state of mind, and in an atmosphere of play, an "important" person may be willing to be playful and to feel a temporary release from some of the behavioral restrictions of everyday social expectations—what Bjørkvold (1989:25) calls "cultural disobedience." (Mans, 2002, p. 55)

Mans research on play also highlights Arnaldi's (1995) position that play is serious and does impact moral values held within the community. Arnaldi (as cited in Mans, 2002, p. 54) states,

> Play is a reflexive activity, and, as most everyone would agree, what is communicated through play, while defined as an amusement, can be quite serious indeed. In the youth theatre, actors use masquerade, dance, music and song to comment upon moral values, the conditions of existence, and the ambiguity and indeterminacies that arise in social relationships in the everyday world of experience. (p. 22)

In other words, without undue distracting insult to self and society, while we play, we are released from restrictions, enabling us to understand what may be wrong and thinking what might be done instead. Similar to the effect we have with our teacher education students, Mans expounds on the benefits of aesthetic and arts education such as cohesion, interpersonal communication, self-growth, and inner awareness, not only for the child but for the teacher.

Amid a time of spiritual crisis, people are looking for hope in new solutions. The antiplay "business as usual" approaches of U.S. educational institutions are increasingly becoming entrenched in mediocrity and have ultimately impacted the quality of our schools and the well-being of our children. Alienation and estrangement from the natural world and one another has become a way of life. Families, communities, teachers, and children are reeling from the effects of a failed economy. More and more children come to school traumatized by homelessness, job loss, divorce, and drug abuse, encapsulated in a nonsustainable rat race that is supporting big business and controlled standardized educational assessments for profit. These societal ailments are present in schools each day and contribute to the alarming increase of aggression, anger, and violence in and around our schools that may subconsciously or knowingly leave teachers with a melancholy, sinking feeling that something is out of place. We feel that children's negative behaviors are expressive and a result of disconnect with the natural world and from the daily suppression and distraction from their inherent, creative, spiritual, compassionate, and innovative powers.

Regardless of our various attuned perceptions of our spiritual crisis, what is needed is a paradigm that does not avoid, skirt, or cast spirituality aside, but embodies, heals, nurtures, and utilizes our endless collective creative soul potential to 'do the right thing." We need a paradigm of hope that mobilizes would-be educators, community, and children to take action with a spiritually powerful morality that creates a better world while simultaneously refreshing our tired minds and restoring our aching hearts. In his article examining spiritual movements, Stuart Smithers (2012) considers what such an uprising might be:

> "A general uprising, as we see it, should be nebulous and elusive; its resistance should never materialize as a concrete body, otherwise the enemy can direct sufficient force at its core, crush it, and take many prisoners. When that happens, the people will lose heart and, believing that the issue has been decided and further efforts would be useless . . . On the other hand, there must be some concentration at certain points: The fog must thicken and form a dark and menacing cloud out of which a bolt of lightning will strike at any time." (Clausewitz, On War) . . . The bolt of en-lightening energy, the sincerity of search for the real, could appear at any moment and from anyone, not just a sanctioned or authorized leader. The dark and menacing cloud is only menacing to the old order, to ignorance and forces of manipulation. The awakening energy of the lightning bolt is nearly invisible in its decent but becomes visible on the uprising as what is called the "return stroke": . . . it will appear in moments when the movement of the real is especially concentrated in an individual; at that moment the group will know the presence of the real.

For us, the invisible spirit of inspiration is the "real." It is a thick bank of aesthetic fog that the status quo does not particularly like, perhaps for lack of experience, but which is never noticeably concrete. It can "en-lighten" an individual to suddenly prompt solution and action by the many. The playful aesthetic solution to any social conundrum, by its very spiritual nature, has already fooled its way past the material and rational barriers of "impossible" hope. Blues music is a perfect example, where musicians and listeners keep their spirits unbroken, even while their bodies and minds may be burdened they continue to "search for the real" (Hoffman, 1967, p. 48). Hoffman (1967) wrote, "The *Real* in art never dies, because its nature is predominantly spiritual" (p. 48).

In our teacher education class course sessions, we too play the blues by providing learning experiences in a subtle, creatively disobedient means and manner, modeling and inviting our students to play within cultural aesthetic spaces of imagination, where we unmask messages in ways that no top-down-telling lecture could ever do. Shown through many illustrations throughout this book (see Sailing to the Lost Island of the Imagination in "The Seed of Play" chapter for instance), one example was the *Obstacle Course of Life*, created to bring to life for children, compassionate heroes from the past and present that never lost hope in their lives' journeys to make the world better for every individual they encountered.

Along the *Obstacle Course of Life,* children witnessed empathic voices from a variety of heroes who shared their stories and invited the children to solve a problem together in a collaborative, experiential way. As children finished the course, they discussed the heroes and empathic voices they identified with and how they touched their hearts, minds, and lives. Compellingly and powerfully, our teacher candidates fully experienced the concept of being ambassadors of hope for children and realized the importance of their responsibility as teachers to design playful problem-solving aesthetic experiences that evoke self-efficacy, empathy, and fill children with feelings of intrinsic hope for their lives. As one teacher candidate stated, "I have gained insight to my vision and beliefs of teaching and [these experiences] helped me bring everything I feel inside to life."

When educators believe that children should feel a sense of hope and perhaps *be* the hope that children need, they open a space for children to feel hope through play and uncover meaning for themselves (Palmer, 1993). As described further below, one child following our *Make a Wave* performance expressed deep emotion from the experience and how he could make a change by boycotting for-profit aquarium entertainment: "Now I am never going to go to a dolphin show, or at least support one. If I [worked in]one of those dolphin jails, I would go on strike and say 'Let them free!'" This child has unmasked a way he can be an agent of hope and change his life in support of a cause he feels passionate about. While his was a singular 2-hour experience in his education, we can only imagine where his thinking would be if curriculum was presented to him in this manner throughout the year, utilizing aesthetic education.

When teachers are not trying to manipulate children or structurally impose and control the outcomes within the learning space, and when they understand how to develop imaginative intelligence with children, they in fact *believe* in giving the space, power, and freedom to children (Glasser, 2010). Then the child can know what hope feels like. In the creative, compassionate space within the KIVA, hope leads to new perspectives. When a teacher practices creative compassionate action, they are not trying to control what a child thinks, hopes and believes. When a teacher believes that play leads to hope, they are resiliently undermining the *status quo.*

Herbert Kohl (1994) created the term *creative maladjustment* in his research to describe how he and children can together navigate the daunting forces of despair in American public education (p. xiii). For instance, as an elementary teacher, Kohl had to fight both the system and his peers to use pastels (chalk) in a writing lesson. In his work, Kohl harnesses Mans' (2002) untamed notion that "play [is] an important component of childhood" (p. 1), juxtaposing it to the usurping nature of American schools, which leaves children devoid of their cultural and spiritual learning rights.

Similarly, creative maladjustment, from our experience working in teacher education (as depicted in the above examples), is a benevolent and truthful practice of the arts and aesthetic to circumnavigate daunting social and ecological ills toward hope, equity, and freedom. Creative maladjustment through the aesthetic guides teacher candidates to move beyond the failed direct attempts of the secular world and toward a deeper knowledge of the child's spiritual domain. The practice of *cultural disobedience* and *creative maladjustment*, garnered through aesthetic play, harbors hope, because it allows teacher candidates to be empathic with their personal worlds.

Focusing on core values of hope and love, the aesthetic allows us to heal from a world-space that has for too long a time been distracted by fear and hate. It permits us means to round time in multiple dimensions toward this end. As beings who are a part of the world, the deep illumination of the aesthetic allows us to hold all of time together. This allows us to create in the present possibilities for the future while drawing upon the roots from the past. The aesthetic permits us means to transform space in multiple dimensions toward this end: whereby universal messages of art crossing all cultural boundaries create compassionate interactive communities of spirit that have resiliency and humor to attain hope amid any social or ecological ill (Berry, 1999).

Hope Found in Spirit and Sacred Space Through Social Imagination and Community

> As soon as a student sees you doubt them or their abilities, they begin to doubt them-selves, making it less likely for them to succeed. It all has to do with what you believe and what you feel in your heart. . . If we can find the spirit in one another, we can help change society and contribute to making every place possible a compassionate commu-nity. (teacher candidate reflection)

As described generally in the *Prologue* and specifically for Chapter 1, "The Seed of Play," community-based aesthetic teacher education (or KIVA) can also open portals of hope. While our KIVA space celebrates and encourages play through diverse aesthetic methods, for nurturance of hope, the KIVA allows for the needed amalgamation of spirit (social imagination) and sa-cred space (compassionate community engagement). As Berry (1999) puts forth, and the above teacher candidate suggests, we have an inherent re-sponsibility for the survival of future generations to be spiritual custodians of the Earth and to develop our imaginations in relation to one another and natural world.

From the places, spaces, and times that we have had to involve our body, mind, and spirit through the aesthetic paradigm, our ambition as teacher educators is the art of creating hope among future educators on how to use the aesthetic to move heart and mindset to new levels for social and ecologi-cal justice. The pedagogy of the aesthetic can be found in the heart of the KIVA paradigm: It is how teacher preparation can find rhythms of unity, of hope, of love, and of possibility.

Finding hope within the spirit of imagination hearkens to Chapter 1, "The Seed of Play," where it was revealed that pretend play is paramount for developing creative intelligence and a child's capacity toward their fullest human potential. As described, taking serious conceptual play and pretend-ing with ideas allows for actual vision to occur. In this regard, the attuned aesthetic practitioner would not only continue enabling playful learning, they would know how to create spaces toward bringing it further to frui-tion. They would examine how there are endless subtle beautiful divergent streams within play that procure possibility. *Social imagination*, as Greene (2001) states below, permits this phenomenon.

> We have to try to move persons to think about alternative ways of being alive, possible ways of inhabiting the world. And then we may be able to help them realize the sense in which an active imagination involves transactions between inner and outer vision. (p. 32)

By contrast, a technical-behaviorist approach would halt playful learning from happening, because it would get stuck on the "misinformation" of "factual" knowledge. But when people reimagine the underlying concepts and systems to provide hope for new learning, such a stringent focus on maintaining "accurate" information becomes moot. As Einstein substantiated, "Imagination is more important than knowledge" (Isaacson, 2007, p. 7). If he had stuck to the "facts" of Newtonian physics, we'd never be closer to a truer nature of our physical and spiritual realities. In fact, Einstein's far-reaching wisdom utilized the aesthetic to create a new theory of relativity. According to Isaacson (2007), when Einstein was asked how he made such discoveries, he explained that his quest began at age 16 when "he imagined what it would be like to ride alongside a light beam" (p. 3). Isaacson explains, "Albert Einstein was a locksmith blessed with imagination and guided by a faith in the harmony of nature's handiwork . . . a testament to the connection between creativity and freedom" (p. 2).

Pretending with new ideas allows fluidity so we have the room to figure things out. And incidentally, the "nuts and bolts" of the "facts" are not thrown asunder within an organic mosaic of the aesthetic, but rather they have a context and reason to be better understood and more importantly, challenged. One child after making a mask with a teacher candidate wrote a reflection stating, "I wish two things in my life. One is to fly. And the other is that there is more art [in my life] and is way more helpful and I am more creative." It is interesting to note how the child is equating the sense of flying with the act of creation. As illustrated below, this can be as true for preservice teachers as it is for children.

Similar to the technical, a critical approach might also be predisposed to stop play as a natural phenomenon from happening, because it may turn a doubtful ear to such irreverence, impatiently insisting on an bona fide "answer" of profound intellectual insight. Yet, entrapped within a critical drive for magnanimity, it could lose sight of the hidden potential energy of the small. The profound, however subtle, is already happening; it is unseen in the invisible world of imagination. If we are allowed to love playing with ideas, we can create new worlds, and this is in actuality a hope of how our own might be. Acted upon, they have an opportunity to come true.

For teacher educators and their candidates, as a continuation of childhood—that which may have been deadened in their own lives and schooling—play equals pretending with vision, where imagination events can become the way out for pedagogical dead-end mediocrity. The aesthetic practitioners truly are the magicians who make hope come alive by activating intuition to illuminate the cognitive realms to a deeper spiritual awakening (French & Clark, 2012; Perkins, 1994). Clark (2005) presents a cognitive symbolic product titled *Although You Can't See Me*, by a 10 year-old child created after viewing *Summertime* by Romare Bearden (p. 431).

Although You Can't See Me
By Teshema
Although you can't see me
There is a whole inside that you can't see
Although you don't know me
And you think I don't have anything
I really do, I got God.
Although you can't see me,
I am your guiding angel.

Clark explains,

> Tashema's cognitive symbolic product, *Although You Can't See Me,* revealed intrapersonal and interpersonal moral thought. She wanted people to think about the idea, as she expressed, "That you can love someone or care for someone without even knowing them." She moved between interpersonal moral thought, stating, and you think I don't have anything/I really do/ I Got God." (p. 431)

This phenomenon of hope found within children's most private thoughts are particularly important for teacher education. Cartwright and Noone (2006), authors of *Critical Imagination: A Pedagogy for Engaging Pre-service Teachers in the University Classroom,* focus upon the nature and content of thinking about teaching with preservice educators beyond failed technical and critical means.

They detail that teacher programs need to go through a process of "jarring" (2006, p. 7) or stirring/shocking students so that they can begin to question their own existence in relation to others. As they explain, such a "jarring" can be done via "critical" imagination, which creates a crisis in which students' current existing thoughts are challenged and become ones of discomfort. Challenge and discomfort can result in feelings of uncertainty that permit a space for students to use critical imagination as a saving grace before falling into *despair* to develop new ideas about how to change the current strain. In short, the imagination provides both the *dissonance* that a technical approach excludes as well as the needed accompaniment of *hope.*

Through semiotic "academic journaling" (p. 10) as one critical imagination strategy, Cartwright and Noone (2006) were able to respond to their students' journals through carefully prepared question cue sets, whose unique nature pushed students to move beyond assumptions to consider ever further possibilities of the relationship between imagination and reality. Not necessarily an informal place for personal thoughts, it gave students a voice while they reflected on their understanding of a particular topic or issue. Thus, students' understandings were probed, but in a manner that prompted them to look past the surface. As such, through this medium of the written word using critical imagination in journaling, Cartwright and

Noone found success in helping their teacher candidates experience "living with the preparedness to withhold judgment and comfort in the face of alternative claims, which is the basis of critical thinking" (p. 10).

For our students, however, imagination development goes well beyond university classroom coursework and academic journal writing. Our preservice teachers are encouraged to utilize mixed mediums in a visual journal as a way of reflecting and symbolizing their frustrations and obstacles that arise in their daily lives and field classrooms. We introduce the visual journal, similar to sketchbooks artists have used throughout time, to record their ideas and thinking. Our teacher candidates use their journal much like a "scrapbook," a reflective synthesis of text and images. However, as illustrated throughout the seed chapters, the *scrapbook journal* is only one of the many aesthetic approaches we use within myriad imagination medium possibilities.

Addressing a particular social and ecological issue in a local or global community context, teacher candidate explorations are encouraged to metamorphose into multiple expressions. Our students are given a full semester-long experience of imagination immersion into a social or ecological issue project where all the other pieces fit in. Created is a tapestry where all the collective threads are woven together to create a lasting imprint that contextualizes every idea, concept, technique, strategy, and method toward a larger vision. Immersed within an omnipresent creative compassionate community, our students, even if they had wanted to, are simply unable to "check out" or "detach" themselves, as they may be more inclined to do within a technical or critical mode.

We have found that nurturing imagination in a multitude of ways unlocks preservice teachers' ideas and beliefs around compassionate learning: It gives them a sense of societal contribution, core values, and conflict-resolution skills and most importantly allows them to hope for change. As one of our teacher candidates related at the end of a semester-long imagination immersion experience:

> In a way, our performance was a chain reaction. We're showing and modeling compassion and kindness, which is put into practice by us and the students. If they show compassion to one another, the classroom will become a great place to grow and learn and play. . . Being the change, is possible and I will be a change agent to carry out the change. Each one of us will be the change and like a chain reaction, change will happen.

Similar to Cartwright and Noone's (2006) findings in using critical imagination to compassionately nurture a critical mind, Shor's (1992) description of "Empowering Education" (p. 15) also found authentic manifestation within our embrace of the critical imagination:

> [Empowering Education] is a critical-democratic pedagogy for self and social change. . . Human beings do not invent themselves in a vacuum, and society

cannot be made unless people create it together. The goals of this pedagogy are to relate personal growth to public life, by developing strong skills, academic knowledge, habits of inquiry, and critical curiosity about society, power, inequality, and change. (p. 15)

But beyond social spheres, freeing the imagination also provides for natural world solutions and hopes whose ailments we have yet to successfully surmise in a socially steeped material industrial culture (French & Clark, 2012) (see also Chapter 4, "The Seed of Change"). Within our deeply embedded social and environmental ecology, we need educators who can interdependently think and act through an "ecology of mind" (Bateson, 1972).

Through activating imagination and nurturing creative skillset capacity, our students are able to achieve empathy, understanding, and compassion for all beings, questioning their own existence in relation to intersections between human and natural worlds (French, 2013; French & Clark, 2012). In this light, we have found that imagination allows for what ecojustice educator Rebecca Martusewicz (2008) calls, a "collaborative intelligence," where "we teach our children and our neighbors as future and current citizens, important ethical choices and responsibilities that recognize those practices that contribute to sustainable healthy communities of life, and those that do not" (p. 27).

As illustrated within our project *Make a Wave,* our students explored the ecological and social atrocities of dolphin slaughter for profit. Over the course of the semester, students revealed new voices that represented awareness, solution, and hope through altering their personal teaching beliefs within the aesthetic mediums of sounds, movement, masks, and poetry. In the design of their final performance, when conveying messages to children on how the dolphin yearly migration has been continually interrupted by slaughter and captivity, they literally became the dolphins (see Figure 2.2).

Audience members were given the opportunity to "not tell the dancer from the dance" (Yeats, as cited in Highwater, 1982). As one member of the 1,000-person-filled auditorium remarked having seen the symbolic portrayal for *Make a Wave,* "I felt a genuine trust between audience and performers, a relationship that could not be duplicated in any 'professional' performance." The idea of hope became visible when preservice teachers stepped into the skin of the dolphin, because by expressing absolute empathy, they were permitted release.

We have found that the creation of a compassionate space through the aesthetic is one that is spiritually sacred and one that heightens the awareness of learning communities far beyond the limits of static approaches. As revealed in the article *Revitalizing the Spiritual Compassionate Commons in Educational Culture* (French & Clark, 2012):

FIGURE 2.2.   Teacher candidates as dolphins: Make a Wave final performance, 2010. To view Teacher Candidates as Dolphins video, visit www.compassionate-teaching.com and click on Our Book tab on home page, then click on Hope tab

> Through metaphysical teaching alternatives and the development of a spiritual-moral commons in education [we] awoke higher consciousness in students' and our own teaching practice, creating, in particular, greater compassion and a renewed hope for a more socially and ecologically sustainable world. . . . Our creation of a compassionate commons was both spiritual and moral, one that transformed the awareness of our learning community. The purpose of education and teaching was no longer a daily material life routine; instead, it had a broader and more sacred connection and purpose: It had vision. (pp. 101–102)

Within each semester's imaginative spiritual creative space brought to fruition, our teacher candidates discover a process of what it feels like to inspire hope. As one teacher candidate shared,

> The performance that our class produced did not only promote a strong message, it was powerful. . . [our professors] tried to explain just how emotional and powerful this experience would be for us, but it wasn't until I actually felt the impact that I really understood this feeling. We worked for weeks preparing our message about compassion, community, peace, love and change. . . The feeling I experienced that day when we sang and danced made me realize just how worth it our message is. To see the looks on the third, fourth and fifth grader's faces brought a smile to my face. . . Their reactions of joy about our message only reinforced my passion about our new ideas this semester.

Closest to the heart of nurturing hope within the KIVA are the interconnected relationships we build with one another as we play together within multiple authentic community and school contexts. Indeed, the need for teacher education programs to engage preservice teachers in multiple contexts beyond traditional school placements has been recognized previously by aesthetic, place-based, and multicultural education research as a key ingredient for fostering teacher candidates' critical thinking and prob-

THE SEED OF HOPE • 55

lem-solving opportunities thus adapting creative, compassionate, culturally responsive, and relevant instruction (Clark, 2009a; Clark & French, 2012; Cochran-Smith, 2004; Darling-Hammond & Fickel, 2006; French, 2012, 2013; French & Clark, 2012; Greene, 2001; Oakes, Franke, Quartz, & Rogers, 2002; O'Grady & Chappell, 2000; Root & Furco, 2001; Sleeter, 2001; Wade, 2000). Involvement of individuals based in the child's larger cultural community is paramount to the quality of teacher candidates' course and field experiences: Teacher candidates placed in collaborative local knowledge community contexts with critical reflection support are more "socially transformative in their beliefs, attitudes and expectations" (French, 2012, p. 19).

Within our course and fieldwork, we have taken to heart these action community engagement findings, involving our students and children in multiple critical imagination aesthetic mediums *as well* as reciprocally across multiple spaces and mentors to engage students' spirits within a compassionate community in addressing both social and ecological issues. Utilizing aesthetic inquiry, our students investigate authentic issues facing their surrounding local and global worlds with culturally creative mentors who reflect the attributes and characteristics described in successful community-based education projects and programs. They explore their cultural biases and stereotypes, values, beliefs, identities, and senses of self as teachers through invited community artists, activists, and educators leading a myriad of arts experiences.

The artistic community forums contribute to a developing sense of the power of aesthetic education that is manifested in the creation and design of symbolic messages using masks, puppets, poetry, dance, music, and theater (Clark & French, 2012). The symbolic ideas carry a compassionate message to build awareness, which is then integrated and shared within the community to empower cutting-edge learning and societal contribution.

In stark contrast to the above literature and our experience, an assistant superintendent of a western suburban Connecticut school district, who came from outside an urban district student's community, said, "Art [aesthetic inquiry] won't work in urban settings." Our school-community–based project described below, a manifest amalgamation of spirit and sacred space, whereby *Hope* grows, provides resounding response to this atypical societal naysayer's hopelessness and predetermination of who can and cannot engage in the aesthetic.

"Steppin' Out" and Into a Kiva of Hope

In *Steppin' Out of a Painting: Releasing a Child's Voice*, an all-White, female cohort of 22 teacher candidates worked in teams with six classrooms of all-Black students to create symbolic expressions representing the diverse voices and ideas of the children. Facilitated by long-term school art teachers, education professors, and community artists, this project focused on

6th graders' visual literacy and language arts skills. During workshops, the children became characters in African artworks to reveal their impressions, opening a multitude of interpretations and realities in relation to their experiences. As testimony to the power of authentic community context and spiritual aesthetic mentorship on the very first day, a teacher candidate read a poem freshly written by one of her 6th-grade students, depicting both pain and hope:

Life Is Hard
by Alexandrea
Life is hard
But you can always overcome your challenges.
Love is the strongest power
and
It only comes once in a lifetime.
I thought I could just push through life
But no,
That's not how it works.
It doesn't work that way
because
There are flaws in everyone
But I try
not to see the flaws.

Reflecting on the moment afterwards, teacher candidates and mentors expressed how within the immediate context, a sacred space was created for not only the child but also for teachers to perceive her in a new way. One of the facilitators, from her experienced community-school insider perspective, exclaimed, "The children are so inspired to share their ideas with teacher candidates." She continued to emphasize the theme of identity embodying the aesthetic project, stating, "We are all flowers of the same tree."

During Saturday morning workshops, children continued to work on their projects with their art teachers, university professors, and teacher candidates. Reflecting the open visibility and inclusivity of the project within the larger school community, one parent attending remarked, while viewing the murals and listening to the poetry, "Look at how much can get done when children are surrounded by community." Another parent was shocked to discover that university professors and teacher candidates worked at the elementary school during their spring break. One teacher candidate shared, "Being here, I am learning so much about the importance of a child's creative voice and critical thinking. Thank you."

In order for a mainstreamed preservice teacher to change self-debilitating perceptions, they must first be exposed to a direct experience and then be encouraged to reevaluate their values and perceptions of the world around them through a supportive format. Rather than the ends in and of themselves, lesson plans and units become a means for us to further engage our students in reflection and practice within the aesthetic paradigm. Working with the children, teacher candidates employed critical thinking and aesthetic methodologies to establish meaningful teaching relationships that celebrated students' identities.

Ultimately, this innovative aesthetic community project was a creative arena for releasing children's feelings and voices, especially children who may have been marginalized academically and socially. Providing preservice teachers such an aesthetic community experience within an alternate context and approach deepens their teaching beliefs. Supported by Yeo (1997), these unique experiences allowed us to start with "the power in prospective teachers' values of compassion, justice, equality, and communication as a basis for beginning to break down defensiveness, build understanding, and strengthen commitment to the values of culturally relevant teaching" (as cited in Bondy & Davis, 2000, p. 55). Through the aesthetic paradigm, *Steppin' Out* teacher candidates recognized the ethical and moral imperative of dignifying cultural differences and identities while working with children of color (Delpit, 1995).

Wynne (2002) states,

> Alice Walker, in *The Same River Twice: Honoring the Difficult* (1996), says that "even to attempt to respectfully encounter 'the other' is a sacred act, and leads to and through the labyrinth. To the river. Possibly to healing. A 'special effect' of the soul." Encountering the other is difficult, for all humans, whether it be in language or in ritual; yet, for me, it sometimes seems the only way we will ever make this democracy work. (p. 216)

A final culminating performance presentation and mural exhibition event came from 6 weeks of apprenticeship workshops with 6th-grade students and teacher candidates at the district's annual arts festival in the grand hall of Hartford, Connecticut's train station on March 26th, 2012. The Arts Festival event featured 6th-grade children dancing, sharing poetry, and presenting three expansive murals about their community and future dreams. One 6th-grade student, age 11, mesmerized the audience with a vocal performance alongside teacher candidates presenting their song/poem.

Our Nature
by Deja
Our nature needs care
With water and light
All through the day and night.
We will have love
No matter what
Even the love sent from above.

Mother Nature calls for us
To care for nature even though we must
Be kind and share our care
All throughout the air.
We will have love
No matter what
Even the love sent from above
For our nature.

The poetry, raps, dance, songs, and exhibition of the children's murals (on display for the community for 2 weeks) were a testimony—borne witness by our students—to the children's multiple talents and abilities. The *Steppin' Out* project paralleled Murrell's (2000) preservice teacher model: that to become a "community teacher," one who honors "collaboration, the humility of practice, and cultural/local knowledge of the people in the community" (p. 55), programs must include educators who have a track record of success working with disenfranchised student populations. To this point, Delpit (1988) argues that "appropriate education for poor children and children of color can only be devised in consultations with adults who have their culture" (p. 32). These are teachers and community educators who often share the same background as their students. For example, one of the elementary teachers in *Steppin' Out* embraced the alternative aesthetic inquiry as an effective way of motivating children to think deeply and divergently.

Our teacher education community projects have been dedicated to revitalizing surrounding communities and developing innovative future educators. In each community project, the focus has been to elicit an intense feeling of inspiration and hope in children's identities as learners, leaders, artists, and writers. CCSU teacher candidates report gaining resiliency, strong personal identities as educators, and cutting-edge educational pedagogy dealing with critical issues in education. Engagement in this process reciprocally helps children in local schools and community venues to create their own artistic representations for the larger community while enabling our students, along with school and community educators, to develop their own understandings and beliefs about teaching and learning.

As illustrated above and throughout the seed chapters of this book, it is crucial to children's and our teacher candidates' power and hope that we provide a vibrant cultural space of hope and community through ecosocial environmental community engagements (Clark & French, 2012; French & Clark, 2012). The underlying aesthetic structure of our course activities and assignments, when enacted within our KIVA paradigm, unlocks preservice teachers' preconceived perceptions of educational practices toward more transformative views and beliefs, which drive instructional decisions and curricular social and ecojustice initiatives. As two of our teacher candidates revealed,

[A] classroom environment should be an environment that strives to bring out the light in every single student by making them reach to the stars and beyond. We feel that when students can show their light and speak peace and love then it will radiate to the rest of the world endlessly.

I have realized that the question is not what we teach but how we teach it. . . This semester was inspirational, showing the endless possibilities that all learners, myself included, can reach. I now know what is possible and will strive for this type of learning in every classroom and school. My professors guided their learners to be the change. . . Our imaginations were the leaders and the possibilities were infinite for our groups and our class.

Aesthetic education provides a portal to empowerment, for not only our preservice teachers' learning but also for classroom students in their fieldwork. The aesthetic awakens the teacher candidate to the true potential that they (and their future students) have. The one-way street becomes a two-way street, where the feelings and learning is mutual, not deficient or compensatory (Delpit, 1988). Students enter and practice building vision and hope with themselves and the children placed within their purview and influence. From a provision of greatness with mentorship, spiritual imagination, and compassionate community context, we have garnered a wellspring of self-efficacy for children and future teachers alike. As one child exclaimed to her peers from interacting with our preservice teachers during a Storybook Character community event to promote literacy and the joy of reading: "I learned that my dreams will come true."

The next seed Chapter 3, explores *Voice* and the expansive river of freedom realized which impacts the sense of self within teacher candidates. Voice once shared within a compassionate community triggers a domino effect of new ideas and possibility shared with one another. As a result of the emerging voice, freedom and love are achieved thus building "an authentic school community which will flourish given it's base in empathic understanding and the students' gradual capacity towards moral intent and the impact their behavior may have on others" (Clark, 2005, p. 444).

Is it possible that I could be for someone the place where hope begins?
—Anonymous

REFERENCES

Arnoldi, M. (1995). *Playing with time. Art and performance in central Mali.* Bloomington: Indiana University Press.

Bateson, G. (1972). *Steps to an ecology of mind.* New York, NY: Ballantine.

Berry, T. (1999). *The great work: Our way into the future.* New York, NY: Crown-Bell/ Random House.

Bhuchung, T. (2012). Fueling creative energy with compassion and emptiness. In John Briggs (Ed.), *Creativity and compassion*. Wayne, NJ: Karuna.

Bjørkvold, J. (1992). *The muse within: Creativity and communication, song and play from childhood through maturity*. (W. H. Halverson, Trans.). New York: HarperCollins. (Original work published 1989)

Bondy, E., & Davis, S. (2000). The caring of strangers: Insights from a field experience in a culturally unfamiliar community. *Action in Teacher Education, 22*(2), 54–66.

Carson, R. (1965). *Sense of wonder*. Retrieved from www.rachelcarsoncouncil.org/index.php?page=about-rcc

Cartwright, P., & Noone, L. (2006). Critical imagination: A pedagogy for engaging pre-service teachers in the university classroom. *College Quarterly, 9*(4) Retrieved from http://www.senecac.on.ca/quarterly/2006-vol09-num04-fall/cartwright_noone.html

Clark, B. (2005). Moral imagination and art: Echoes from a child's soul. *Forum on Public Policy: Issue Child Psychology, 1*(4), 428–446.

Clark, B. (2009a). Aesthetic education and masked emotions: A model for emancipatory teacher preparation. *Critical Questions in Education, 1*(1), 40–50. Retrieved from http://education.missouristate.edu/AcadEd/75534.htm

Clark, B. (2009b). Mustard seed: A personal search for "Ahimsa" (The truth of nonviolence). *Closing the Circle Exhibition*. B. Clark & M. Cipriano (Artists). New Britain, CT: New Britain Commission on the Arts.

Clark, B. (2013). Breaking the culture of silence in schools: Children's voices revealed through moral imagination. In D. G. Mulcahy (Ed.), *Transforming schools: Alternative perspectives on school reform*. Charlotte, NC: Information Age.

Clark, B., & French, J. (2012). ZEAL: A revolution for education, unmasking teacher identity through aesthetic education, imagination and transformational practice. *Critical Questions in Education, 3*(1), 12–22.

Cochran-Smith, M. (2004). *Walking the road: Race, diversity, and social justice in teacher education*. New York, NY: Teachers College Press.

Csikszentmihalyi, M. (1996). *Creativity: Flow and the psychology of discovery and invention*. New York, NY: HarperCollins.

Cullum, A. (1971). *The geranium on the windowsill just died, but teacher you went right on*. New York, NY: Harlin Quist.

Darling-Hammond, L., & Fickel, L. (2006). *Powerful teacher education: Lessons from exemplary programs*. San Francisco, CA: Jossey-Bass.

Delpit, L. (1988). The silenced dialogue: Power and pedagogy in educating other people's children. *Harvard Educational Review, 58*(3), 280–298.

Delpit, L. (1995). *Others peoples children: Cultural conflict in the classroom*. New York, NY: New Press.

French, J. (2005). *Culturally responsive pre-service teacher development: A case study of the impact of community and school fieldwork* (Doctoral dissertation). University of Connecticut, Storrs. Retrieved from Dissertations and Theses: Full Text database. (Publication No. AAI3167589).

French, J. (2012). Creating eco-social culturally responsive educators with community. *Green Theory and Praxis, 6*(1), 17–34.

French, J. (2013). Methods & mindsets for creating eco-social community educators. In D. G. Mulcahy (Ed.), *Transforming schools: Alternative perspectives on school reform* (pp. 37–66). Charlotte, NC: Information Age.

French, J., & Clark, B. (2012). Revitalizing a spiritual compassionate commons in educational culture. *Religion and Education, 39*(1), 93–108.

Gandhi, M. In Attenborough, R. (2000) *The words of Gandhi.* New York: Newmarket Press.

Glasser, W. (2010). *Choice theory: A new psychology of personal freedom.* New York, NY: HarperCollins.

Greene, M. (2001). *Variations on a blue guitar: The Lincoln Center Institute lectures on aesthetic education.* New York, NY: Teacher College Press.

Haberman, M. (1993). Teaching in multicultural schools: Implications for teacher selection and training. In L. Kremer-Hayon, H. Vonk, & R. Fessler (Eds.), *Teacher professional development* (pp. 267–294). Amsterdam, The Netherlands: Swets and Zietlinger B.V.

Haberman, M., & Post, L. (1992). Does direct experience change education students' perceptions of low-income minority children? *Midwestern Educational Researcher, 5*(2), 29–31.

Highwater, J. (1982). *The primal mind: Vision and reality in Indian America.* New York, NY: Meridian.

Hoffman, H. (1967). *Search for the real and other essays.* Cambridge, MA: MIT Press.

hooks, b. (1995). *Teaching to transgress: Education as the practice of freedom.* New York, NY: Routledge.

Isaacson, W. (2007). *Einstein: His life and universe.* New York, NY: Simon & Schuster.

Kohl, H. (1994). *"I won't learn from you" and other thoughts on creative maladjustment.* New York, NY: New Press.

Land, G., & Jarman, B. (1992). *Breakpoint and beyond: Mastering the future, today.* Champaign, IL: HarperBusiness.

Mans, M. (2002). To pamwe or to "play": The role of play in arts education in Africa. *International Journal of Music Education, 39*(1), 50–64.

Martusewicz, R. (2008). Educating for "collaborative intelligence:" Revitalizing the cultural and ecological commons in Detroit. In H. Bai, M. McKenzie, P. Hart, & B. Jickling (Eds.), *Fields of green: Re-storying education.* New York, NY: Hampton.

Merton, T. (1951). *The ascent to truth.* Orlando, FL: Harcourt Brace.

Murrell, P. (2000). Community teachers: A conceptual framework for preparing exemplary urban teachers. *Journal of Negro Education, 69*(4), 338–348.

Nouwen, H. (1983). *Compassion: A reflection on the Christian life.* New York, NY: Doubleday.

Oakes, J., Franke, M. L., Quartz, K. H., & Rogers, J. (2002). Research for high-quality urban teaching: Defining it, developing it, assessing it. *Journal of Teacher Education, 53*(3), 228–234.

O'Grady, C. R., & Chappell, B. (2000). With, not for: The politics of service learning in multicultural communities. In C. J. Ovando & P. McLaren (Eds.), *The politics of multicultualism and bilingual education: Students and teachers caught in the cross fire* (pp. 209–224). Boston, MA: McGraw-Hill.

Palmer, P. (1993). *The violence of our knowledge: Toward a spirituality of higher education.* Paper presented at the the Michael Keenan Memorial Lecture, the 7th Lecture, Berea College, KY. Retrieved from http://www.kairos2.com/palmer_1999.htm

Perkins, D. (1994). *The intelligent eye: Learning to think by looking at art.* Santa Monica, CA: Getty Center for Education in the Arts.

Robinson, K. (2010). Changing education paradigms. *RSA animate: The Royal Society of Arts, London.* Retrieved from http://www.youtube.com/watch?v=zDZFcDGpL4U

Root, S., & Furco, A. (2001). A review of research on service learning in preservice teacher education. In J. B. Anderson, K. J. Swick, & J. Yff (Eds.), *Service-learning in teacher education: Enhancing the growth of new teachers, their students, and communities* (pp. 86–101). Washington, DC: AACTE.

Shor, I. (1992). *Empowering education: Critical teaching for social change.* Chicago, IL: University of Chicago Press.

Sleeter, C. E. (2001). Preparing teachers for culturally diverse schools: Research and the overwhelming presence of Whiteness. *Journal of Teacher Education, 52*(2), 94–106.

Smaller, H. (2007). Moving beyond institutional boundaries in inner-city teacher preparation. In R. Solomon & Sekayi, D. (Ed.), *Urban teacher education and teaching: Innovative practice for diversity and social justice* (pp. 89–108). London, UK: Lawrence Erlbaum.

Smithers, S. (2012, June). The spiritual crisis of capitalism: What would the Buddha do? *Adbusters.* Retrieved from https://www.adbusters.org/magazine/102/spiritual-crisis-of-capitalism.html

Wade, R. C. (2000). Service-learning for multicultural teaching competency: Insights from the literature for teacher educators. *Equity and Excellence in Education, 33*(3), 21–29.

Wardle, F. (2003). *Introduction to early childhood education: A multidimensional approach to child-centered care and learning.* Boston, MA: Allyn & Bacon.

Warhol, A. (2013). *On working in the studio.* Retrieved from crystalbridges.org/blog/blankcanvas/

Wynne, J. (2002). We don't talk right. You ask him. In L. Delpit & J. Dowdy (Eds.), *The skin that we speak: Thoughts on language and culture in the classroom.* New York, NY: W.W. Norton.

Yeo, F. (1997). *Inner-city schools multiculturalism and teacher education: A professional journey.* New York, NY: Garland.

Zajonc, A. (2006). *Love and knowledge: Recovering the heart of learning through contemplation.* Retrieved from http://www.arthurzajonc.org/Teaching.php

Zeichner, K. M. (2003). The adequacies and inadequacies of three current strategies to recruit, prepare, and retain the best teachers for all students. *Teachers College Record, 105*(3), 490–519.

Zeichner, K. M., & Hoeft, K. (1996). Teacher socialization for cultural diversity. In J. Sikula, T. J. Buttery, & E. Guyton (Eds.), *Handbook of research on teacher education* (2nd ed.). New York, NY: Simon & Schuster/Macmillan.

CHAPTER 3

THE SEED OF IMAGINATIVE VOICE

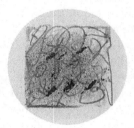

Seed of Voice Painting
(Clark, 2009)

Courage doesn't always roar. Sometimes courage is the quiet voice at the end of the day saying, "I will try again tomorrow."

—Mary Anne Radmacher

UNMASKING THE KIVA TO RELEASE A VOICE OF EMOTIONAL IMAGINATION

How do you feel about the condition of society, education, and the future of the next generation? Do you think about the 16 million homeless chil-

Hearts and Minds Without Fear: Unmasking the Sacred in Teacher Preparation,
pages 63–83.

dren in America? Do the poverty, violence, injustice, and ecological ravages growing at an ever-increasing rate each day outrage you? Many of us bury our emotions regarding these issues that face us repeatedly through media exploitation and the repetitive display of images portraying tragic events, such as 9/11, the Oklahoma City bombing, and the Columbine and Newtown school shootings. So many teachers, parents, and citizens are facing what is now being called "compassion fatigue." What is the ultimate consequence when we bury our emotions? What happens when our young children and teachers practice hiding their emotions each day in schools behind a psychological mask or with the help of the drug induced fog to "control" attention deficit/hyperactivity disorder (ADHD)?

We propose that the arts and aesthetic experiences are critical in training teacher candidates to learn how to *release their critical and emotional voice* in order to reveal and exhibit their outrage and concern for the social and ecological nightmares currently exploited by the media for profit in the 21st century. Unmasking the sacred in teacher preparation also unmasks the emotional imaginative voice to address our current injustices. It is our premise that we are spiritual beings, and at the sacred core of our humanity, we do care about others and about the condition in which we leave our world for future generations. After all, what is education for? Can we risk ignoring one another and the societal and environmental ills that afflict so many in our country and around the world? Are not the perceptions and powers of emotions essential in the development of creative and innovative thinkers?

Having experienced the Civil Rights Movement and Vietnam War as kids, now we have taught in classrooms during the Space Shuttle Challenger explosion (while children watched it live), the Oklahoma City bombing, the 9/11 tragedy, the devastating tsunamis, the slaughter of dolphins and whales, the pollution of our water and food supply, the wars in the Middle East, Clinton's impeachment, and on and on. As we watch new societal tragedies become the emotional weight of our teacher candidates, they are learning that society's issues enter the classroom each day on the backs of children (Elkind, 1981). And while children try to hide their emotions, in most instances these emotions are revealed in multiple ways, either through bullying, violence, drug use, or self-mutilation.

In this chapter, several aesthetic strategies utilizing the arts will be presented that address the *emotional imagination* in response to social and ecological issues by *releasing the imaginative voice*. The arts and aesthetic experiences, like mask-making, act as the vehicle to carry difficult emotions and address our deepest fears. The teacher candidates we work with practice critical and imaginative thinking through the arts so that they can implement these aesthetic strategies with their students. We must practice our *emotional imagination* and, in that practice, develop a prophetic voice that releases the

UNMASKING
IMAGINATIVE VOICE

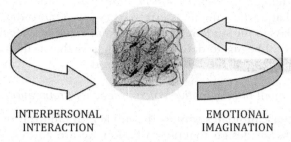

INTERPERSONAL   EMOTIONAL
INTERACTION   IMAGINATION

FIGURE 3.1.   Unmasking imaginative voice concept map.

imagination to perceive each other and the world in new ways (Greene, 1993; McElfresh-Spehler & Slattery, 1999).

Our teacher candidates must learn how to address and teach children to understand the power of their imaginative voice when released in a safe, trusting, and compassionate learning environment—the KIVA. As the *emotional imagination* is developed and released into the compassionate KIVA learning environment, teacher candidates working with children learned to listen to a spiritual, moral, empathic, and compassionate voice that otherwise would have remained silent and buried in the darkest corners of their sacred core.

Simultaneously, when the voices are shared, hope and love emerge within the community. Thus, forgiveness may be achieved (Weil, 2001) and action is taken to improve our relationships with one another and our daily habits that may contribute to the economic exploitation of others and the ecological devastation of our earth (Coles, 1987; French, 2013; French & Clark, 2012). Hammarskjöld (1964), points out the importance of forgiving a child and being a witness in the child's life; and perhaps the child's life is a mirror to our own. A child will mask her voice if she is fearful of rejection. He states,

> Forgiveness is the answer to the child's dream of a miracle by which what is broken is made whole again, what is soiled is again made clean. The dream explains why we need to be forgiven, and why we must forgive. In the presence of God, nothing stands between Him and us—we *are* forgiven. But we *cannot* feel His presence if anything is allowed to stand between ourselves and others. (p. 124; emphasis in original)

The KIVA allows for play, experimentation, innovation, diversity of ideas, cultural relevancy, and a celebration of imaginative possibility as individual voices are heard. As the scaffolding process unfolds, teacher candidates must be in a mindful state and forgiving of each other's human idiosyncrasies.

The concept map for the seed of voice (Figure 3.1) depicts the critical agency by the teacher to utilize aesthetic methods that instill trust within the child. Meditate on the *Seed of Imaginative Voice* painting (Clark, 2009) above: Shadowed portraits depict how when finding your own voice it mirrors the imprints of shared experiences and memories with others. This seed is reciprocal in that as the student asserts his/her power and who they are, the teacher displays to the student how that power of choice is received and nurtured. The child begins to define their self-knowledge as their sense of self, their imaginative independent voice, is realized.

The Development of Imaginative Voice in Teacher Preparation

Our teacher candidates witness the impact on children in the community programs we design together; whether we are addressing homelessness, compassionate action, or ending the slaughter of dolphins for profit. When the teacher candidates witness the transformation of children as they release their imaginative and prophetic voice through their poetry, masks, or skits, they are amazed that these abilities may have forever been dormant within the child, if not triggered by the aesthetic and guidance from the teacher. We have to ask ourselves as educators, what is happening to children when imaginative voices become dormant, shadowed, covered, and caught in web-like testing nets? If these imaginative voices are allowed to surface, we have so much to gain as a future, healthy, compassionate society. Figure 3.2 is a painting created by an 8-year-old child inspired by our teacher candidate's lesson exploring homelessness.

As you examine the painting, it is interesting to examine the composition and how the child used the entire paper to paint a home with the entryway at the heart of the paper. The focus of the painting is the entrance

FIGURE 3.2. "It Is Important to Have a Place to Go So That You Can Sleep Well and Feel Loved." Painting by Jesarry, Age 8

into the home. Jesarry's imaginative voice is revealed, expressing that the importance of a home is being a place to not only feel safe but to also feel loved.

As professors of teacher preparation, we understand the urgency to create a space, so we simulate a KIVA on campus for teacher candidates to understand how to transfer the aesthetic ideas that release a child's imaginative voice. Throughout the creative process however, the teacher candidates participating do not fully realize the depth of transformation aesthetic methods have on children's sense of personal voice until they witness it in real time, enacted side by side with children.

To model an example of the depth of a child's sacred core and potential to release the emotional and imaginative prophetic voice, the following poem by a fourth grader is presented. While reading the poem, the voice of the child emerges and astounds adults, a deeply critical voice exposing the depth of the child's perceptive and spiritual awareness. The below poem (1998), by Evan (age 9, from Newtown, Connecticut) was composed instantly without revision after viewing *Starry Night* by Vincent van Gogh (1889) and while participating in a visual thinking exercise and discussion of Vincent's search for love throughout his life:

The Spirit of Vincent's Painting
I am the voice behind the door,
I may be a spirit,
with tricks in store,
or a mask of two colors very much the same.
But who's behind it?
Is this a game?
Here I am,
but what am I?
Can you see?
Can you fly?
Can you see through my empty eyes?
Could you guess?
Just one guess?
. What I am,
in this mess?
Ancient children
play in my mind,
the door is open,
but what's behind?
Take a step,
Don't be scared,
do you
hear the whispers
of secrets shared?
As the blanks of

tomorrow,
Of happiness
and ancient sorrow
come together,
like a quilt,
Is this innocence?
Is this guilt?
But the only way
You'll find out,
Is to step inside,
What's this about?
Don't be afraid,
to be late,
if you go forward,
Wonders await.

As was done with Evan and her class, the utilization of aesthetic works of famous art (Clark, 2005) are also used with teacher candidate college students who may not perceive themselves as writers or poets. Through a series of arts-based workshops presenting aesthetic methods (see also other *Seed* chapters), preservice teachers learn to release their voices through playful imaginative experiences that are metaphysical in nature. This allows them to develop an innovative repertoire of inspirational strategies for children. The following pieces (Figures 3.3 and 3.4) were composed by two of our teacher candidates after making masks and then using the mask as a metaphor for beliefs on becoming a teacher through learning how to release a child's voice.

FIGURE 3.3. Mystery mask.

FIGURE 3.4.   Burning With Passion.

Mystery
By Stacey
Pure gold adorned with turquoise gems.
Eyes are the window to the soul.
Silent but powerful.
Beautiful but strong.
Mysterious on the outside.
Look closer.
Quiet but full of ideas.
Look deeper
Once afraid to speak now with a voice.
Awakened.

Burning With Passion
By Laura
My fire burns hot and bright.
Carrying everyone to the light.
My fire burns unstoppable and consuming.
Grabbing hold of the mind and taking it zooming.
My fire burns with love and passion
Capturing the heart in the gentlest fashion.

Our teacher candidates are startled to perceive themselves and each other in these new ways. We all have hidden potential. The aesthetic holds a mirror to the soul and says "look at me—you have ignored me for so long—now I am appearing—will you accept me as part of you?" Our imaginative core is our soul—the very depths of our soul. This is the sacred core and the mystery of our humanity. Our endless search for meaning is one of the recurring mysteries in our lives; it is as if we are continually trying to find our way—our way home.

If only we could all realize our potential, to unlock the door to the imagination and let go of fear and allow possibilities to take wings and fly. Our *soul force* or, as Gandhi (1957) also calls, our *love force*, "the search for truth" (p. 276), illuminates the gifts we have and can give to others, especially when working with children and the necessary nurturing they need and deserve to develop emotionally, physically, socially, creatively, and spiritually (Greene, 2001). Why has the understanding of the importance of our scared imaginative core not been perceived as important to develop in teacher preparation? Exploring the related consequences in the following poem, titled *Puzzle*, a teacher candidate describes the many negative marks made on a child by a series of teachers who did not know the child and the devastating landscape of darkness that has been left behind, as also illustrated in Figure 3.5:

Puzzle
By Nicole

Chalky white, dusty gray, and matte black cover a bumpy, broken, plaster student.
He tries to speak and reach out, but he cannot break through the paint of past teachers.
His plaster soul shines through, but all you see are the marks other teachers have left on him.
He is distraught, saddened and confused.
Why has everyone given up on him?
He wears the black mistakes and white triumphs of his past education, but he is mostly gray.
Through his face you can see a silver sparkle of hope.

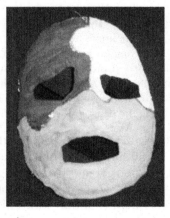

FIGURE 3.5.   Puzzle of Confusion.

It is a critical task to mentor preservice teachers to develop compassionate voices that echo softly to children; velvet words that speak of self-respect, hope, imagination, and dignity. As the above poem depicts, even in a neglected and abused child, there is always a "silver sparkle of hope" present, waiting for a compassionate and imaginative teacher to ignite! Our preservice teachers must know how to place "oneself in the shoes of others, especially children, absorbing their needs, their vulnerability, their weakness, and their suffering" (Anna Freud, as cited in Coles, 1993a, p. 205).

Their voices must speak to be continuously empathic in nature, so as to slide through the cracks in a child's armor of fear to light up the heart, mind, and soul. One child told me that her idea of the color blue was her sense of rejection by herself and others "in herself, her life and her soul." She had no friends, no loving teachers, and the more she broke into violent rages and temper tantrums in schools, the more that rejection and her sense of the rejection by others continued to develop. She was engulfed in an ocean of despair as she clung to a lifeboat of creative encounters that revealed her depth of pain. When her imaginative voice was revealed through aesthetic encounters with great works of art, her teachers and peers began to perceive her in new ways, and relationships began to change. She began to understand her pain and that she had a voice, and it was powerful.

Such experiences with children who have been rejected in public schools have inspired, motivated, and fueled the innovative design of several compassionate community events. The events explored throughout this book were designed to inflame the imaginative realm that unites teacher candidates and children for a community purpose. The results of the aesthetic community projects (social or ecological) revealed preservice teachers' unique voices expressing joy and a sense of contribution to a creative community. Through collective imaginative voices, a shared aesthetic action for change revealed creative and innovative thinking from our teacher candidates within a compassionate community—the KIVA.

We utilize a combination of artistic methods in our university KIVA classroom. A social or ecological theme is introduced to the teacher candidates via a painting, a skit modeled by their professors, a film, or a documentary such as *The Cove* (www.thecovemovie.com). After the introduction of the aesthetic as a motivating force for discussions of the theme or issue and how they impact our lives, teacher candidates begin to prepare symbolic skits, dances, and poems to teach children about the social or ecological issue. The multimethods of aesthetic layers allow the teacher candidates the freedom to explore a variety of creative and innovative landscapes of expression.

The teacher candidates then share and discuss the progression of the ideas in design. However "messy" at first, as the creative and emotional voices emerge, divergent thinking is developed and perceived as important to candidates. They begin to discover possibility in themselves while learning with and about each other, appreciating the diverse talents they have. We ask them to think about utilizing these methods with children. Many of our teachers transfer these methods to the field experiences and instantly understand the power of the aesthetic in releasing a child's imaginative voice. Our classes become much like the 20th century artists who were drawn to the primal mind for inspiration and connection to the sacred. Ideas such as storytelling around community fires or, in this instance, our KIVA classroom, are passed on from teacher candidates to the children in the classroom.

At one time, art was sacred and necessary for the survival of the culture. Currently in the 21st century, art has become a commodity; electronic and unnatural. Photographer Thierry Cohen (2013) blends city scenes to illustrate the degree of pollution in our cities' night skies. Cohen says the urbanites "forget and no longer understand nature." Likewise, by juxtaposing Cohen's city scenes to *Starry Night* by van Gogh (1889), are we actually viewing the brilliance of our Earth's skies at one time before modern pollution? Is our Earth's beauty diminished to such an extent that we no longer know of nature's true beauty and the beauty of our humanity? So too is the case in teacher preparation. Our teacher candidates are coming to us at the university feeling that they are void of an understanding of the aesthetic, the organic, and the natural world. Their voices have been replaced by text and electronic mediums in short, quick sound bites.

As authors of this book, we practice each day to live the aesthetic paradigm and immerse our students in the aesthetic so that their beliefs may be realized within the aesthetic. Our hope is to unlock our preservice teachers' fears and potential, and teach them to utilize their imaginative voice in order to champion children's voices when they become teachers. Their senses of self as a creative people have been shellacked, hardened, and disguised from years of neglect. Art is a foreign language and a critical medium for cultural expression. Hearing their voices within new worlds, our students are at first startled, but then empowered to perceive themselves in new ways.

Greene (1993) stated that

> encounters with the arts can awaken us to alternative possibilities of existing, of being human, of relating to others, of being other, that I argue for their centrality in curriculum. I believe they can open new perspectives on what is assumed to be "reality". . . Consider the advancing invisibility of the homeless or how accustomed we have become to burnt-out buildings. (p. 214)

The imagination is a key aspect of a teacher's potential. Teaching preservice teachers to understand how their imaginative voice will impact a child's

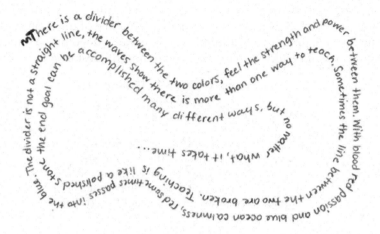

FIGURE 3.6.   Waves of Emotion by Leah.

engagement and sense of civic responsibility to the community and to each other must be part of the preservice teacher's development (Boyte, 2008).

As a teacher candidate, Leah illustrated her voice forming into a labyrinth of space and time, which is an ancient practice (Figure 3.6). Among the Celts, "imagination" means soul. Celtic scholar John O'Donohue (1997) points out that in the Celtic way of seeing, "everything in the world of soul has a deep longing and desire for visible form; this is exactly where the power of the imagination lives" (pp. 50–51). The imagination operates at a threshold where light and dark, visible and invisible, possibility and fact come together.

> The linear, controlling, external mind will never even glimpse the gift that imagination is. The revelations of nature come to us by way of imagination— that is, what expands the soul. In a culture where anthropocentrism does not reign, imaginations still does. For imagination needs the cosmos to feed on. It longs for relationships that stretch the soul. (Fox, 2004, p. 63)

Imaginative Voice and Social Possibility

As explored in previous seed chapters, for part of our methods coursework in elementary education, preservice teachers were immersed in a public school community that faced homelessness in their surrounding university environment. Preservice teachers constructed compassionate messages as a result of their participation and created the compassionate community curriculum for children using the arts to unmask the critical neglect of homeless children to paint a new face of homelessness. A teacher candidate composed the following poem in the first sequence of the professional program. His imaginative and humble voice reveals a deep understanding and importance of believing that children are our greatest teachers.

Piecing Together the Classroom
By Ian

My students are not there for me only to teach
My students are there to teach me.
When I look at the class it's all individuals
Each piece adds something to the whole
Looking at the puzzle there is a piece missing
The missing piece is me, the teacher
I start everyday wondering what I'll learn today
As much as I may teach
Equally I will learn
I can never forget that my students
Are also my teachers.

Preservice teachers explored puppets, pop culture characters, masks, and movement to construct new ways to perceive the stereotyped homeless individual in America today. Their imaginative voices were released as the generative topic of homelessness was discussed and symbolic ideas explored using aesthetic methods. They asked each other in small groups the questions: How do we get children to understand the homeless and to want to be involved with civic engagement? How do we change the stereotype of the homeless person? How do we inspire children to become civic agents?

After a series of six workshops utilizing spontaneous play, reflective think-writes, and poetry, preservice teachers discovered that the power of diverse symbolic messages may change the face of homelessness and simultaneously teach children to utilize compassionate action in their community. These aesthetic actions impacted preservice teachers' "voice" in relationship to their sense of self as teachers and beliefs about teaching children. Teacher candidates revealed the critical importance of nurturing and exercising the imaginative realm. As one preservice teacher said, "Learning was not dictated from a book—it was real—we acted it out and the children responded." When the preservice teachers unmasked the stereotypes regarding homelessness, their voices revealed a depth of awareness and empathy.

The teacher candidates' voices acknowledge the critical importance in shaping how preservice teachers perceive themselves as creative, compassionate teacher leaders of change in education. One future teacher stated, "We as future teachers can change the world. The idea starts small and grows." Shared imaginative action within a compassionate community reveals creative and innovative action. Eisner (2002) supports this perspective, stating,

Imagination, that form of thinking that engenders images of the possible, also has a critically important cognitive function to perform aside from the creation of possible worlds. Imagination also enables us to try things out—again in the mind's eye—without the consequences we might encounter if we had to act upon them empirically. (p. 5)

Figure 3.7 depicts three teacher candidates after performing in the community project to end homelessness. Identifying the best aesthetic methods to utilize to communicate compassion for the homeless in the local urban area, they discovered the power in trying out possible ideas, coming to a consensus, and revealing possibilities for transformation. One preservice teacher voiced,

> I have found my inner light and it makes me want to go out there and make a difference. Since I was a very young girl, I knew that I have always wanted to be a teacher. But now I feel even more than that. I feel like I can be a teacher and change the world. I want to show students how school can be a learning celebration rather than something they have to attend everyday because it's mandatory. I want to create a classroom that is memorable. My students will be able to count on me for anything because I will never speak negatively of a child. When learning is memorable to students they will remember what they have learned for the rest of their lives. As a future teacher, I want to be the change I wish to see in the world. Can you hear my voice? (Clark & French, 2012, p. 17)

Yet even with such eventual roars of spirit, our preservice teachers have an enduring crisis of "creative confidence" (Kelley & Kelley, 2012; see also

FIGURE 3.7. Creating a Compassionate Community: Preservice Teachers Sharing an Imaginative Voice, 2009.

Chapter 5, "The Seed of Inner Awareness") when they are first asked to expose their imaginative voice. They can even lapse back into their original shell afterwards, when they are "required" to go back to default outside our KIVA space. Candidates reveal in words and action that they do not understand why elementary teachers need to be creative and understand the arts as mediums for learning. Our teachers need support and guidance to attend to their confidence crises and must be led through a series of baby steps and successes that will ultimately build confidence and a community of teacher artists. Our students learn in a "social context that provides interplay of two or more people, including the professor," to create a sense of possibility and innovation (Efland, 2002, p. 36). Through this, preservice teachers learn how to create cutting-edge ideas about teaching complex concepts to children.

But these barriers to "authentic speaking" (Greene, 1978, p. 61) are, it must be stressed, enormous. As illustration, Greene presents Dewey's description of the modern life wherein steam and electric machines have invaded society and oppressed "the silent ones" (Dewey, as cited in Greene, 1978, pp. 61–62). Science fiction literature from the 20th century has warned us about the possibility of machines taking over our lives. More and more impersonal forces are invading our cultural ways of thinking and doing, and eroding the quality of human life. Could one say that the machines now in the 21st century have continued to promote conformities, isolation, and oppression—especially for those who do not possess the machines? Greene (1978) states,

> My point is that teacher educators ought to work to combat the sense of ineffectuality and powerlessness that comes when persons feel themselves to be the victims of forces wholly beyond their control, in fact beyond any human control. The explanations of inflations are not the only ones that breed powerlessness and self-interest. They are not the only ones that turn people towards a kind of lifeboat psychology that makes impossible any tuning-in relationship, any sense of interdependence or common life. (p. 64)

Many of our teacher candidates have forgotten how to communicate and fall into awkward silence during our introduction of the aesthetic. Many express that using masks, dance, or poetry is outside their comfort zone. We created the concept of the compassionate KIVA in our classes as a way for students to understand that their voices that have long ago been silenced and forgotten will emerge once again while facing one another, reading one another's emotions, applying emotional imagination, studying voices of others in the past, and using masks to face off with one another. The KIVA space allows their voices to be expressed and bear witness to one another—to their hopes, fears, and dreams.

We must turn around in education the existing "media of exploitation" amid unequal educational opportunities. The meritocratic paradigm must be questioned (Davis, 1995). Those children who have been living in a culture of silence and oppression must be given pathways to release their imaginative voices (Clark, 2005).

According to McElfresh-Spehler and Slattery (1999), the most important voice that emerges through exposure to the arts is the prophetic voice addressing our complex modern challenges with environment and economics, power and poverty. The prophetic voice, when revealed, is the ultimate unmasking of the sacred within us. It holds the responsibility we must all carry to help one another and respect all of life and nature as we live our lives on earth. Like us, McElfresh-Spehler and Slattery believe that the pursuit of social and ecological justice in our public schools is invariably invisible in curriculum. The authors ascertain that a prophetic voice leads to social change and is revealed through exposure to the arts; otherwise, "students and citizens become hollow, stuffed, and dead" (p. 2).

When preservice teachers are "personally engaged with the subject matter and with the world" they begin to awaken their own beliefs and values (Greene, 1978, p. 48). As said, preservice teachers come to us with certain indifference to the arts and to creativity. They struggle with social play and social community events that should awaken their perception and beliefs of how children learn best. It is our goal to awaken the preservice teacher's voice and imagination to, at the very least, guide them to see one another, hear one another, and care for one another. In Coles (1993b) book titled, *The Call of Service,* he questions one's commitment to their work. Do our teacher candidates perceive their work as a calling, or as a career?

If our preservice teachers are not awakened and go into teaching in a type of sugared fog of unreality and stereotypes, they will struggle, or worse, begin to blame the children and their families for the lack of learning. Dewey called for "choice of action" (Greene, 1978, p. 47), implementing one's own resources and knowledge of self-efficacy. How do we get teachers to see that children are active and continually change as they grow and develop through various stages? "Engaged with the environment, each one must effect connections within his or her own experience and . . . perceive the consequences" (Greene, 1978, p. 47).

Voice and Innovation: Transfer of the Aesthetic to the Field Classroom

Greene (1978) is concerned with curriculum that is finding meaning and sense-making (p. 169). One preservice teacher, Courtney, developed a holistic science lesson utilizing aesthetic methodology to study the rotation of the Earth, moon, and sun. Using a classroom SMART board, the

5th-grade children were asked to view Monet's haystacks projected on the screen (Figure 3.8):

The children were captivated with the colors and light and shadow. Courtney questioned the children asking, What do you see? Where is the shadow? What time of day was Monet (1891) capturing? How did he paint light? Courtney then had the children create sculptures of haystacks. Using small flashlights, the scene that Monet painted was re-created by the children through the interplay of light and shadow dancing upon their clay sculptures. The children worked with partners to discuss how the shadow changed depending on the direction of light and time of day.

As Courtney continued to develop the lesson, the children were asked to record their observations in their journals. The last part of the lesson had the children create masks symbolizing the sun, moon, or Earth and wrote poetry. The science lesson captivated the children's imagination through the aesthetic lens. Nature and art merged to build science concepts and were authentically connected to the children's lives. Our methods are designed so that our teacher candidates begin to perceive their beliefs and discover their individual voice and diversity of possibility as they share with one another a unique sense of passion and zeal (Clark & French, 2012). As a preservice teacher, Courtney's values and voice shaped this unique lesson. She wanted the children to experience the world through their senses and art, revealing their innate talents and potential. Incorporating a playful strategy to study light from the Earth and sun's rotation inspired children to recognize that learning is full of miracles and that nature abounds with

FIGURE 3.8. Morning Snow Effect by Monet (1891).

inspiration. Aesthetic methods naturally focus on the whole child, being particularly aware of the child's imaginative and spiritual realm of understanding connections to their world and others.

Like Courtney, many of our preservice teachers emerged with strong imaginative voices in that they were able to transfer their values and beliefs to their field experience classrooms. Their voices emerged also during the design of various skits and then performances, teaching children themes of social and ecological justice issues. One preservice teacher, Yesenia, made her first debut solo singing (see Chapter 8, "The Seed of Love," for lyrics) to over 1,000 children. She was so passionate about the dolphin slaughter in Taiji, Japan, that she wanted to inspire the children. On her way home in her car from a class workshop with us, she wrote lyrics releasing her voice to depict her beliefs regarding an ecological disaster. She courageously presented her lyrics and sang for her peers the next week in her methods class.

Yesenia literally found her voice and made a transformation motivated directly in order to impact children's perception of their world. About 1,000 children viewed a future teacher giving her heart and soul to stop the dolphin slaughter. The children may not remember the lyrics, but they will remember the passion and imaginative voice that echoed throughout the auditorium. A voice was inspired from within Yesenia's sacred core, a transformative voice emerging from her soul-force, her love-force, for future teachers and for children learning from what we do.

Another preservice teacher as a freshman encountered aesthetic education and unmasking children's emotions. This young man, Wellington, was inspired after taking on a role as a jester, leading 60 children through a series of spontaneous movements. This was Wellington's first semester working with children and the arts. He said, "I am a creative being. I see myself in new ways I never imagined." He also perceived the children in new ways, understanding deeply that children wonder and worry about very similar issues in their lives as compared to his. He found his voice; he found his spirit, his imagination, and hope through play and innovative actions with children. Similarly, a preservice teacher, Yvette, recognized the power of aesthetics to impact and release an imaginative voice in children. After participating in a community project titled *Echoes from a Child's Soul,* with 160 fifth-grade children, she stated,

> Before we started this project the students were very quiet and closed up when it came to sharing their emotions. Through working with the students I found that they became more trusting of us as teachers and they started opening up. The students felt as though they could express their emotions appropriately. The students in our group became very close like a family and everyone respected each other's feelings and emotions. After the performance the students were very sad because they found out that it would be the last time that they would be working with the CCSU students. I think they really enjoyed

working with us. Some of the students said to me, "I wish we could go up on stage again" and "That was really fun! I wish it wasn't over." I really enjoyed working with these students, and I learned more from them than they learned from me, I think.

Yvette went on to utilize the unmasking of ideas in her field experience with 5th-grade children. She was astounded to find parallel results in a suburban classroom. She said that this experience impacted her teaching beliefs and that she was confident to share the message that the arts and aesthetic methods get to the very core of children's hearts and minds, to their innate abilities, to possibility, through play and invention.

Voice and Culturally Responsive Teaching

A 5th-grade student from a dual language public magnet school created the following poem/song in an urban setting. Her teachers did not view the child at the time as gifted or as a risk taker, but Karen wanted to share her dream with others and asked to be able to sing her song at the *Echoes from a Child's Soul* community forum. She revealed through her experience with mask, movement, and poetry that she had a voice and had a lot to say to the world about her life and feelings. She stepped out onto the stage and sang *a cappella*. The world stopped for those moments as the 10-year-old child's voice was revealed. The audience was amazed. After Karen completed her song, a burst of applause rang out.

At the time of the performance, we did not know that Karen was a child with an incarcerated parent. Karen revealed to a preservice teacher her frustration that her mother was not present. She was proud of herself. She grew that day. Her voice had been shared within a compassionate community setting, and she found out what happens when the imaginative voice is released: possibility and hope abounds. Here is Karen's song:

On Top of the World
I don't have the balance,
Think I'm gonna fall.
Why did I think I could do this?
I don't belong here at all.

Drowning in the pressure,
In over my head.
Why did I think I could do this?
Could have walked away instead.

This is my chance to break free
Everything's depending on me

And if I keep trying,
I'll be on top of the world.

Where I can see everything before me.
Reaching out to touch the sky,

On top of the world,
All of my dreams are reaching toward me.
Stretching out my wings to fly,
On top of the world.

At the same time that our teacher candidates are working to release children's voices, we are working with our teacher candidates to teach them that they also have a voice. As seen below, the following mask pictures (Figure 3.9) and poem by Sarah, models the passion and spirited voice that symbolizes her views as to the force of a teacher when they focus their work as writers, dreamers, artists, speakers, and creators.

I love to learn and play   I am flying through life   I am falling, falling, falling
   A celebration,   A journey of free imagination   But I'm not scared
Bursting with new feelings.   All year long.   Everyone is here to catch me.
We Are All Changing
Constantly Evolving
With Each Other.
We Are All Unique.
We Are The
Writers, Dreamers, Artists, Speakers, Creators
Of Life's Greatest Moments.

In stark contrast to the emotional voice within Sarah, what we currently mutter in schools is just not good enough. If public schools in America continue to base their curriculum implementation on technical strategies that only prepare our children for the workforce, we are at risk of being at a diminished capacity to nurture the imaginative, physical, social, emotional, and psychological well-being of our children and our future teachers.

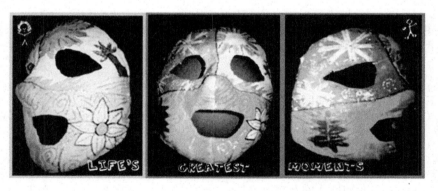

FIGURE 3.9.   Three Mask Perspectives: Life's Greatest Moments.

As will be further explored in the following Chapter 4, "The Seed of Change," to enact change in their future classrooms and education, teacher candidates must unmask indifference and status quo and not accept mediocrity as a standard for children. Urging the call for change, the sacred imaginative voice and emotional voice explored in this chapter must first be renewed as a critical platform of basic beliefs by teacher candidates in the development of the whole child.

REFERENCES

Boyte, H. (2008). *The citizen solution: How you can make a difference*. St. Paul: Minnesota Historical Society.

Clark, B. (2005). *Moral imagination and art: Echoes from a child's soul* (Doctoral dissertation). University of Hartford, Connecticut. Retrieved May 10, 2012, from Dissertations & Theses: Full Text. (Publication No. AAT 315 7797).

Clark, B. (2009). Mustard seed: A personal search for "Ahimsa" (The truth of nonviolence). *Closing the Circle Exhibition*. B. Clark & M. Cipriano (Artists). New Britain, CT: New Britain Commission on the Arts.

Clark, B., & French, J. (2012). ZEAL: A revolution for education, unmasking teacher identity through aesthetic education, imagination and transformational practice. *Critical Questions in Education, 3*(1), 12–22.

Cohen, T. (2013). Starry, starry, starry night. *New York Times*. Retrieved from http://www.nytimes.com/interactive/2013/02/03/magazine/look-stars.html?_r=0

Coles, R. (1987). *Simone Weil: A modern pilgrimage*. Reading, MA. Addison-Wesley.

Coles, R. (1993a). *Anna Freud: The dream of psychoanalysis*. New York, NY: Perseus.

Coles, R. (1993b). *The call of service*. New York, NY: Houghton Mifflin.

Davis, K. (1995). Multicultural classrooms and cultural communities of teachers. *Teaching and Teacher Education, 11*(6), 553–563.

Efland, A. (2002). *Art and cognition: Integrating the visual arts in the curriculum*. New York, NY: Teachers College Press.

Eisner, E. W. (2002). *The arts and the creation of mind*. New Haven, CT: Yale University Press.

Elkind, D. (1981). *The hurried child: Growing up too fast too soon*. Redding, MA.: Addison-Wesley.

Fox, M. (2004). *Creativity: Where the divine and human meet*. New York, NY: Penguin.

French, J. (2013). Methods & mindsets for creating eco-social community educators. In D. G. Mulcahy (Ed.), *Transforming schools: Alternative perspectives on school reform* (pp. 37–66). Charlotte, NC: Information Age.

French, J., & Clark, B. (2012). Revitalizing a spiritual compassionate commons in educational culture. *Religion and Education, 39*(1), 93–108.

Gandhi, M. (1957). *Autobiography: The story of my experiments with truth*. Boston, MA: Beacon.

Greene, M. (1978). *Landscapes of learning*. New York, NY: Teachers College Press.

Greene, M. (1993). Diversity and inclusion: Toward a curriculum for human beings. *Teachers College Record, 95*(2), 213–221.

Greene, M. (2001). *Variations on a blue guitar: The Lincoln Center Institute lectures on aesthetic education*. New York, NY: Teacher College Press.

Hammarskjöld, D. (1964). *Markings*. New York, NY: Alfred A. Knopf.

Kelley, T., & Kelley, D. (2012). Reclaim your creative confidence. *Harvard Business Review, 90*(12), 115.

McElfresh-Spehler, R., & Slattery, P. (1999). Voices of imagination: The artist as prophet in the process of social change. *International Journal of Leadership in Education, 2*(1), 1–12.

Monet, C. (1891). *Meule, Effet de Neige, le Matin* (*Morning Snow Effect*) [Painting]. Retrieved May 22, 2013, http://commons.wikimedia.org/wiki/Monet#Wheatstacks_.26_Haystacks

O'Donohue, J. (1997). *Anam cara: A book of Celtic wisdom*. New York, NY: Harper Collins.

Radmacher, M. (2013). *Artist, author, apronary*. Retrieved from www.maryanneradmacher.net.

Weil, S. (2001). *Waiting for God*. New York, NY: Harper Perennial.

CHAPTER 4

THE SEED OF CHANGE

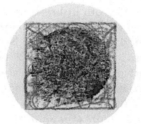

Seed of Change Painting
(Clark, 2009b)

I suspect that many of the great cultural shifts that prepare the way for political change are largely aesthetic.

—J. G. Ballard

You cannot point out one thing that is not here—
time, space, the earth, the rain, the minerals in the soil,
the sunshine, the cloud, the river, the heat.
Everything co-exists with this sheet of paper.
As thin as this sheet of paper is,
it contains everything in the universe in it.

——Thich Nhat Hanh

Hearts and Minds Without Fear: Unmasking the Sacred in Teacher Preparation,
pages 85–117.

Where did we come from, who are we, where are we going and how will we get there? U.S. educational curriculum and teacher preparation has yet to be able to envision and act for change in children's education for what Earth and interdependent human and ecological communities need to thrive. In an effort to explain why, societal philosopher John Saul (2012) asserts,

> Our reality is that several generations have refused to imagine themselves making changes. Modern society is built upon a war between rationality and superstition . . . but the real point here is that the either/or reason of life—of how we imagine ourselves, doesn't work. There are other options.

We agree: Our failure to act for change is due to our refusal to recognize the infinite domain of the imagination. Pushing aside the enactment of moral imagination through the arts instantly marginalizes children as at-risk rather than at-promise (Clark, 2005b). Beyond the simultaneous failed potential of our educational systems to address needed change in their societal mindset, with coldly rational educational accountability, curriculum and pedagogy standing idly by, our hubris-driven postindustrial experiment on the national and global stage continues to bring massive social and ecological devastation (French & Clark, 2012). Nonpossibilizing creative options, as the pop song lyrics of John Mayer (2006) so aptly condemn us or confirm for us, we instead are "*Waiting on the world to change.*"

As a society, in the last 400 years, we have increasingly gone against the natural laws of creativity and the hunger for a connection to the spiritual within. The Celts lived close to the water and the essence of creation was celebrated with a profound respect for the "elements of wind, storm, rain, and snow, as well as the glorious beauty and warmth of sunlight (when it finally appears)" (Sellner, 1999, p. 137). We hear endlessly about healthy relationships on talk shows or individuals bragging about the number of friends they have on virtual social media outlets, yet these are hollow and shallow relationships "in a world that is internetted, but in reality, all they deliver is a simulated world of shadows" (O'Donohue, 1997, p. 17). O'Donohue believes that "real intimacy is a sacred experience. It never exposes its sacred trust and belonging to the voyeuristic eye of a neon culture. Real intimacy is of the soul, and the soul is reserved" (p. 17).

Yeats celebrated the Celtic spiritual traditions in a book titled, *The Celtic Twilight* (1902). In Yeats' poem, "Into the Twilight" (1893), he captures the desire for a time long past, a sacred time where possibility was infinite within ones imagination (Sellner, 1999):

Into the Twilight
By William Butler Yeats
Out-worn heart, in a time out-worn,
Come clear of the nets of wrong and right;
Laugh, heart, again in the gray twilight;

Sigh, heart, again in the dew of the morn.
Thy mother Eire is always young,
Dew ever shining and twilight gray,
Though hope fall from thee or love decay
Burning in fires of a slanderous tongue.
Come, heart, where hill is heaped upon hill,
For there the mystical brotherhood
Of hollow wood and the hilly wood
And the changing moon work out their will.
And God stands winding his lonely horn;
And Time and World are ever in flight,
And love is less kind than the gray twilight,
And hope is less dear than the dew of the morn.

Many of these so-called primitive cultures, like the Celts, whose embodiments recognize creative law as inherent, have sustained longevity well beyond our own meager timeline, due to the practiced knowledge that the very essence of life is formed within the creative spirit. Nonlinear and inclusive, they see themselves as a part of the natural world. Their perspectives match the simultaneous, intricate, complex, and interconnected realities of nature (see spiral concept map in Figure 4.2). Their spiritually informed and imbedded sustainable cultural worldviews provide synergistic truths and explanations, while our postindustrial despondent logic can only produce thin, artificial, oversimplified manipulations to further reinforce our false sense of superiority and hubris.

Our lack of concordance with creativity and compassion has reinforced individualism, competition, and destruction. Aggressive mindsets of material wealth and practice have been introduced physically and ideologically into what we have condescendingly labeled the "third-world" (Norberg-Hodge, 1991). Through the brute force of our dysfunctional "free-market" systems within multiple historic colonization and present-day international globalization contexts, our postindustrial "progress" has also simultaneously eradicated the wisdom of countless communally "shared life-sustaining skills, knowledge, and natural environments into monetized and privately owned commodities" (French & Clark, 2012, p. 97).

Meanwhile, running out of time, unable to digest other "radically" different perspectives in our freefall ecstasy we call flying (Quinn, 1995), our linear infrastructures stupefy any possibility for change. Distracted by the material, we have forgotten how to honor nature. In the face of rigorous rationality and the drive for profit, progress, and success, creative spirituality is cast aside as optional rather than perceived as essential for a thriving culture.

Allowing our rational mindsets to artificially distance our perceptions from one another, we have convinced ourselves that nature and aesthetics are somehow separated from daily life. This is evident in many ways: While the masculine mind is hard at work, the objectified feminine form is deemed weak—we do our jobs rather than celebrate our connection to nature in daily life and learning; we routinely complain instead of ceremoniously regard our very conception as a creative force; we find inconvenience in lieu of celebration of our children and planet. As the Dalai Lama observes, we live our daily lives in self-centeredness rather than through a realized vision that we are all one, sharing the same mind, spirit and body (2012).

Briggs (2012) believes that in order to address our tumultuous problems of the 21st century there must be "a dynamic conjunction between compassion and creativity. . . . Compassion for all sentient beings, as the Buddhists put it, may provide the only sensible framework and enabling force that will allow our overflowing creativity to function sanely" (p. xix). If we want to really create peace in our world, creativity and compassion must be dynamically united within the individual and practiced with others.

Many people are not aware that the Celts revered women for their creative gifts, compassionate action, and leadership. Women had specific legal rights in Ireland that allowed for divorce of a husband and to protect their inheritances. St. Brigit was a part of the community, preaching sermons, hearing confessions, and healing the sick. Throughout history, accounts are made that attribute miracles to St. Brigit's creativity and compassionate action combined. Her leadership qualities are legendary and she remains a female hero in Irish spiritual literature.

St. Brigit became the most blessed woman among her male and female followers throughout the entire island of Ireland. St. Brigit is one of many ancient examples wherein creativity and compassion changed the lives and mindsets of so many who struggled with the "dark night of the soul." The Celts lived so close to nature and were constantly at risk for homelessness and poverty. However their natural perspective regarding life as a gift to be treasured led them to compassionate outreach toward others who were deemed outcasts. St. Brigit was an example of compassion as stories from long ago detail her ministry to the homeless, the lepers, pregnant young women, the old and weak (Sellner, 1999, p. 139).

Yet, when any plausible attempt is made to address our 21st century mindset and approach, such compassionate intentions are labeled as a romanticization, or that to change our ways would be to move society backwards into a harsher, archaic lifestyle. When presented with the opportunity to create, we often refuse to enter the imaginative realm, because to reimagine would mean to break away from what we have convinced ourselves is the only right way. The aesthetic and the arts are seen as a threat and are continuously marginalized. Fearful of the unknown, we cling to this paradigm. Fearing reprisal and criticism, we propagate a continual disruption of the sacred.

The aesthetic provides the means to reimagine ourselves alongside sustainable creative culture wisdoms, but instead, our selfish patriarchal fast-car culture has disrupted and dishonored our creative cultural potential for true joy and change. In our self-induced perception and negation of creativity born from the spirit, we further alienate ourselves from nature and one another. We multiply the effect even more so with our efficient emphasis on technology and medications, which only compounds a further loosening of any emotional and intellectual connection to essence through our senses. Along with destroying our own longevity as a postindustrial society, our insatiable self-destructive consumerisms have taken countless other sustainable cultures and ecosystems (French & Clark, 2012). At home, the consequence has been a disruption and dissolving of community and family bonds that result in continuous trauma for the child.

It would seem that given such suffering, we should be rushing to imagine and practice alternative sustainable ways of knowing to nurture, grow, support, and revitalize our creative spirits as a society. Countless individuals have pointed out the means to changing mindset through education, begging for the purpose of teacher education—how should teachers be prepared to impact children's and our future lives? Given our current mindset predicament, how might we change ourselves through education, if not for an unyielding adult society, but for our children, youth, and teachers?

We believe that the KIVA paradigm, which manifests educators who understand natural and creative potential beyond our toxic secular climate, is essential for enacting true change. As a society, and within our educational institutions, we must examine and embrace other lived cultural practices and perspectives to address our catastrophic consequences of "rational" materialistic thinking. We must reimagine ourselves beyond a false propagated linearity to instead embrace a spiraled reality, which ancient and exceedingly fewer present-day sustainable cultures have already recognized as a means of life and survival. With help to gain awareness and perspective of our elusive addiction to our positivist stupor, we can begin to reimagine ourselves and revolutionize our educational system to embrace forgotten, pushed away possibilities that have always been with us. In short, we cannot continue to ignore the vast imaginative capacity that every child holds.

For example, we can bring to our learning, to the so-called democratic pillars of the long-standing American public education system, a counter-narrative that reverses the artificial socially constructed limits of privatization. Aesthetic educator Elliot Eisner (2002) states, "Transforming the private into the public is a primary process of work in both art and science. Helping the young to learn how to make that transformation is another of education's most important aims" (p. 3). We must shore up destructive rhetoric to pave the way for privatization of the public sphere magnified by media, of U.S. public education being a "total failure" (Ravitch, 2011). At least in our institutions of education, to fully begin any fundamental authentic transformation of our mindset and identity as teachers and learners, and to provide a real buttress of hope for public education, we must embrace the aesthetic as a means, not as a disposable extra, but an inherent form of teaching and learning. As Greene implores,

> For those authentically concerned about the "birth of meaning," about breaking through the surfaces, about teaching others to "read" their own worlds, art forms must be conceived of as ever-present possibility. They ought not to be treated as decorative, as frivolous. They ought to be, if transformative teaching is our concern, a central part of curriculum, wherever it is devised. (1988, p. 131)

Indeed, any serious consideration of an alternative aesthetic paradigm demands a shift in societal perspective and relationship with the arts. Given the psychological market influences in our society (i.e., mass-produced kitsch art), the aesthetic provides a powerful counterremedy to question prevailing values and power and ultimately leads us toward a greater truth about our existence. Great art throughout history has always been on the front lines of any radical movement. The aesthetic provides multiple alternate pathways that open invitation, exposure, time, and personal choice, and moves people into actions that lead to change.

By implementing the aesthetic paradigm of experiencing, learning, and knowing within our teacher education courses, we have discovered that the aesthetic nurtures reconnection to nature and humanity. Planting the aesthetic within a teacher preparation course curriculum critically awakened our students to SEE with respect, heart, and soul to imagine, a "wide-awakening" (Greene, 2001) of what could be possible in educational practice when engaged in the community. Within the space of KIVA, we were able to reimagine ourselves and thus what our world could be and how we could get there.

By the means of radically changing how we can imagine ourselves through aesthetic education, we have found ways to bring about vision and action for change in children's education. As we detail within this seed chapter, when given multiple opportunities for innovative curriculum design to promote imaginative social and eco-action through aesthetic scaffolding, our elementary preservice teachers revealed their emerging sense of identity as creative compassionate teacher leaders.

The critical importance of nurturing and exercising the *emotional imaginative* realm will be explained systematically with specific examples of activities highlighting both social justice and ecojustice themes. When introduced in the aesthetic domain to community efforts that embraced a sense

UNMASKING
CHANGE

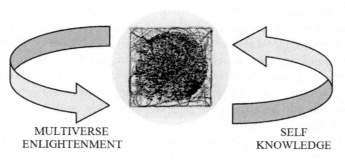

MULTIVERSE   SELF
ENLIGHTENMENT   KNOWLEDGE

FIGURE 4.1. Unmasking Change Concept Map.

of possibility, through aesthetic civic engagement, social imagination, and empowerment, future educators made evident the beliefs and possibility to change their own and other's behaviors and mindsets (Clark & French, 2012; French, 2013). Experiencing an aesthetic compassionate learning community methodology, our students realized they were imaginative, innovative, and inspirational teachers of children and citizens of change.

The above conceptual map presents the *Seed of Change* (Figure 4.1).The seed of change inherently implies that humans, whether teacher or student in this context, are not stagnant. The teacher's responsibility will stimulate the sense of enlightenment toward a multiverse of persons, realities, concepts, ideas, and multidirectional consequences through the aesthetic. In other words, the reciprocal interaction of this seed between the teacher and learner illustrates the diversity of people's perceptions throughout the world when they encounter the aesthetic such as a mask, a dance, a poem, and such. When students are confronted with concepts of transformative change through encounters with the aesthetic, knowledge of self and others grows. The aesthetic is the universal bridge connecting to all cultures and realities the imaginative seed we all carry at our very core. This is truly a reciprocal seed, as consciousness grows when learning in a multiverse of possibility engaged in artistic expression. Teacher candidates begin to see in new ways in which ecological and social issues (self, school, community, worldviews) are impacted. Aesthetic methods promote divergent thinking, no end to the possibilities, and an infinite number of answers to problems. The aesthetic is the precursor to political change. Meditating on the *Seed of Change* painting (Clark, 2009b), one can see the deep values blending, merging, and building power toward change.

Change: Reimagining Teacher Education and Natural Worlds

As was detailed in Chapter 2, "The Seed of Hope," the whole of our revolutionary place-based aesthetic curriculum leap frogs over the mediocre hopelessness of teaching-to-the-test mandates. True transformative learning happens when we are able to reimagine the possibilities of what we can do and by going against learned top-down testing psychosis. In this frame of reference, *doing* rather than *letting things happen*, the enactment of the aesthetic is a natural outlet opportunity within the teacher education context, whose core should be a group of people engaged in finding out *what they can do* to help people learn.

From previous chapter discussions, it should come as no surprise that our entrenched testing paradigm fits perfectly as a means to preserve segregated schools, bias, and racism. It allows for uninspiring, unintuitive, unimaginative teacher education and teaching practice. It permits the continuation of students' learning for grades rather than for personal transformation. It perpetuates mediocrity and fear of the "unattainable" heights of knowledge and power. It induces hubris, self-centeredness, and false superiority. Teacher evaluations based on test scores reinforce meritocratic myths within the endless cycle of continued bias against immigrant children, children with disabilities, and children living in poverty. Ultimately, narrowing our mindsets to a rational positivist industrial logic of the status quo, ingrained pedagogies may be continually distracting us from *reimagining what we could be* in relation to our children's natural and social worlds.

Aesthetic Conceptual Framework Spiral

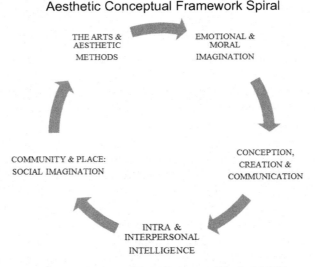

FIGURE 4.2. Aesthetic Conceptual Spiral Map #1 (Clark, 2005b).

Below we reveal a concept map diagram (Figure 4.2) illustrating how the aesthetic paradigm can authentically inspire a deeper knowledge of eco- and social-justice issues and awareness. Instead of just waiting around for change, we activated and instilled the imperative goals of social and ecojustice *by doing*. Through a continuation of the aesthetic in full form and force, beyond just an attractive "initiation" or "hook," we were able to continually reinforce inspiration, motivation, awareness, and action.

Alongside children, we were effectively able to impact our teacher candidates' ideas and beliefs about transformative learning, their sense of imaginative societal contribution, core values, and abilities to cope with institutional conflicts within local, national, and international social- and ecojustice issues. Galvanized by the paramount compelling spiritual force of the aesthetic, preservice teachers' beliefs and identity were inspired. Through their emotional imaginations, they addressed the collective community social and ecological issues they would face in their field experiences and future teaching.

Traditionally, academia relates new ideas in a linear fashion. But while this may be comfortable and familiar to some, such an approach is impossible in the case of the aesthetic paradigm unmasking the sacred core. As already shown, the purposefully created and placed Seed Painting concept maps that have introduced and framed each chapter of this book have authentically contributed to demystifying our paradigm. The aesthetic conceptual framework (see Figure 4.2) continues this process by using a spiral to specifically depict the aesthetic paradigm change process (Clark, 2005b) as described in this chapter.

As shown above, the aesthetic (i.e., painting, poem, video, dance, story) is introduced so that the emotional imagination of the learner is triggered to critically dissect all aspects of the theme or topic, whether it is socially or ecologically based. The emotional imagination evokes in the learner a set of feelings based on memories and prior experiences that simultaneously surface with their emotions. The learner will utilize reflective intelligence to examine the feelings that may possibly hold bias, stereotypes, and/or lazy dispositions to ignore or be passive (Perkins, 1994).

This visual thinking process utilizing the complex language of the aesthetic results in a deepening of self-knowledge (interpersonal intelligence) and simultaneously builds upon intrapersonal knowledge when feelings, emotions, and common experiences are shared with a group. Once feelings are examined and discussed with the continuous support of the aesthetic theme, new concepts, ideas, and possibilities originate from the learners, both as individuals and as a group. These concepts and ideas are then communicated and shared with the community, wherein social imagination is revealed (Gardner, 1982; Langer, 1957).

Make a Wave Project: Example of Aesthetic Community Impact on Moral and Social Imagination

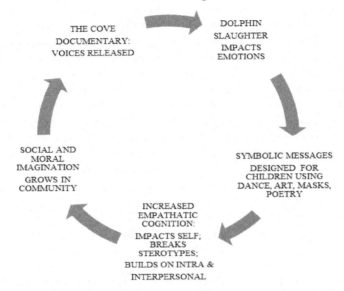

FIGURE 4.3. Aesthetic conceptual spiral map #2 (Clark, 2005b; Clark & French, 2012)

The aesthetic paradigm promotes individual and community growth at the same time. It provides an instant trigger because the nature of the aesthetic holds instant access to the myriad themes, ideas, and relationships that the viewer can explore. As a visual metaphor, the whole of the concept map is drawn as a spiral to reflect the reciprocal nature between intra- and interpersonal relationships that leads to an empathic sense toward others and nature and to increased compassionate action for the well-being of a social or ecological community. In this instant, simultaneous, and reciprocal manner, the aesthetic brings about the change and deeper knowledge of social and ecojustice as related in a holistic and authentic learning experience approach.

To further illustrate the above aesthetic paradigm's effect on change within an artistically imaginative ecocritical curriculum imbedded in community action (Clark & French, 2012), the Make a Wave Project conceptual framework map (Figure 4.3) is the same spiral shape, but we have replaced the labels with a specific KIVA project contextual example from one of our course semesters.

FIGURE 4.4. "You are the Change!": Our students with children on stage in the finale of *Make a Wave* project (Photo by Craven, 2010).

In *Make a Wave*, we addressed ecological change through reimagining our natural world relationships. As part of their work, preservice teachers designed, performed, and hosted a theatrical piece addressing the dolphin slaughter for profit (depicted in the documentary "The Cove" [www.thecovemovie.com], whose compelling nature was used as an initial aesthetic experience with our students). Some 1,000 urban children from the surrounding public school community came to our college campus and learned about the dolphin slaughter for profit through puppets, dance, and poetry. Portraying their own desire for freedom and hope as teachers and artists, preservice teachers danced the dance of the dolphin, enacted an acknowledgement of human shortsighted cruelty, and offered a song to take compassionate action.

This one-semester course's final performance is an example of how the innovative methods of aesthetic education encompassed our student selected ecosocial justice topics and simultaneously addressed our preservice teachers' ideas and beliefs about new learning, their sense of imaginative societal contribution, core values, and coping with institutional conflicts (Figure 4.4).

Similar to the aesthetic scaffolding described for other KIVA spaces throughout this book (like the *Creating a Compassionate World Community Project* depicted below), leading up to this final performance, pre-service teachers utilized creative inquiry to investigate the authentic eco-social issue facing their surrounding local and global community. They explored their beliefs and identities on this issue by inviting community artists and activists to contribute to the creation and design of symbolic messages using masks, puppets, poetry, dance, music, and theater.

FIGURE 4.5. Dolphins in Captivity: *Make a Wave* project, 2010. To view *Dolphins in Captivity* video, visit www.compassionateteaching.com and click on *Our Book* tab on home page, then click on *Freedom* tab.

As shown in Figure 4.5 photographs taken during the final performance, composite, multiple symbolic ideas carried a compassionate message to build awareness of the particular ecosocial issue, which was then integrated and shared within the community to address transformative learning and societal contribution.

As an instance of the emotional imagination KIVA space within the *Make a Wave* semester's project, our students reimagined themselves and effected their empathy and compassion through the aesthetic medium. Layering symbol upon symbol, they not only literally became the dolphins, the trainers, and the killers but also expounded their message by performing in a public pronouncement. The possibility of change was realized as symbolic messages were shared in order to end the dolphin slaughter, thus capturing an emerging sense of self as a teacher agent of change. Our students and children were indelibly transformed from this experience. As two children in the audience wrote us following the performance,

> Things I thought about during the performance was how dolphins could become extinct. When I thought that, I thought WOW! This is so sad. What I did learn was that dolphins are dying because of people hunting them and making them practice for big shows.

> The thing that I learned by watching the performance is that you can make a change and to not keep dolphins as a pet because they need to be with their family. The feelings that were evoked by watching is they gave me a message that really touched me. Save the dolphins. Make a change!

As shown in the children's voices above, we see how individuals in the community are impacted and start to change their perspectives when new aesthetics are introduced (*Make a Wave* performance). As perspectives change and social and ecological consciousness grows empathically, change continues to occur. The community begins to imagine a better world to live in, and each individual has a responsibility to contribute to that change each day of their life.

The aesthetic paradigm described above allowed our preservice teachers to reveal and release their identities as people and future citizens toward ecosocial consciousness and expression, thus enabling them to contribute to social and ecojustice action in their pedagogy and practice with children (French, 2011; French & Clark, 2012). The emotional imagination, when activated through art, impacts the seeing, thinking, and feeling systems wherein moral imagination can develop (Clark, 2005a). Dewey (1980) struck a heightened awareness that through art and experience, art and morality are by nature linked. We are imagining a revolution of change through the aesthetic whereby the imagination reveals itself to be deeply spiritual, moral, and empathic.

Ultimately, a key message that can be taken from the above spiral concept maps we create for our students is that eco- and social-justice goals cannot be realized at the higher level of thinking (or later acted upon) without the aesthetic. The aesthetic moves our students creatively, emotionally, and spiritually, enabling them to become increasingly aware of the power of their *emotional imaginations* that create new ideas and take actions for change. Aesthetics and imagination are synonymous as the "Gestalt" of body and soul (Arnheim, 2004; Clark, 2005b; Eisner, 2002). It is the aesthetic that ignites our imagination, which allows for true creation, possibility, and change.

Imagination –> Creativity + Innovative Action = Change

As educators, there are many potential places and spaces for us to effect community revitalization both within the natural world as well as in the interplay between our social infrastructure and the natural world (Bowers, 2006; French, 2013; Martusewicz, Edmundson, & Lupinacci, 2011). Our KIVA model depicts a space where learners can feel safe sharing and creating a multiverse of reality (Highwater, 1982; Perlmutter & Lenzer, 1996) (see also Chapter 7, "The Seed of Freedom") like our ancient sustainable cultures. The KIVA also mirrors the types of spaces that have been continually rediscovered within postindustrial culture by many artists, activists, and change-makers, such as Thoreau, Frost, Whitman, and Graham, who were thereby able to develop profound emotional and spiritual intelligence and knowledge that ancient cultures such as the Celts and Native Americans have always understood.

Capoeira for instance, a martial art but also a religion, education, and philosophy, embodies the KIVA concept. Disguised as a dance and developed as a means of survival by African slaves, present-day Capoeira in Brazil and beyond has become an institution that continues to emphatically empower millions whom adversity has dealt a tremendous blow, including the enormous Brazilian orphan population (Capoeira, 2002). In this cultural space, protected from the highly toxic outside culture, children and adults have found sanctuary in Capoeira by intergenerationally exploring self, community, and world potentials. At the heart of the Capoeira movement is the power of immersing one's self into the aesthetic spiritual "zone" of a creative community.

Closer to home, within the 1930s progressive schools community, in one such school affectionately known as *Little Red*, teachers and students were engaged in bringing great compassion, care, and construct to what and how they were learning (Martin, 2011). Despite the misleading manipulative academic criticisms of the day that marginalized these communities through a sexist discourse (which continues today), where the masculinized "three Rs of reading, writing and arithmetic" (p. 186) of "real learning" was trumped over the "weak," "effeminate" "three Cs of care, concern, and connection" (p. 181) "nonlearning" arts, *Little Red* took on a mesmerizing space of true learning, with full support of their local community.

Even closer to home, like the teachers in *Little Red,* three retired teachers, Agatha Meyer, Lillian T. Clark, and Clare Torre, also experienced spiritual and creative community classrooms in their Long Island, New York, one- and two-room schoolhouses, their careers spanning from 1920 to 1970. Pat Clark Smith (2000)[1] invited the three retired teachers to share their personal stories with her faculty and staff, emphasizing the following: a love of teaching and learning; the critical urgency to perceive each child as unique; dignifying each child; designing lessons tailored for individual children; and the importance of play, the arts, and community in learning. Meyer, Clark, and Torre's unique professional presentation to elementary educators stressed the importance of the teacher as artist.

In her presentation, Meyer shared her joy of playing with the children outside and having coloring parties. Meyer's passion for children and love of teaching was depicted in her descriptive activities to involve children organically in the learning experience. Like Meyer, her sister Clark described the effects of the Great Depression on children in her classroom:

---

[1] Pat Clark Smith, Lillian T. Clark, Agatha Meyer, and Clare Torre are the sister, mother, and aunts, respectively, of Barbara Clark (co-author). *A Past to Remember . . . A Future to Mold* (professional development presentation, September 7, 2000) was at Pine Grove Elementary School in Avon, CT. and designed by Pat Clark Smith (Assistant Principal & Supervisor of Reading and Language Arts, 2000).

Over 50% were farming children up from the South . . . the rest were local farmers' children . . . so many of the families and children had so little. That year, I and the other schoolteacher, with whom I shared our two-room schoolhouse, decided to help the poor children of the migrant farm workers. We put on a play with the children; she did the music and I the sets and costumes, and we charged 50 cents for adult admission. With the money raised, we bought cocoa, evaporated milk, and Campbell's Soup for the children every day of the winter. Soon the children were working better and seemed happier . . . I learned from them and hopefully they learned from me . . . it was like a large family. (Albertson, 2000, p. 8)

The last sister, Torre, explained working with children "whose families had been affected by World War II who perhaps lost a father or brother overseas." Torre continued, "These children needed lots of activity" (Albertson, 2000, p. 8). Torre believed that, "Education rediscovers itself often going off on tangents trying new approaches—backing off and starting again . . . It is a maze with many different paths leading to the child . . . We reach the children when we best discover how s/he learns best." Torre passionately shared a core belief with the teachers in the professional development audience, stating, "The biggest resource is you, the teacher. I salute you" (Albertson, 2000, p. 8).

Community centered and aesthetic, the teachers and children within these one- and two-room schoolhouses and *Little Red* simultaneously explored multiple places and perspectives where empathy, understanding, and full awareness for the interconnectedness of social and ecological world contexts were held sacred and revered. One child graduating from *Little Red*, now an adult, attributes her education experience there as having saved her life, meaning through this seed chapter lens, that *Little Red* had given her a voice and an opportunity to preserve her reimagination potential (Martin, 2012).

The KIVA represents a space of what happens for our teacher candidates when they reimagine themselves, society, and natural world relationships. Creating the KIVA space allows them to step into an ancient holistic circular, inclusive, and intricate learning community culture where they can freely possibilize with their imaginations. And our preservice teachers are simultaneously given opportunity to experience this space by gradually scaffolding themselves away from our toxic secular culture. This scaffolding is particularly necessary for our teachers, who, distracted by layers of their own life experience and schooling (see Chapter 5, "The Seed of Unmasking"), move much more slowly than the children they will teach.

In ultimate outcomes of having been engaged in the aesthetic experience, we observed that making new ideas visible and creating possibilities to envision a world that could be better or fairer was a level of consciousness that could not have been reached without the shared realities through the aesthetic entry point (Greene, 1995). We guided our students in building their creative inner space to help lead them to profoundly creative and spiritual expressions that shaped their identity, relationships, and capacity to see themselves as teachers for ecosocial change.

Change: Reimagining Confidence and Self

"I can't draw anything right!" A little boy crumples his artwork and throws it away in disgust, adding to the other rumpled balls of paper abandoned on the floor. He resolves at that moment to quit for good. His little sister, watching him, picks up the crumpled paper and brings it to her room. Following her, the boy finds all of his previously thrown away work now smoothed and hung up in open pride upon the walls. "It's a museum," she shares. Frowning, the boy replies, "But I can't draw." He points to a drawing, "This doesn't even look like a vase." His sister again gazes at the picture in adulation: "But it looks vase-ish. And I love it. It's my favorite."

Titled *Ish* (Reynolds, 2004), this illustrated storybook continues with the little boy picking up his drawing tools once again. He begins to draw everything and anything, where each subject or object isn't exact, but *–ish*. With budding pride and conviction, he then starts to compose poetry to go along with his pictures. Poems about the sun or peace, all of which he writes confidently knowing that while they are not exactly the "sun" or "peace," they *are* sun-*ish* or peace-*ish*. The book closes with the boy growing up in the world that has now become one of his -*ish* drawings. He is calm, serene, and happy; sometimes creating, sometimes just being, and we know by the final page that his life will be meaningful, peaceful, and full of love. The book closes with a dedication from the author to a teacher who inspired him.

This remarkable story speaks directly to how children (who might want to throw away their artwork) and adults (who may have stopped practicing their art of creation) *must* create to find true happiness. Beyond drawing, singing, acting, painting, sculpture, problem-solving, innovating, or any form of expression, the human need to create is universal. And to do so with conviction, pride, and confidence, or with what Dr. David Kelley has called "creative confidence" (Tischler, 2009) is paramount. Dr. Kelley offers a sad anecdote, similar to the little boy in *Ish*, of how we crush creative spirit; when in third grade, Kelley's best friend, Brian, was prompted to "opt out" of creativity.

In our work with children in schools, alongside our teacher candidates within the spiral aesthetic paradigm, children can instead have inspirational life experiences, as depicted in an elementary student's words after he had participated in the *Echoes* project: "My mask was about all my feelings and being proud about myself. I felt really happy about myself and happy for everybody."

We simply will not feel complete with our day and indeed our lives if we have not engaged and perceived success with our inherent creative core. As people, children, adults, and especially as educators, there must be a thriving sense of self-efficacy to possibilize and change the world. Dr. Kelley, in addition to defeating diagnosed cancer, has gone on in his life, through his company, *Ideo,* to revolutionize countless businesses and universities (Kelley & Kelley, 2012) through his design-thinking model. He also has completed several school projects demonstrating how we might generate creative confidence in children, school staff, and community.

As Kelley embodies, we must live our own lives and teach our children to sustain the joy and spirit of believing ourselves to be, and to practicing being "creatives." We become empowered when we can see our successes. Illustrated throughout this book in the many studio projects we have done with children, when a child holds a creation or mask that they made, they feel proud. The children are hopeful that they can become anything, do anything, and surmount any obstacle; because they, in a sense, have poured their own identity into the form of the mask, and it is there, looking back at them. It can do things they cannot and by that same token, they can do what the mask can.

So too, an enormous part of the creative confidence process for our teacher candidates is to discover that they have, within our studio paradigm, a new skill and ability to create and self-express. With their teachers as guides, it is ultimately the children who tip the balance in this awakening. Adults have to hearken back to what they know or remember from childhood. When we are able to connect ourselves with doing and creating in a place and context, we become hopeful because we are engaged in a very concrete fundamental way. When we are given the opportunity to create, we are bringing to fruition what we have in this world.

Art takes time and commitment because it doesn't happen instantly. It is by its very nature an experimental process that is highly reflective, and through the process of critique, the creator must stay body, mind, and soul in the moment. Being "in the now" forces us to see and hear one another's truest reality. So too the art of teaching is being in the moment, sensory engaged, with the teacher as artist working with children who are already inherently in the moment. The aesthetic paradigm in teaching places the teacher in an artistic realm with children.

Indeed, the key to the experiences we provide our teacher candidates is like a lighting of the imagination that stirs the spirit. Brain-based research scientists are now discovering what artists have known since the beginning of recorded timelines in art history. From viewing the ancient fertility sculpture, the *Venus of Willendorf,* or seeing Jackson Pollock's expansive action paintings from the 1940s, "molecules of emotion" (Pert, 1997, p. 25) are activated. This physical world discovery by science, while not popularly said as such, has always had universal connections when art was at one time sacred to the spiritual and emotional imagination. How else would we make sense of the world and our existence if it were not for art as created by humans over time? "The artist is never happy until he finds the well of the unconscious; then if he has a life force, there is engagement, an encounter, and he becomes illumined by the generating forces as an icon (Carone on Pollock's work with Yung, as cited in Potter, 1985, p. 197).

Through our work, we discovered that the aesthetic was essential in bringing to fruition, or "possibilizing" (Greene, 1995) what are and can be social- and ecojustice curricula goals for our teachers. Similar to all the KIVA spaces described in this book, our learning community was very much like an artist's studio where multiple ideas were tested and discussed. Multiple methods and media including technology were integrated during problem-solving studio sessions, wherein songs, skits, dance, and a variety of eclectic symbolic messages were created to inspire children.

Aesthetic education releases an endless wellspring of methods and strategies to be used with children. Through the KIVA, we inspired our preservice teachers to address collective social and ecological issues that impact their daily lives, communities, and world. Working in cooperative teams, our students' views and beliefs were unlocked to investigate ecologically and socially sustainable teaching practices that drove their instructional and curriculum development. Our teacher candidates began to perceive themselves as creative thinkers and resilient future teacher leaders. In short, providing the opportunity for our students to drink deeply from the cool waters of their spiritual and imaginative consciousness, they were able to reimagine themselves to realize their endless capacity for greatness as educators.

Change: Reimagining Scaffolding and Society

As revealed in Chapter 2, "The Seed of Hope," the aesthetic helps adults remember how to round time and space in multiple dimensions, something that children can do effortlessly. Once the artist-teacher steps with their students into this invisible realm, wherein realities that are not yet realized are revealed, the artist-teacher begins to see the sacred both within themselves and also within the children. By their very craft and skill, teachers are always looking for ideas on how to teach subjects. Incidentally, through practicing the aesthetic, they become instant interdisciplinarians.

However, for any of us coming up from a secular toxic market-culture destructive low, it takes small steps to attain an emotional intelligence within the KIVA space. As guides for our students, we were thus very careful and deliberate to structure aesthetic mini-experiences where our students would be pushed to reach the creative high. So as with children in the stu-

FIGURE 4.6.   Studio Paradigm in Action: Dr. Joss French and Teacher Candidates Creating *Make A Wave*, 2010.

dio paradigm, albeit in a more gradual way, we start with the small: music, poetry, visual, skits, dance, and theater.

Thus, in our studio paradigm teacher education experiences, we are scaffolding all the time to foster creative confidence and creative skills. These experiences scaffolded by design are described throughout this book, as depicted in both above and below events, but also in "Rat/Honey" (see Chapters 5, "The Seed of Unmasking" and 1, "The Seed of Play").

As described in *Make a Wave* (see Figure 4.6), the studio paradigm was used in the creation of a purposeful community event for 1,000 urban children in our surrounding city that addressed awareness of the dolphin slaughter in Taiji, Japan. Leading up to what was perceived by our teacher candidates as an almost "impossibly" big show, teacher candidates were engaged in diverse aesthetic experiences that provided multiple small successes and critically identified the causes behind the dolphin slaughter. These experiences included role-play, movement, poetry, visual imagery, and drumming. In the many instances of building creative confidence in these scaffolding experiences, our students practice metacognitive approaches that "get messy" and appear to be lacking in "control," but in actuality are modeling possibilization in the studio structure. Greene (2001) explains this aesthetic journey of self-discovery within the heart of the KIVA as "a process of initiating persons into faithful perceiving, a means of empowering them to accomplish the task—from their own standpoints, against the background of their own awarenesses" (p. 45).

Following the contours of our above aesthetic system map, to illustrate in greater detail how we scaffold the aesthetic process within a studio paradigm toward change, below we describe one mini-experience which was ultimately used to prepare our students for their end-of-the-semester performance project addressing the societal issue of homelessness. Effectively, with this example as one mosaic tile within a larger aesthetic scaffolding, we gradually enacted the KIVA for teacher education students to successfully reimagine their relationship to people who are homeless. After some very brief "toe-dipping" into the aesthetic realm, including a reading of *Fly Away Home* (Bunting, 1991), a children's book depicting the story of a homeless father and son as they struggle to survive in an airport, we were ready to take a swim in a mini-aesthetic event through the creation of group collages and skits.

Using collaged visual imagery and scrap material from assorted newspapers, photos, the Web, *Adbusters*, paintings, literature and poetry from pop culture focused on how the media affects people's relationship with one another and the natural world, along with other mediums of paint (found and donated), and large cardboard foldouts, and with musical accompaniment of live social human rights songs on banjo[2], teacher candidates in groups were asked to create compassionate messages for one another.

Collage posters were formed outside (on the loading dock of the education building), where student groups started to focus their critique around the crisis and issues children are facing in society. As they were asked to manifest a visual message, students had to delve headlong into critical conversations to truly symbolize their ideas and thinking. In discussion, finding that their own experiences with life coincided with others' perspectives, student ideas took strength and interconnected to ultimately create a mixed-media collage.

With the multiple and constructed images of society provided, students had props to begin building confidence in voicing their ideas with one another; putting brush to canvas, juxtaposing and layering photographs, pictures, and text. When the collage was complete, groups were asked to write about their experience and then synthesized their interpretations into a skit-discussion-presentation for the larger class, which were then expressed in the shade of a nearby tree. The images of this mini-aesthetic activity are shown and described in the below series:

> Peace smells like the tulips, spring and the morning.
> I find myself thinking about what it means to fight for something.
> I am only one, but still I am one.

[2] Union and international folk song musical accompaniment during teacher candidates' design and expression of their social and ecological justice poster collages (see Figures 4.7–4.14) and other KIVA events during the project was offered by Tom French (music teacher and composer), father of Joss French (co-author).

FIGURE 4.7.   Be the Change: Teacher Candidates Composed Thoughts and Ideas Along the Purple Curls (4'x 5' acrylic and mixed media).

Farewell false love. Can you make a change?
It's not enough to be compassionate, you must act.
There is no future without forgiveness.
Peace shouldn't be hard to find. (Figure 4.7)

As the creators of *Be the Change* (Figure 4.7) confided in their discussion that explained their experience, they had spent most of their time searching for a message and in the process realized that the very struggle of that search could be embodied as a visual symbolic representation in their ultimate collage creation. In their discussion, the students said that although they had struggled to find something to show, they were proud of what they had done, particularly with their added symbolic layered hint of depth with the purple strand saying, "*Peace shouldn't be hard to find*" ending at an actual peace symbol.

The work points to some of the realities already described at the beginning of this seed chapter concerning our struggle with waiting rather than acting upon or of realizing our powerful capacity. The group's work refrains a message from chapter 3, "The Seed of Voice": that a realization of our proclivity for change can come only through allowing our imaginative voice to sound. The heart will move the mind from one line of questioning to another thought. So too was this possibilizing represented in the students' creation.

In the cold light of day, it's society's mask, it's society's way,
And the truth is, it's all a façade.
The lie he will tell you. Hypocrites! Hypocrites!
This disease that we've got, has no ready cure.

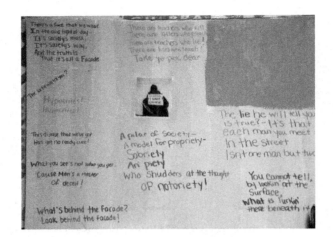

FIGURE 4.8. Modified Lyrics of *Façade* (Bruicusse, 1995) From the Musical *Jekyll & Hyde* Were Placed Over a Money Flag, With a Collaged Visual Image At Center Depicting a Shadowed Figure Holding a Sign Which Reads, "I Want Change" (4'X 5' Acrylic and Mixed Media).

> What you see's not what you get—cuz man's a master of deceit.
> What's behind the façade? Look behind the façade?
> There are teachers who talk. There are teachers who preach.
> There are teachers who lie! There are liars who teach!
> Take yer pick, dear. A pillar of society. A model for propriety.
> Sobriety. Piety. Who shudders at the thought of notoriety!
> The lie he will tell you is true?
> It's that each man you meet in the street, isn't one man, but two.
> You cannot tell, by lookin' at the surface, what is lurkin' there beneath it?

In the above image (Figure 4.8), beyond the larger critique of society, what was perhaps most startling was when one member of the student group revealed in discussion that the inspiration for the piece came from their own experience of singing the song at Disney World and making new connections to social justice. Hearing this, we asked if the student would be willing to sing us the song, which he did. Following singing the song, the student said about his creation within the context of our class, "I never realized the full meaning of the words from the musical when I had sung it, until now."

Overall, the student groups' images (see Figures 4.7–4.14) and the expression of their creations offered pointing out a mixture of social and ecological injustices, prompted from human greed, with a call for taking action. Where at first it might be easy for a decontextualized passerby to write off the above student poster creations as trite, ill-conceived, or as a

FIGURE 4.9.   Drawn In, the Eyes Have It: A Collaged Visual Image Surrounded With Words: "No One Can Make You Feel Inferior; Use Your Voice; You Have a Choice; Educate Your World; Have No Fear" (4'X 5' Acrylic And Mixed Media).

FIGURE 4.10.   Rainbow Colors With "New Beginning" and Collaged Visual Images With Gandhi Quote Running Throughout Collage: "If We Are To Reach Peace In This World, We Shall Have To Begin With The Children" (4'X 5' Acrylic and Mixed Media).

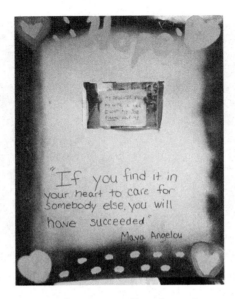

FIGURE 4.11.   Under Title Of "Hope": Collaged Visual Image Of Homeless Person Holding Up Sign Which Reads, "My Daughter Died. My Wife Is Sick. I Lost My Job. Please Help Me." With Quote Below Image From Maya Angelou: "If You Find It In Your Heart To Care For Somebody Else, You Will Have Succeeded" (4'X 5' Acrylic And Mixed Media).

FIGURE 4.12.   Teacher Candidates' Creation As a Result Of Being Stunned By Collaged Visual Image Of Anorexic Elite Consumer Fashion Culture and Juxtaposed With the Resultant Extreme Of Starvation From Poverty Asking, "What Have We Done?" (4'X 5' Acrylic And Mixed Media).

FIGURE 4.13.   Upon a Background With Prominent Word "Greed" and Leaves (In Corner) Are Pasted Two Images—One, a Bansky (2008) Graffiti Image (Of a *Mr. Rat,* See Chapter 5, "The Seed Of Unmasking") Saying "Let Them Eat Crack," and Two, a "Name These Brands. Name These Plants" Activity Image With Commercial Icons and Natural Tree Leaves. Quote From Elie Wiesel Reads, "There May Be Times When We Are Powerless To Prevent Injustice, But There Must Never Be A Time When We Fail To Protest" (4'X 5' Acrylic And Mixed Media).

Figure 4.14. No words, just joy of possibility and each student group members' hand-identity imprints. Flow of creativity and symbols of promise and love (4'x 5' acrylic and mixed media).

charitable releasing of guilt, at a closer examination (and realized contextual experience), students are expressing their sincere compassion and reaction. They are stating their thoughts, and composite to their creation of a performance addressing homelessness, these beginning thoughts through the aesthetic scaffolding process were brought to fruition.

The aesthetic compels us to wonder deeply and to stay with the pain and the issue until we do something about it. We cannot stop thinking of that song, of that movie, of that poem, of that play, of that concert, of that painting, creating that moment for another. A child too, the artist-creator, is further drawn into the issue, and through the social-interpersonal between one another, awareness-building becomes action. We are mirrors to one another. This is done collectively. You are having a shared experience through the aesthetic, which sends the cognition soaring because the *emotional* piece is there. You are hooked through shared conversations.

Social imagination impacts change and begins to grow according to Greene (2001) when we begin to see one another and hear one another. Community "has to be achieved by persons offered a space in which to discover what they recognize together appreciate [and have] in common. It must be a space infused by the kind of awareness that enables those involved to imagine alternate possibilities for their own becoming, and their group's becoming" (Greene, 2001, p. 146). Social imagination comes from the aesthetic and through the aesthetic being shared with one another. This is the formation of the KIVA. Social and moral imagination comes from the shared empathetic living, sharing of pain, love, and experience enabled by the emotional imagination. Art and the aesthetic now have regained their sacred position (rather than being marginalized and treated as a frivolous commodity). The work of art is no longer an accouterment; it is paramount for helping us understand who we are and where we are going, allowing us to act for change.

As illustrated within this mini-aesthetic KIVA space instance, there was a turning point: The groups had effectively created a reality that they could act upon with their hearts and not just intellectually dwell momentarily upon. Multiple student groups expressed sincere gratitude for their experience that day, saying, "We wish we could live in this class all day." Effectively, they were saying that their hearts and minds were lifted from the mediocre to the sublime, and it felt great. Through this "series of aesthetic commons educational pedagogical practice course experiences, pre-service teachers' beliefs were 'unlocked' leading to the revitalization of creative teaching skill sets supported by values and beliefs regarding teaching and learning" (Clark & French, 2012, p. 15).

It is from this gradual uplifting into the aesthetic conscious and unconscious realm, where students can get their feet wet with success, and then gradually find that they are able to swim freestyle as if crossing the English

Channel. This sense of power that change inspires in an individual impacts their beliefs as a result of social cooperative play (see Chapter 1, "The Seed of Play"). The culminating opportunity to express, with the aid of creative force and gravity from their peers, children, and community, guides their own thoughts to be channeled to resonate with various themes. Utilizing multiple approaches while keeping it real ultimately reveals new creations and symbolic messages that are communicated—not as statistics, but as something tangible that impacts our emotions and meaning of life.

The symbolic messages (Figures 4.7–4.14) carried a compassionate message to build awareness, which was then integrated and shared within the community to foster a socially just democracy. In a culminating performance titled *Creating a Compassionate World Community*, these collage posters provided the stage backdrop. Our teacher candidates designed a compassionate interactive message for elementary school children to understand and created a new face for homeless awareness and poverty in the community. After the performance, teacher candidates had students drawing and writing in a workshop that inspired a locally authentic, genuine, and heartfelt understanding of compassion and justice within the students' lives.

In the enactment of this performance and in the follow-up revelations, teacher candidates simultaneously both experienced and witnessed the impact of the aesthetic. As was realized when teacher candidates and children witnessed and reimagined themselves, during the performance, several elementary students who had been labeled autistic inspired their classroom teachers with unprecedented communication and interaction. Another student, who had been engaged in bullying behavior, also took an active role by creatively reflecting on his actions on stage. A school staff member also took the initiative following the performance to visit each class, building her identity and relationship with students and staff. It is interesting to note that this performance started to alleviate in students and teachers their artificially imposed labels. Those punitive shackles no longer had their weight. Is it really the fault of a child to be perceived as if they possess some fault of nature? In some instances, these children continue to be labeled to further increase the monetary capacity for schools to receive national funding.

Following the performance, the school principal approached our practicum sections and thanked our teacher candidates for giving her "hope for the future of education." She explained that the performance had given her staff an exemplary model of what higher order thinking through the arts can be for children. Outcomes like this remark from the principal, the compliments and actions from staff, and the expressions created by the students empowered our teacher candidates' resilience and confidence toward becoming teacher leaders. The performance our students demonstrated to themselves, school staff, and children showed that a learning environment based on compassion and community constructs can increase opportunities for children to unite socially, empathically, cognitively, and spiritually for the greater good.

Beyond portraying the new face of homelessness message for children and their school, and beyond our teachers' own reimaginings of themselves of what could be possible in teaching and relationships, the larger social community was, within one hour; literally transformed and changed. As articulated in their final course reflections, the process and outcomes of our teacher candidates' performance illustrated not only that they could work together toward a goal that was creative and important, but that their beliefs and actions could go on to empower elementary school children, fellow teachers, and administrators. Embodied within this performance at the school, preservice and in-service teachers were given a vision of how they *see* their class as a compassionate community, showing greater leadership to promote social justice and build upon their students' strengths, which unites everyone's potential toward cooperation, collaboration, and change (Clark & French, 2012).

Change: Reimagining Relationship and Role

Our preservice teachers provided student testimony to their reimagining of self, society, the natural world, and relationships with one another and children. One future educator, a participant in *Make a Wave*, illustrates how aesthetic teacher education pedagogy practice guided her to unmask conflicts between her beliefs and the realities of educational and societal institutions, revealing her emerging sense of identity as an imaginative and compassionate teacher leader for ecological and social change. Below, her words embody how aesthetic methodology and experiences promoted her intra- and interpersonal reflection with regard to traditional educational pedagogy and how they challenged her to develop reflective dispositions and apply ecocritical creative thinking to the development of transformative instruction for elementary age children.

Q: Do you think you could have taught that level of ecojustice without the arts to the children?

A: I mean, you can teach it . . . whether or not they would learn it and really be able to experience it is another thing. . . You could teach it by maybe having them read a book or watch a video, but, having performed it and learned through the arts, it is ingrained. . . It is something you experience through your senses, other than just . . . reading about it or listening to your teacher talk about it . . . it is not the same at all.

Q: A lot of people don't think concepts of care and compassion is important in creating a learning environment.

A: I don't see how you could create one with out it . . . because if you
      don't have compassion, you don't care for one another, and then
      you are not going to be able to be yourself. You are not going to be
      able to bring forth ideas. You are going to be closed in. . . . I didn't
      come. . . . to this school or to this program thinking that I would
      have these experiences and meet these people who I feel so close
      to and I don't think it would have been possible if we did not learn
      the way we learned and feel that this is our purpose to teach. . . . I
      know more about them intimately. The arts allow that to happen
      because you get to express yourself in a way where you know where
      words can't express. Sometimes words can't express how you feel
      what you are thinking, as well as a movement for some or a piece of
      art for others, things like that, music.

As seen from the teacher candidate's words, she expresses her shared experiences within the dwelling of the KIVA. She shares a very personal awakening as a result of learning within the nonmaterial, intangible spiritual
space of the KIVA; one that cannot be quantified or measured. Outside the
KIVA, within teacher education programs or further within our data-ridden
culture, such personal aesthetic experiences are relegated to an inferior
status rather than as a sacred, revered space to attain.

In other words, to make true meaning, to make true interconnections
with one another and our world, to have sense of purpose and empowerment, we must create together. It completes us. It is part and parcel of our
relationship with "God," with all living beings, and with nature. It fulfills the
sacrament and purpose of why we are here (see also Chapter 8, "The Seed
of Love"). It provides us interdependent authentic genuine reliance and
fulfills the need we have for one another. As the above teacher candidate
shared about her fellow classmates in interview from having engaged in our
KIVA,

> I don't even see them as my "peers," I see them all as my brothers and sisters.
> They are like family to me and I know having done all that with them even
> this semester, I know I can count on them for anything, whether it be school
> or personal. I know they are there for me like I am there for them . . . and if
> we didn't have that experience we wouldn't be as close as we are.

Hearkening back to the spiral concept map process, creating and engaging our students within this sacred space of inter- and intradevelopment,
where moral imagination is heightened (Clark, 2005b), is ultimately what
fostered change within our students to engage with social and ecojustice.
Providing an in-depth multifaceted studio paradigm (Clark, 2005a, 2009a;
Clark & Ritzenhoff, 2008), while simultaneously immersed in a community
context and with intergenerational skill mentorship (French, 2011, 2012,

2013), students' senses were filled to realize inner awareness phenomena. Greene (1988) believes that developing social intelligence leads to imaginative creative action, therefore increasing our collective potential to envision fairer learning and living conditions by aesthetic means of artistic investigation. Aesthetic education theory combines with the creation of a compassionate community celebrating unique perspectives and diversity (p. 157). As told in *Zeal*:

> Having seen their influence upon affecting children's interest to learn, pre-service teachers stated that they felt more likely to promote eco and social justice issues that connect to students' community towards transformative thinking and creative collaborative group potential. . . . As a result of participating in an aesthetic educational approach imbedded in community action, pre-service teachers transferred and implemented aesthetic creative commons experiences into their field instruction (Clark & French, 2012, pp. 17–19).

To truly enact real ecological and social change, as people, students, and educators, to begin to undo self-induced atrocities, we need to experience our epistemological beginnings of true expression and spirituality. In other words, to get right down to the point, we need to diminish our cold material and rational distancing from one another to embrace dance; make masks; sing; create tools, clothes, and costume. And that, in our small time and space of the universe, is exactly what we do and inspire for our teacher candidates.

In our realized interdependent KIVA space, we had the power to leave our personal ego-centered troubles behind for a while, to bring compelling desire from the heart to address a larger vision of social/ecojustice issues (homelessness, greed, destruction of the environment for money, and so on). In so doing, we brought to fruition an awareness to question consumptive behavior and praxis of responsibility to be caretakers and advocates for one another and our interdependent human and natural world cultures and communities. As one of our teacher candidates revealed in her dreams for aesthetic community change,

> In my student teaching, I hope to do what was done for me. I want to be able to teach, to focus on a particular concept that's maybe happening currently so that way . . . we could be more involved in the community and kind of bring the community in because I think that it is really important to do that because I think that a lot of students' kids' schools are not able to do that. And all through the arts. Have them learn, put themselves in the shoes of the other so they get to understand and be more compassionate of others. And with art, visual, movement, music and everything, have them show me what they've learned and have them be able to express themselves so they are comfortable, not only with me, but with each other.

The next chapter, "The Seed of Unmasking," will continue to explore the impact of the KIVA paradigm on teacher candidates' beliefs and values. It was found that the underlying aesthetic structure of course activities and assignments, when enacted within the aesthetic KIVA, unlocked preservice teachers' preconceived perceptions of educational practices toward more paradigmatic views and beliefs that blossomed into innovative instructional decisions and curriculum initiatives. Significant to teacher education's role in training and retention, we revealed that aesthetic education could provide preservice teachers the needed social reimagination level of consciousness to allow their education experiences to have impact upon their identity as resilient future teacher leaders for ecosocial change. Let the unmasking begin.

REFERENCES

Albertson, K. (2000, September). From the 20th century to the 21st, teachers reflect on all they share. *Farmington Valley Post* (Avon, CT).

Arnheim, R. (2004). *Art and visual perception: A psychology of the creative eye.* Oakland: University of California Press. (Original work published 1954.)

Ballard, J. G., as cited in Orrell, D. (2012). *Truth or beauty: Science for the quest for order.* New Haven, CT: Yale University Press.)

Bowers, C. A. (2006). *Revitalizing the commons: Cultural and educational sites of resistance and affirmation.* New York, NY: Lexington.

Briggs, J. (2012). Introduction: The origns of our inquiry. In John Briggs (Ed.), *Creativity and compassion.* Wayne, NJ: Karuna.

Bruicusse, L. (1995). Façade. In F. Wildhorn & R. Stevenson (Eds.), *Jekyll & Hyde: The gothic musical thriller: Vocal selections.* Cherry Lane Music.

Bunting, E. (1991) *Fly away home.* New York, NY: Houghton Mifflin.

Capoeira, N. (2002). *Capoeira: Roots of the dance-fight-game.* Berkeley, CA: Blue Snake.

Clark, B. (2005a). Moral imagination and art: Echoes from a child's soul. *Forum on Public Policy: Issue Child Psychology, 1*(4), 428–446.

Clark, B. (2005b). *Moral imagination and art: Echoes from a child's soul* (Doctoral dissertation). University of Hartford, Connecticut. Retrieved May 10, 2012, from Dissertations & Theses: Full Text. (Publication No. AAT 315 7797).

Clark, B. (2009a). Aesthetic education and masked emotions: A model for emancipatory teacher preparation. *Critical Questions in Education, 1*(1), 40–50.

Clark, B. (2009b). Mustard seed: A personal search for "Ahimsa" (The truth of nonviolence). *Closing the Circle Exhibition.* B. Clark & M. Cipriano (Artists). New Britain, CT: New Britain Commission on the Arts.

Clark, B., & French, J. (2012). ZEAL: A revolution for education, unmasking teacher identity through aesthetic education, imagination and transformational practice. *Critical Questions in Education, 3*(1), 12–22.

Clark, B., & Ritzenhoff, K. (2008). UMC New Britain collaborative on the cutting edge: University museum community collaboration. *The International Journal of the Inclusive Museum, 1*(2), 63–78.

Craven, J. (2010, May 14). Students teach students. *New Britain Herald.* Retrieved from http://www.compassionateteaching.com/NEWSPAPER%20PAGES/students%20teach%20student%20NBH.html

Dalai Lama. (2012, October). *The art of compassion.* Lecture presented at the Embracing the Challenges of the 21st Century conference, Western Connecticut State University, Danbury, CT.

Dewey, J. (1980). *Art and experience.* New York, NY: Macmillan.

Eisner, E. W. (2002). *The arts and the creation of mind.* New Haven, CT: Yale University Press.

French, J. (2011). Revitalizing community based language arts curriculum practice through ecojustice education. *New England Reading Association (NERJA), 47*(1), 43–50.

French, J. (2012). Creating eco-social culturally responsive educators with community. *Green Theory and Praxis, 6*(1), 17–34.

French, J. (2013). Methods & mindsets for creating eco-social community educators. In D.G. Mulcahy (Ed.), *Transforming schools: Alternative perspectives on school reform* (pp. 37–66). Charlotte, NC: Information Age.

French, J., & Clark, B. (2012). Revitalizing a spiritual compassionate commons in educational culture. *Religion and Education, 39*(1), 93–108.

Gardner, H. (1982). *Art, mind, and brain: A cognitive approach to creativity.* New York, NY: Basic Books.

Greene, M. (1988). *The dialectic of freedom.* New York, NY: Teachers College Press.

Greene, M. (1995). *Releasing the imagination.* San Francisco, CA: Jossey-Bass.

Greene, M. (2001). *Variations on a blue guitar: The Lincoln Center Institute lectures on aesthetic education.* New York, NY: Teachers College Press.

Highwater, J. (1982). *The primal mind: Vision and reality in Indian America.* New York, NY: Harper & Row.

Highwater, J. (Writer), Perlmutter, A. (Producer), & Lenzer, D. (Director). (1996). *Primal mind: Alternative perspectives on self, environment and the development of culture* [Documentary]. Primal Mind Foundation.

Kelley, T., & Kelley, D. (2012). Reclaim your creative confidence. *Harvard Business Review, 90*(12), 115.

Langer, S. (1957). *Philosophy is a new key.* Cambridge, MA.: Harvard University Press.

Martin, J. R. (2011). *Education reconfigured: Culture, encounter, and change.* New York, NY: Routledge.

Martin, J. R. (2012). *Keynote address.* Paper presented at the New England Philosophy of Education Society conference, Central Connecticut State University, New Britain, CT.

Martusewicz, R. A., Edmundson, J., & Lupinacci, J. (2011). *Ecojustice education: Toward diverse, democratic, and sustainable communities (sociocultural, political, and historical studies in education).* New York, NY: Routledge.

Mayer, J. (2006). Waiting on the world to change. On *Continuum* [CD]. New York, NY: Columbia Records.

Norberg-Hodge, H. (1991). *Ancient futures: Learning from Ladakh.* San Fransciso, CA: Sierra Club.

O'Donohue, J. (1997). *Anam cara: A book of Celtic wisdom.* New York, NY: Harper Collins.

Perkins, D. (1994). *The intelligent eye: Learning to think by looking at art*. Santa Monica, CA: Getty Center for Education in the Arts.

Pert, C. B. (1997). *Molecules of emotion: The science behind mind-body medicine*. New York, NY: Scribner.

Potter, J. (1985). *To a violent grave: An oral biography of Jackson Pollock*. Wainscott, NY: Pushcart.

Quinn, D. (1995). *Ishmael: An adventure of the mind and spirit*. New York, NY: Bantam.

Ravitch, D. (2011). *The death and life of the great American school system: How testing and choice are undermining education*. New York, NY: Basic Books.

Reynolds, P. (2004). *Ish*. Somerville, MA: Candlewick.

Saul, J. R. (2012, June 19). Canada's spiritual quest: Learning to imagine ourelves. *Adbusters*, (103). Retrieved from www.adbusters.org/magazine/102/john-ralston-saul.html

Sellner, E. (1999). Celtic Christian spirituality: Intimations of the future. *Spiritual Life: A Journal of Contemporary Spirituality, 45*(3), 135–145.

Tischler, L. (2009, February). Ideo's David Kelley on design thinking. *Fast Company, V*(I). Retrieved from www.fastcompany.com/1139331/ideas-david-kelley-design-thinking

Yeats, W. B. (1902). *The Celtic twilight*. Retrieved from sacred-texts.com/neu/yeats/twi/index.htm. (Original work published 1893.)

CHAPTER 5

THE SEED OF UNMASKING

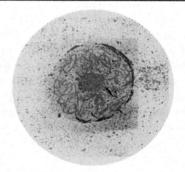

Seed of Unmasking Painting
(Clark, 2009)

We are supposed to be the light of the world. We are supposed to be a light to ourselves and to others. That may well be what accounts for the fact that the world is in darkness!

—Thomas Merton (1955)

The mask has been in all cultures throughout history as a universal symbol of creativity, but also a symbol that humans have used to survive, cover, hide, protect, disguise, and transform our true sense of selves (Highwater, 1982).

Art at one time was sacred, however due to industrialization, it is now considered a commodity, investment, decoration, or purely for pleasure.

In education, we have many children who have "masked" themselves in order to protect and hide from teachers, and we also have teachers who have "masked" themselves to hide behind educational standards and testing mandates. As a result, children and teachers are suffering behind both self-imposed and institutionalized masks. This paradox however should not exist in an educational setting. As teacher educators, we have to unlearn our teacher candidates' preconceived notions of education in order to unmask a fresh sense of what the best practices are for children.

Many of our students begin their teacher preparation program with a "thick plastered mask" that has grown over time, wherein perceiving and thinking in new ways is in actuality locked out and covered up. We have discovered that our preservice teachers who were born around 1986 have not experienced aesthetic education methodology in their own K–12 public education. This comes as no surprise, as we continue to be driven by the resurgence of our modern standards movement originating with the corporate federal rally call: *A Nation at Risk* (Shor, 1992), with *No Child Left Behind* and *Race to the Top* as the most recent manifestations (see Prologue),

Pressured local school administrative decisions are made not for children but for incommensurate adult economic and political world factors (Elkind, 2007; Ravitch, 2011). In this vein, the opportunity for aesthetic place-based approaches within schools are under pressure with *Smarter Balanced Assessment* and new teacher evaluation system (Calkins, Ehrenworth, & Lehman, 2012). Local schools are under such stress at this time that they are actually considering not having teacher candidates and aesthetic programs as part of their curricula. The psychological mask of misplaced top-down management power effects are thickening at an alarming rate as teachers and administrators scramble to address new mandates that are being institutionalized before schools have the proper resources. Testing mandates are attached to teacher evaluations, causing some teachers and administrators to cheat (Gillum & Bello, 2011; Jonsson, 2011). As *Smarter Balanced Assessment* is being tested on 8-year-old children, teachers are reporting, "Our children are hanging their heads in despair and frustration."

Beyond our public schools, the accountability movement has also burdened possibilities for our increasingly corporatized universities and colleges in teacher education. Standards and controlled evaluations have stagnated academic freedom, creativity, compassionate approaches, and innovation:

> With iron-clad federal policy shackles like *No Child Left Behind* and *Race to the Top* holding public schools in check, schools of education have followed suit, limiting what teachers must be able to do to foster myopic parameters of student achievement. The importance of involving teachers and students

with the truly essential progressive issues of equity and diversity within social and ecological community spheres are being diminished alongside hollow remediation reform and high stakes standardization. Implementation of alternative community practice based education programs for our teachers and thus their students are not only becoming increasingly difficult to do within this climate, they are being pushed out as superfluous. (French, 2012, p. 18)

Colluding with societal pressures and toxicity, which both teacher candidates and educators bring into the classroom; department faculty and students are additionally further steeped in their larger university cultural experience, which shows little promise for redemption. As former Harvard dean Harry Lewis makes plain in his book *Excellence Without a Soul*:

Universities have forgotten their larger educational goal for college students . . . Rarely will you hear more than bromides about personal strength, integrity, kindness, cooperation, compassion, and how to leave the world a better place than you found it. The greater the university, the more intent it is on competitive success in the marketplace of faculty, students, and research money. And the less likely it is to talk seriously to students about their development into people of good character who will know that they owe something to society for the privileged education they have received. (Lewis, 2006, p. xii)

Imagine a new teacher, masked, looking out at a room full of masks, molded from cursory public education mandates and reinforced with a dog-eat-dog exclamation point from their college and teacher education experience. Under the vise of "accountability" and the compassion-consuming competitive "free market," society has distracted us from our emotive cores to meet institutionalized assessments and profit margins. Educational institutions utilizing testing software for profit has resulted in even larger "waves of fear, animosity, and upheaval that directly clash with students', future teachers', and our own learning and teaching needs" (French & Clark, 2012, p. 94).

How can we build strong educators at this time of upheaval in education? We hope that teacher preparation certification programs, students, and children will look to the light of aesthetic education rather than the dark of overemphasis on testing, by desiring to enter the KIVA paradigm, wherein there is no need to hide behind the mask when the learner and teacher realize together the power of *emotional imagination*, where humans have always transformed through the arts and their hearts. It is our goal that teacher education candidates are not increasingly distracted from embracing the quintessential questions of emotional imagination: *How do your students feel about learning and how do you feel about teaching?* Otherwise, they may become at risk of losing their moral compass and direction as an educator.

Given the unresponsive process and pressures of our educational institutions, we may at moments marvel at why so many teachers have distanced themselves from potential meaningful feeling and empathic thought. Examples of and opportunities for unmasking are all around us; all we need is a perceptual shift that the aesthetic can provide. Hemingway once admitted that he could write his masterpieces only when he had fully engaged in the creative process. Emotional imagination for Hemingway was attained only after he lived it, and so he immersed himself fully in the experience of the blood of a bullfight or the isolation of a boat at sea, as if "the sentences are there waiting for me, shouting to be set down" (McLain, 2011, p. 226). So too, we may seek fiction and fantasy of the fantastic that pull on our *archetypes of the imagination* to jolt us from our false, one-sided reality (French & Clark, 2012; Pinchbeck, 2007).

Creating such an "impossible" space amid unforgiving societal and institutional strife, we have witnessed our students "unmask" fears, doubts, self-consciousness, prejudices, and anger when engaged in compassionate community aesthetic methodologies. Amid layers of experience and memory, the composite eight seeds of compassionate action instantaneously reveal the true sense of self in the preservice teacher through "unmasking," which is the focus of this seed chapter. The spiritual activity of unmasking within the KIVA is a messy, layered, transformational experience for all, as are most things inventive and creating "new" (Csikszentmihalyi, 1996; Gardner, 1994).

Emotional imagination surfaces as masks are dissolved and the seeds of *Play, Hope, Voice,* and *Change* are simultaneously triggered and modeled. By unmasking self and society, history and culture, and allowing ourselves and others to be open to these possibilities, we reveal the invisible within us, which we embrace as a form of communication, social imagination, and teacher identity (Clark & French, 2012).

The Mask is our symbol and archetype for the concept of unmasking in preparing teachers. Encompassed within the title of this book, with our students, we have drawn upon the unmasking metaphor using the poem by Rabindranath Tagore titled, *A Mind Without Fear* (1913). Tagore himself began a school (*School of Wisdom*) that used the aesthetic (particularly through music and poetry) to learn, seeking an exodus from India's institutionalized schooling, of self-imposed and societal constraints on teachers and student learning (Yogananda, 1946)[1]. Embodying how both our teachers and students can become unmasked together, Tagore writes,

Where the mind is without fear and the head is held high
Where knowledge is free

---

[1] See also http://www.schoolofwisdom.com/history/teachers/rabindranath-tagore/.

Where the world has not been broken up into fragments
By narrow domestic walls
Where words come out from the depth of truth
Where tireless striving stretches its arms towards perfection
Where the clear stream of reason has not lost its way
Into the dreary desert sand of dead habit
Where the mind is led forward by thee
Into ever-widening thought and action
Into that heaven of freedom, my Father, let [the children] awake

What is at risk if we do not understand our emotional imagination and allow it to surface? Imagine for instance how a victim of racism *feels* or how a community that has undergone a tragedy *feels*; going beyond the right or wrong of moral imagination to an empathetic imagination that travels to the depths of how we all experience things. Emotional imagination is the empathic precursor to moral imagination, which, as was explained in Chapter 4, "The Seed of Change," allows for social and ecojustice action to occur.

Simultaneously establishing the many masks we bring to learning and teaching as educators from our societal and institutional life experiences, this chapter will explore the transformational experiences we used to unmask toward the seeds of *Inner Awareness, Freedom,* and finally *Love* to all involved. The mask and unmasking awareness provided new faces of homelessness to shatter stereotypes. We used the mask and unmasking to expose cruel human atrocities upon the natural world so that we might collectively take responsibility and action, and it was also used to allow the adult world to hear children's voices, identities, and supreme potential and power. We unmasked conflicts between beliefs and the realities of educational institutions and identified prejudices and judgmental attitudes to then embrace instructor freedom, autonomy, and new ways of teaching.

The masks that we all wear, we peel off in stages. We are ultimately trying to get to the sacred, a "heart and mind without fear," the core of being who we want to be. As one of our 5th-grade students from the *Echoes from A Child's Soul* project reveals in the following poem,

Mask Poem

You can only see half of me.
The good side of me.
The good side of me is the side that I show people.
I can only reveal the other side of me when I am with a good friend.
I hide behind my mask the side of me that I don't want people to see.
That is my bad side.
What I hide is my anger and my sad side.
I think that when I put on my mask now I can just hide my emotions.
You can only see half of me outside, the side you can't see all of me

UNMASKING

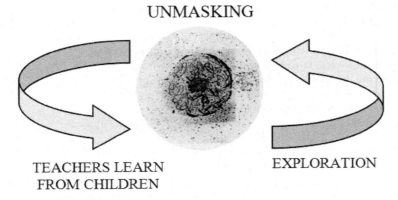

TEACHERS LEARN
FROM CHILDREN

EXPLORATION

FIGURE 5.1. Unmasking Concept Map.

In order to "unmask" the sacred within oneself, the learners and teacher must explore with each other (Figure 5.1). Exploration is not necessarily easy. The student has to overcome obstacles of permission from oneself and the larger status quo to explore identity. The general connotation of a "mask" is that it is hiding something; for example, war masks, Halloween masks, and even masquerade masks lend to the idea of "exploring new worlds with different norms, and such" via a mask. Imagine that the teacher is closer to accessing the student's LOVE of learning (the final seed), and the teacher has to help the student channel a message. For example, a student who has incarcerated parents can still write poetry (can dance, etc.), which in turn is the "Way" to unmasking one's true identity. Hence, the teacher must provide responsible guidance in their ethics of exploration through questions, moral aptitude, and the ability of the children. Teacher candidates and children may have no fear at this point, and truly show who they are. Beliefs express through moral imagination and unmask their deepest fears, allowing an opening for people to *see* and *hear* them. As you meditate on the Seed of Unmasking painting (Clark, 2009), focus on the dissolving of the outer hard edge of the seed, exploding with possibility into the universe. This symbolizes the new perception gained along with new awareness, freedom, and power.

Unmasking Fear of the Aesthetic

The process of unmasking begins by unlearning doubts, fears, and prejudices so that truth can be revealed like a refreshing breeze. It is a classic opening of the trumpet call for unleashing creativity and imagination upon a stagnant, unaware and unawakened world of highly rigid onlookers. This is an audience who, while they may pose their persona to be aloof and removed from their innate fascination and engagement with the aesthetic, are in their core transfixed and mesmerized by such vivid and surprising forms of expression. In their hidden, reserved, but profound appreciation of the arts and the aesthetic, they may clap wildly in spite of themselves, only to turn a dour face when asked to reciprocate creatively or provide compensation for the gifts of such joy and compassion that stirred their spirits.

Why do some reject and fear aesthetic genius? Why have artists like Henry Moore, Martha Graham, or Jackson Pollack throughout history been relegated to the margins of society when they have revealed the invisible and allowed us all a glimpse into the sacred? Why have they all been rejected or parodied by *status quo*? Why are we so uncomfortable with invisible possibility? Perhaps it is because it reminds us of our own spiritual prisons. Have we, as Highwater, Perlmutter, and Lenzer, (1996) have proposed, become the proverbial "Crabs in the bucket?" According to Kohan (2013), art was sacred when shared as universal truth. Kohan's website is specifically designed to "recover a lost way of looking," feeling, and thinking about art (http://sacredartpilgrim.com/).

The bucket of the "crabs in the bucket" metaphor can symbolize to name a few: racism, classism, patriarchy, anthropocentrism, consumerism, globalization, heterosexism, or "technopoly." Take your pick; it is a one-size-fits all attitude and disposition, which is the undoing of culture and humanity. The bucket-crab metaphor helps us appreciate why Thomas Merton (1955) observed that "the world is in darkness" and why, as told below, there are *Mr. Rats* among us that creep around, keeping genius repressed to maintain status quo. To varying degrees, while some may claw and pinch more than others, by sharing the same bucket, we may allow the collective toxins to seep into our own hearts and minds if we are not careful to focus on the light of possibility. Teachers especially must be resilient and brave enough to climb out if they have accidently fallen into the bucket of peer pressure that accepts the fatalistic whisper, "Like it or not, we are all going to stay in here together."

But what have we become as teacher educators and what will our students as future teachers become, if in fact they do not see or accept the inherent value of aesthetic education for a healthy child's development? Why would one want to become a teacher for children if they have not realized the very essence of being a child? Why are we so afraid to break into song-dance-paint; to create poems, stories or, as Albert Cullum (1967) exclaims, "Donning a feathered cap, wav[ing] a wooden sword, and push[ing] back [our] desks" (p. 21)? Why? Some educators may be hesitant to venture into the unknown landscape within a child's heart and mind because they may have throughout their own education experienced the same noncompassionate teachers in their own training and preparation.

For hope to continue, it is paramount that we do not succumb to the fear perpetuated by industry and individuality. Logic and reason have created monsters that emotion and empathic imagination have thus far managed to keep at bay, or at least not let destroy us. As artists (like the impressionists) and scientists (like quantum-spiritual physicists), in every discipline throughout history has done, so too in teacher preparation: We must just leave the bucket completely. We live in a multiverse; there are always ways out. We do not have to tolerate the bucket; we can jump out. And as we describe in our unmasking methodology below, we teach our students how they, now that they've unmasked societal and personal ills, can leave too.

Of course, despite our successes, there is the learning curve as well, for school zombies who are looking for that familiar end-fix satisfaction. For example, in the *Echoes* project described below, there were students who, when pressed to engage in the aesthetic and were no longer able to invest energy into their accustomed but heart-numbing spoon-fed assignments, rallied together around the tried and true "arts are weak" scapegoat. This "crabs in the bucket" toxin leaked to some other students, who felt the pressure and sting as well, tethering their spirits for fear of peer pressure approval.

Indeed, *Unmasking* is a war and tension between the sacred divine gift of spirit we were born with and the man-made pressures and constraints that suppress it and contain us to fit into a false persona. You can't be you because you won't fit in. A "mask" can hide something, but also reveal or explore new worlds within different norms. Kids know that war is wrong, and they also know that they have a sacred seed they were born with. We need teachers who know how to access students' *love* of learning (the final seed) by unmasking (Figure 5.2). We need teachers who can help students navigate their soul-force messages. To do this takes supreme confidence. And what is confidence but to become something that you once were not?

FIGURE 5.2.   Homeless Video: University, Museum, Community Project, 2013.

FIGURE 5.2a.   Unmasking Homelessness: University, Museum, Community Project, 2013.

As the ancient Chinese art form of Face Changing (*Biàn Liǎn*) illustrates in the magical seamless transformation from one identity and emotion to another: How do we get our students to practice trying on and taking off multiple masks with creative confidence so that they can bring to surface their true selves, their empathic and emotional imaginations, and then to use this wisdom to transform their reality around them?

Teacher candidate Rich designed his mask to portray the isolation that homeless children feel in school (Figures 5.2 and 5.2a). Rich unmasked any preconceived bias regarding homeless children and why they can struggle to learn. For teacher candidates, this critical process of examining beliefs and stereotypes will always be a challenge. Exploration is not necessarily easy. The student/teacher has to overcome obstacles of permission to explore identity. As the status quo of society steeps arts as "weak," we also find that our students must endure a struggle of unmasking their preconceived notions of seeing themselves stigmatized as a *Teacher-Artist*. The dearth of "creative confidence" (Kelley, 2012; see also Chapters 3, "The Seed of Voice") in macrosociety increasingly becomes an obstacle we face as we implement our ideas in the micromoments of teacher education with our students. From sheer lack of exposure, which is self-society induced, many of our students beginning to notice their masks, find themselves just as entrenched, and unable to be spontaneous with their expression, movement, or voice. They fear playing and performing.

Merton (1955) describes our "false self" as prejudices and judgmental attitudes that inhibit compassion. Teachers who have upheld teaching as a spiritual practice believe that an aesthetic educational experience within a compassionate community may lead to the unmasking of our false self (Eisner, 2002; Fox, 2004; Gardner, 1993; Greene, 2001). In order to "unmask" the sacred art of learning/teaching, the student/teacher must have a space to explore, with guides to help navigate the turbulent waters between self and society. As illustrated with aesthetic scaffolding in previous chapters, creating this KIVA space is compassionate, tender, deliberate, and highly intricate. Among children, aesthetic education guides preservice teachers to unmask the conflicts between their beliefs and the realities of educational institutions, revealing their emerging sense of identity as creative compassionate teacher leaders.

Unmasking the Institutional and Professional Stereotypes Through Archetype

As introduced previously for illuminating the *Seed of Play*, one of the unmasking techniques we use to metaphysically reveal existing toxicity and possibility within our educational climate is to use archetype characters that portray the contrast of light and dark in the educational arena. At a spontaneous, but carefully psychologically chosen point in the semester, two characters entered our university classroom: *Miss Honey*, full of light, hope, imagination, and compassion; and *Mr. Rat*, a vessel of darkness, despair, hatred, and scorn for children's imaginations. The aesthetic performance is an effective symbolic unmasking message designed to promote preservice teachers' reflective and social intelligence regarding current political educational laws and events. It presents our teacher candidates the opportunity for reflection and revelation of their own and others' masks borne of personal schooling experience and their developing roles as future professionals.

Cloaked, with bristling snout and whiskers protruding from a dark hood, *Mr. Rat*, given orders from yet another removed level of authority (a larger-than-life video screen projection of a bulging-eyed purple-cloaked puppet), swiftly kidnaps *Miss Honey*, who is trying to teach a group of students/children (our teacher candidates seated on the floor). He returns with chains, and turning his twitching nose to the air, smells in disgust, "What is that *smell?* Is it imagination? It *reeks* to high hell!" With a hunched back straggling forth, he begins to lay heavy chains upon the children's heads and shoulders. Examining the chains on their necks, our students see each link is inscribed with current standard-based anachronisms like *CMT, NCLB, SRBI, SBA,* and such. Cackling maniacally, *Rat* makes no secret of his evil intentions: "Yes, yes, yes," he croaks, "I will lay the chains upon the children's hearts and minds. I will crush their spirits!"

With chains secured, he bends down to an artificial flag spread upon the floor (with corporate logos instead of stars) (Adbusters, 2013), and procures two string marionette-children (teddy bears attached to string and popsicle sticks). Laughing wickedly, noisily bragging and shouting about his total dominion and control over the children, he dances the puppets about until suddenly, bright music is heard.

Rat freezes and jaggedly crocks an ear to the heavens, when suddenly *Miss Honey*, the "angel of inspiration" breaks through (see Figure 5.3). With a flourish of her wand, she banishes *Mr. Rat*, who screams, drops his mario-nette children, and flees. Our students spontaneously cheer. *Miss Honey* lifts the chains from their shoulders, lights a single candle, and reads a poem of hope. She immediately engages our teacher candidates, dressed as sto-rybook characters, in a joyful learning experience. One teacher candidate described the emotional impact the aesthetic had upon his perceptions of power relationships:

> "Chaining" us down with the chains of NCLB was powerful. The high-stakes testing weighs down learning and the students, as it did to us for that period of time. Miss Honey, the angel of inspiration, saved us. We, as pre-service teachers, are angels of inspiration. Miss Honey spread her inspiration by lift-ing off the chains and allowing us to be creative and free. We learned through play, by creating puppets and parading them through the hallways of Bar-nard. Our spirits and our minds were lifted. (Clark & French, 2012, p. 14)

While this particular version used the concrete onslaught of standardized test terror in teaching and learning, we have adjusted this aesthetic perfor-mance to fit other contexts, including our own struggle within teacher educa-tion, at varying levels of abstraction, unmasking, and creative maladjustment. In another variation, *Miss Honey* begins by singing the blues to our teachers, warning them of the ever-present possibility of falling into the fear and de-

FIGURE 5.3. *Miss Honey* confronting *Mr. Rat* As Preservice Teachers Watch, 2009.

spair of *Mr. Rat.* With the hint of *Rat* lurking nearby (his tail and cloak seen twitching in a dark corner), *Miss Honey* sings, "Mr. Rat: He's in your heart; He's on your mind . . . I'm singin' the blu-uu-uu-uu-ues." Sure enough, lights dim, dark music plays and *Rat* appears—but this time for an interview.

This particular interview version coincided with a university "Excellence in Teaching" event, which sent a videographer to film our class for a university promotional piece, showcasing "model" teaching at our university. Taking the opportunity for a teachable, creative maladjusted moment, we decided to make our class into a TV studio. *Miss Honey* was having future educators come in for interviews to express why they wanted to become teachers, while *Rat* wreaked havoc trying to instill doubt and fear into student responses. Students, under intentional duress, were pressed to defend their beliefs, apparently, on television. In preparation, we had asked our students to come prepared with their own statements of belief garnered from readings of Robert Coles *Spiritual Life of Children* (1990), Ruby Bridges *Through My Eyes* (1991), and Albert Cullum *Push Back the Desks* (1967). With the dichotomy of *Rat* and *Honey* framing the TV studio, during the event our students experienced a playful realm of imagination to hear each other articulate, defend, and unmask their beliefs as future advocates for children's learning.

Meanwhile, within our own subcontext as teacher educators, the CCSU videographer filmed everything (with, impressively, only a slightly raised eyebrow behind the camera), and by taking some choice footage in other more typical university classroom lectures, we thus appeared teaching as *Rat and Honey* at the *Excellence in Teaching* (EIT) gala event. As the clip played out during the EIT program, we glanced at the audience taking it in and noticed visible outrage from a few of the university faculty that this would even be considered *excellence* in teaching.

Indeed, as a stage upon a stage, for both our students and ourselves as teachers of teachers, *Mr. Rat* is real and always lurking somewhere, especially in one's self-doubt, which has rejected their sacred potential and true self. But rather than live with a heart and mind in fear, it is always a satisfying relief to name, confront, and take off *Rat*'s mask in whatever corner of the heart he may be hiding, to strengthen conviction, confidence and hope. What may be viewed as cultural disobedience, while teaching our teacher candidates about character and compassion, are actually authentic methods modeled for our students, which are public and playful, and unintentionally unveil masks of mediocrity and hypocrisy within our own institutional boundaries. This is important to reveal because often times the *Rats* don't even know they are wearing a mask.

Beyond revealing the standardized test mandate pressure on children's learning and our own teacher education program pressures on aesthetic education, we have also used the infinitude applications of *Honey* and *Rat* to help our students make instantaneous and powerful personal connections to the everyday realities of public school classroom teaching, which no amount of critical theory text reading could ever do. As such, in a purposeful preamble, another method designed as a simulation in our coursework was utilized so that our teacher candidates could experience the feeling when witnessing the crushing of a teacher's spirit, in a dramatic reenactment of a negative "teacher evaluation." We wanted our students to understand why teachers may start their profession optimistic, full of light and compassion but, for some, the psychological mask is donned as protection and defense.

A teacher is beginning her class with a "great idea" that she "can't wait to share," when an unwelcomed evaluator bursts into the classroom—masked. Observing from the back, sighing loudly with disgust, leaning over students, noisily scribbling notes, and making cross marks on a clipboard, he documents everything that is missing from his prescribed checklist of standardized items. The evaluator is distracting students from their learning. The teacher, also distracted and distressed, starts to become self-conscious and slows in her energy and enthusiasm.

Seeing her fear, the evaluator takes this opportunity to lambaste the teacher in front of her students for not adhering to standard school classroom policy. Shaking his clipboard, he leaves with the threat of a documentation of negative job performance. Visibly shaken, the teacher continues, but now with a monotone quality of voice. Void of her previous energy, she starts to direct children in a strict manner with a larger-than-life checklist of standards now projected on the screen. Lights go out, dark music and the master puppet come on, blending the preamble skit into the next sequence where, when *Miss Honey* liberates the children learning from *Mr. Rat's* control; in this particular version, she pulls back *Mr. Rat's* hood, to reveal once again the evaluator. The evaluator, in turn having been exposed, who had all along been hiding behind the mask of *Rat*, is now the one who is visibly shaken and runs screaming from the room.

Through the powerful aesthetic impact and invitation to unmask, these various versions of *Rat and Honey* archetypes are created with purposeful prop and playful dramatic exaggeration, allowing for our students to formulate immediate beliefs and powerful connections to self-identity. *Rat* and *Honey* have appeared in our final semester performances with and for elementary school children as well (Figures 5.4 and 5.5). Bringing to life current political educational laws and events, the lasting archetypes of *Rat and Honey*, meaningfully galvanize the core of similar messages from interactive course sessions (see Chapter 1, *Seed of Play*), literature, scrapbook response and field experiences for our students.

From the university classroom, our students take these core messages to further imbue with awareness, enlightenment, and caring to authentically

FIGURE 5.4. *Miss Honey* Confronting *Mr. Rat* With Masked Teacher Candidates In a Community-School Performance On Homelessness For Children, 2009. To view *Miss Honey confronting Mr. Rat with masked teacher candidates* video, visit www. compassionateteaching.com and click on Our Book tab on home page, then click on the Play tab.

contextualize any "strategy, method, assessment approach, etc." that would normally in a technical-behaviorist model be regurgitated (French, 2005). Quite literally, creating the stage with *Rat* and *Honey*, among other aesthetic events, our students' learning immediately becomes more meaningful and significant in the process of unmasking.

FIGURE 5.5. *Miss Honey* leading Teacher Candidates In A Parade Of Creativity Through University Education Building, 2009.

Through the aesthetic, we model in real time with and in front of children, the energy necessary to inspire, so that our preservice teacher candidates might believe they can do the same by applying aesthetic methods in their field experience classrooms. Making the masks visible, preservice teacher candidates write of their awareness and desire to take action:

> When Miss Honey and Mr. Rat came into our classroom, my eyes sparkled. I felt like I was in a make-believe world in which I was a storybook character. It did not occur to me that throughout the performance, I would walk away with valuable knowledge that I learned from this role-play.

> From the experience with Miss Honey and Mr. Rat it was *obvious what style of teaching creates a positive environment.* A caring and encouraging teacher makes her students feel more comfortable and accepted in the class. Even though we knew Mr. Rat . . . brought a completely different tone into the room. We are all adults, yet we were anxious and actually scared of him. Mr. Rat was focused on testing and limiting our imagination. The mood of the entire room changed, though, when Miss Honey stepped into the picture. She accepted all of our thoughts and we as students were excited by her enthusiasm. She allowed us to use our imagination and creativity without judgment or criticism. I have been able to bring this knowledge into my fieldwork classroom. (Clark & French, 2012, p. 14)

The teacher candidates above express their emotional imagination and understanding that they have to unmask their fears if they are going to become motivational teachers for children. Additionally, experiencing these aesthetic methods in a community and then sharing their experiences and new ideas, our teacher candidates come to know and understand the powerful and transformative concept of social imagination at work (Clark & French, 2012). According to Greene (1998), social imagination leads to social action and involves looking at the world in new ways. She concurs that developing emotional intelligence through the aesthetic leads to imaginative creative action, therefore increasing our collective potential to envision equal learning and living conditions by aesthetic means of artistic investigation. Strengthening students' spirits, naming the masks that they, we, and others wear is a humbling relief and brings us face to face with our own spirits (as our ancestors did so long ago), where true learning and teaching can take place as they become teachers and advocates for children.

Unmasking Emotional Imagination for Teacher Candidate Communities

In this process of unmasking, of which the aesthetic archetype window of *Miss Honey* and *Mr. Rat* are an integral part, we continually ask our students to face their fears. Each semester brings a new social or ecological theme enabling teacher candidates to learn how to create their own masks.

Ironically, this allows them to further realize and perhaps remove their own preconceived psychological identity masks. Although it may seem paradoxical, we take off our invisible masks by putting our created visible masks on.

The metaphysics of unmasking empowers our students to release their voice, choose to symbolize personal stories that are protected and may remain unknown, and possibly to disguise themselves as they work through the emotional complexity of their fears, bias, and self-imposed stereotypes. When our students make their masks, they are pouring into its form their fears, hopes, and joys. As is true for children, the aesthetic domain also permits our students to put a secret ingredient into their creation or mask, which gives them permission to reveal this both privately and publically, intra- and interpersonally (see Chapter 4, "The Seed of Change"), and who they are or what they want to be. The beauty is that inside the creation, only the divine artist/maker truly knows (see also Chapter 6, "The Seed of Inner Awareness").

We have made various types of masks with our teacher candidates: plaster, burlap, found objects, but regardless of the medium, they make their own masks with guidance from us, their mentors, guest artists, and one another. As was described within Chapter 4, "The Seed of Change," creating interdependent learning from artist mentors and one other is integral for an authentic and genuine compassionate community. While we may provide some of the harder-to-get items, we ask that students meaningfully gather materials and make major decisions as to the content and expressive quality of their masks.

The plaster mask medium is a prime example of the interconnectedness that is generated immediately and so we often begin the semester with our students applying plaster masks to one another's skin. Students are asked the previous week to come to class with three items: a trash bag poncho, old clothes, and lots of Vaseline. We provide the plaster strips. Coming in a bit earlier, some students always ready to go, we set out the warm water, plaster strips, and newspaper. Class begins and students pair up. We ask the "maskee" and the masker to communicate their individual and expressive ideas, of shape (e.g., raised eyebrow) or coverage (e.g., half or full mask).

The classroom instantly transforms into an artist's studio as tables are pushed to the side, plastic bags are donned to protect their clothing, and students partner off with excitement. Then plaster strips are adhered to one another's faces. After some gasps and cries for help and guidance, some of our students jump in, while others might be reluctant, but the physicality joyfully always holds sway. By smoothing wet strips around the contours of a person's face, the activity is intimate; there is touch, recognition, and close examination. There is an authentic conversation of how the maskee feels and of what shapes the masker should furrow are genuine and needed.

While adhering the mask material, the masks of surface societal artificial interaction and tension start to peel and fade away. Physically, mentally, and spiritually, our teacher candidates grow closer and for the first time really SEE each other. Each time we have done this, watching our teacher candidates after about half an hour with laughter, intention, care, and purpose, the energy of the room is transformed from when they otherwise may have sleepily entered at 8 a.m. This is the beginning of the paradox of how the aesthetic process of making a mask actually unmasks preconceived notions and awakens and models authentically the compassionate community classroom.

When masks are dry, we then ask students to apply color and texture according to their own artistic sense and come to the following class with a sound, depicting the voice of their mask—a poem, props, or role-play that will help further convey their mask's message. The final masks are magnificent: Whether made from plaster or burlap, with paint and found objects imbedded, each is designed accordingly by the individual representing how they perceive themselves as compassionate artist-teachers. The following week, we then play with the masks created (using techniques as described in Chapter 1, "The Seed of Play"), trying on one another's; experimenting in an expressive way, the voices of the masks; role-playing as students and teachers; reading a piece of literature; and taking on multiple perspectives. Slowly but surely, by using the masks, beliefs are unmasked.

In promoting truth without fear, there is a compassionate influence on those who are witnessing and sharing. What may not have worked out due to inexperience in the arts and not knowing how to manipulate new material is profoundly effective in critiquing how children feel when challenged by teachers to take risks and try new experiences. As the teacher candidates become more open minded, understanding the underlying point of these aesthetic experiences, they begin to freely express using descriptive metaphors and composing poetry that would have otherwise lain dormant within them. As students share the poetry inspired by their masks, the invisible within each other is now made visible through the aesthetic. The following poem, titled *Hope*, by a teacher candidate, Briana, expresses a brave viewpoint to others asking them if they "see" her. She unmasks and asks for help, stating in the truest sense that she needs your "love, comfort, and guidance."

Hope

Eyes wide open
Clear to see right through
Do you see me? Because I can see you.
I see you pass me by, like another lost cause
Doesn't deserve the time of day, doesn't deserve your attention at all
I may come off as angry, ungrateful maybe sad

But what I really need is your love, comfort and guidance
So please help me see my potential
Because with your help, I can make something of myself.

The aesthetic methods used in our class studio environment give our teacher candidates the opportunity and choice to reveal the underlying truth from behind their psychological masks and their made masks. In a poetic way that aesthetic methodology supports, what was once private and hidden now becomes public for all to witness. This phenomenon occurs from trusting relationships developed between teacher candidates and professors who have modeled the process side by side. Our students thus continue to find deeper meaning in their own creative mask forms and one anothers'. They begin to collectively consider these methods with children, especially with literacy skills and more importantly in some ways, by enhancing the learning of social and behavioral skills in children that further builds healthy communities.

Unmasking Emotional Imagination for School Communities

When the seed of compassionate action grows as a belief within a pre-service teacher, the mask of indifference and prejudice (which they don't even know they have for children) melts away. When face to face with others, witnessing together a new paradigm of hope, creativity, and compassionate action within a community, our teachers can begin to anticipate what such an unmasking/masking process might be for a group of children in a classroom or community. As with *Rat* and *Honey*, the teacher candidates' first epiphany of personal transformation within the unmasking creation process, other aesthetic methods are layered to continue developing their sense of self as educators. Through further unmasking and solidifying conviction, understanding and beliefs of becoming teachers, our students have gone on to create masks with their fieldwork students. In order for our teachers to understand how these aesthetic methods can be transferred to the classroom, we work with school partners and classroom teachers within a specified grade level to design a community program for children and teacher candidates to work together and experience the unmasking process (see *Echoes* project below).

One of our students, John, had his elementary students make their own metaphysical masks, "pouring their deepest self-understandings of the world into their form" (French & Clark, 2012, p. 104). As was done for John and his teacher candidate peers, children in his field classroom were given the opportunity to make masks and to express who they were. They loved him for opening the door for them. In fact, John arrived an hour early before school started to work with individual students and parents. His classroom teacher supervisor did not want her classroom to be messy, and even the school art teacher was not willing to collaborate with John as a teacher candidate. How-

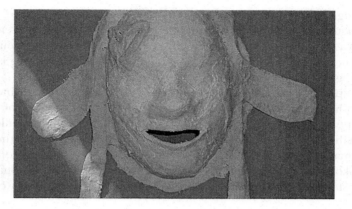

FIGURE 5.6.   Child's Mask: "I Cry When I Am Not Filled With Happiness."

ever, as the masks were drying in her classroom, several art specialists in a meeting saw them and praised the work.

John presented to his peers his joy, conviction, and evidence documented on how this aesthetic experience in making masks greatly influenced the children's literacy skills and use of metaphor in their writing. For example, one of John's students said, speaking of his relationship to his metaphorical mask, "I cry when I am not filled with happiness" (see Figures 5.6 and 5.7).

Unmasking through the aesthetic presents all of us with the opportunity "to free ourselves of the constraints of our abbreviated and constricted material world-view" (French & Clark, 2012, p. 107). This awakens the imaginative inner core dwelling within every individual, and opens up the possibility for a metaphysical life imbued with relationship, interconnection,

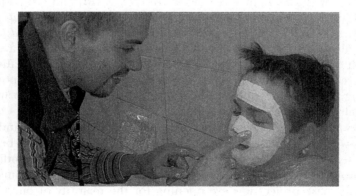

FIGURE 5.7.   John In Hall Outside Field Classroom Applying a Mask To One Of His Fieldwork Students, 2008.

meaning, and love. When we see evidence of children's inspired writing, as depicted above in John's lesson, one has to wonder why children are reported as "failures" in writing. Actually, the problem is that children hate to write because of their frustrating experience with the way writing is taught in segregated literacy strands.

Encapsulated in John's final beliefs project, he was firmly convinced that the aesthetic was essential for inspiring a child's voice and love of writing. His experience, shared with our class, prompted our teacher candidates to see aesthetics at the center of education. With themselves and their society unmasked, they in turn could see the potential for children to become unmasked; the community now could be viewed as a compassionate one, where stereotypes, prejudices, false judgments, and accusations once existed.

> Reflecting upon the mask-making experience with his students, John observed how competitive assessment approaches and labeling had no place in the experience. He found that the previously affixed Connecticut Mastery Test labels high, low, and middle no longer applied: "A student labeled low was suddenly no longer 'low.' Everyone was successful in expressing themselves." When John applied his experienced belief that people need to belong, embodied his belief within the mask-making with children, there simply was no opportunity for his students to feel isolated or made to feel inferior or superior; they were celebrated for who they were. (French & Clark, 2012, p. 104)

UNMASKING TEACHERS AND STUDENTS AS ARTISTS: ECHOES FROM A CHILD'S SOUL—A COMMUNITY PROJECT

At the core of course and fieldwork effect upon our students, authentic space for new engagement to reveal the *Teacher as Artist* identity was opened. The project, *Echoes from a Child's Soul: Children of Incarcerated Parents Release their Voices through Art, Music, Dance, Mask Making, Movement, and Creative Writing* illustrates this effect directly. Based on author Dr. Barbara Clark's research on moral imagination and art (Clark, 2005), this innovative aesthetic creative community project promoted the transformative power of releasing children's feelings and voices, especially children who may be marginalized academically and socially.

Echoes from a Child's Soul was specifically designed for teacher candidates to work with children of incarcerated parents (CIP). This project bridged, for our teacher candidates, a means to utilize and transfer their individual mask projects and lessons into multiple 5th-grade field classrooms. This particular mask project was eye opening for the majority of our teacher candidates as they were unaware and had never experienced this social justice issue. *Echoes* enveloped complex school policies wherein CIP children are not identified by social workers, teachers, and principals. Because many children are fearful of school officials or teachers finding out their family members are in prison, CIP children wear thick masks of fear and are oftentimes known only if they choose to self-identify.

In this particular semester project, elementary education teacher candidates and first year freshmen teamed with 160 children from the fifth grade from two New Britain Elementary Schools. The project culminated in a compassionate community performance at the university's main auditorium, portraying a series of symbolic artistic messages encompassing poetry, dance, visual imagery, masks, and music to release the children's voices. Masks were then exhibited and featured at the downtown Community Central gallery in New Britain uniting myriad community members, artists, university students, principals, elementary school students, parents, and teachers (Figure 5.8).

The performance presentation and mask exhibition culminated after 10 intensive weeks of apprenticeship workshops within the classrooms, hallways, auditoriums, and gymnasiums of the two elementary schools. In one school, 5th-grade children, teacher candidates, and first-year freshman teams were mentored by Teacher Education and Art Education department professors. In the second school, on the other side of the city,

FIGURE 5.8. Showcased masks on stage anticipating the *Echoes* Performance, 2011. *Showcased Masks on Stage Anticipating the Echoes Performance* designed by Dr. Jerry Butler and teacher candidates.

teacher candidates worked with a partner and between 8 and 10 bilingual children in teams. The teacher candidates designed a series of lessons using the masks with the children that culminated into the community performance.

Following a mask-making workshop, international artist Larry Hunt, of Masque Theatre Company (http://masque-theatre.org/) then lit up the schools' stages demonstrating mask possibilities and universal cultural interpretations to examine human emotion and identity (Figure 5.9). Teams of university students and fifth graders then constructed, through the aesthetic process, symbolic representations of their dreams, hopes, fears, and challenges they face each day (Figure 5.10).

At one point during the 10-week workshop sessions, within an aesthetic minimask brainstorm, our teacher candidates in groups with children discussed what they thought masks were for, where the first mask was made, and why. These open-ended questions and ideas, and the excitement of what was to come, prompted children's responses that were full of core honesty and soul searching. In one instance, children offered a reflection of having to hide their first language (Spanish) with a mask of English.

Following our teacher candidates' minilesson, this seminal moment of unmasking language and culture was reexamined, not only for what was revealed of this (and others) in students' identities or perception of school and society, but how the aesthetic effortlessly allowed this belief reality to surface in the school context. To further help teacher candidates navigate the teacher-artist identity, they compared and contrasted how the current status quo approach versus the aesthetic education methods and studio

FIGURE 5.9.   Larry Hunt of Masque: Echoes Fom a Child's Soul Project Community Workshop, 2010. To view *Larry Hunt of Masque: Echoes from a Child's Soul Project* video, visit IMRP Video at http://vimeo.com/34858804

FIGURE 5.10. Who Am I?: First-Year Freshman and 5Th-Grade Student Share Mask Ideas, 2011 (Photo Used With Permission From Central Connecticut State University).

classroom approach that they witnessed had a direct impact on a child's language and cultural identity preservation in school.

We continued to critique how traditional schooling approaches could even further repress and suppress (however inadvertently) a student's sense of self-worth, especially a CIP child or other children who have trauma in their lives. Wisdom from both candidates' engaged contextualized aesthetic applied experience and from our postreflection as a class afterwards was then brought back into the project, where candidates were able to bring out their core identity even further through masks, poetry, and performance (see aesthetic spiral map in Chapter 4, "The Seed of Change").

Navigating the complex web of societal constructs that unjustly marginalize children who are labeled "at-risk," motivated specific teacher candidates to take leadership roles in the project. The aesthetic methodologies utilizing the mask to release a child's voice was revealed, at the end of the project, to be a powerful medium for children. For the first time in their lives, they stood on stage, using a mask, danced, sang, and read poetry. They expressed later that they saw themselves for the first time the way they wanted others to see them, but had previously been afraid to try. The mask helped them express what they felt and who they wanted to become (see Figure 5.10 and 5.11).

Implemented authentically with professors and preservice teachers in a community engaged context (see also Chapter 2, "The Seed of Hope") for children, the unmasking process continues into the larger world community and opens new, vibrant possibilities for our students to take social and ecocommunity action (French & Clark, 2012; see also Chapter 4, "The Seed of Change") with children.

These types of art projects are also transformative for children as they see themselves in new ways and perceive new possibilities. Muralist and professor Dr. Jerry Butler was involved in the project and shared in one of his workshops that the arts inspire us to "reengineer ourselves," to be the person we truly want to be. Teacher candidates, classroom teachers, and university professors expressed how, within the context of this project and series of workshops, a transformative space was created for not only the children but also for teachers and peers to perceive each other in new ways (Clark & French, 2012).

As depicted, unmasking truth and freedom was paramount during the *Echoes* performance. Children were free to express their views and perceptions of their life and community with strength, pride, and conviction. Through a tapestry of masks, music, poetry, dance, and acting, intense emotional responses of respect, compassion, hope, anger control, and confidence were released. Future teachers developed new realities of education and unmasked beliefs that they can empower elementary school children. Parents and family members recorded the performances to be cherished and shared with their larger family and neighborhood friends. One community member wondered, after seeing the performance, "Why are the test scores in [our city] low when the children here show that they are talented, bright, and expressive in so many ways."

Working with the children, elementary education teacher candidates employed critical thinking and the arts to reveal meaningful teaching relationships that celebrated students' identities and cultural wellspring. One

FIGURE 5.11.   Celebrating Identity: Fifth Grade *Echoes* Performers On Stage, 2011.

teacher candidate shared, "Being here, I am learning so much about the importance of a child's creative voice and critical thinking. Thank you." Another candidate, stemming from her exploratory minimask lesson experience with bilingual elementary children, said, "It's critical that we learn a second language to be effective teachers. We are working with children who are bilingual, and we are not."

Beyond the culminating event, in a follow-up investigation of the *Echoes* project, focus groups were held in participant schools with professors, children, and teachers to assess the long-term impact of the project on the children's critical thinking, sense of self, and resiliency. One child expressed, 4 months following the performance event,

> I can be myself now. I have friends that I didn't have before the program because now they want to know me. I was afraid before to show my feelings and the mask helped me show that there are two sides to me. Sometimes I am happy. Sometimes I am sad.

Another child stated, "I knew my teacher liked me before, but after the performance, I think they know more about me." In further revealing relationship-building and unmasking identity between teachers and students, beyond our preservice teachers, an in-service 5th-grade teacher at one of the schools commented on the effect that this particular mask project cumulatively had on some of the children over time:

> I'm thinking of students from the year before, who have come back, and they are so much more confident. I see the impact in the long run. He's in sixth grade now, he has more self-assurance of who he is. He talked about it. It's self-confidence. I . . . see it with some of the girls [as well].

When asked if there was any student who surprised her during or after the mask project, this teacher described a surprising personal transformation that occurred with one child:

> There was one student who contributed quite a bit in one of the performances and she tends to be a child who does not have a lot of friends—she's a child that stays by herself. She'll grab a book, stay and sit, and read instead of going to play at recess, but she had a starring role in one of the performances. I thought that was great. I think that that really helped her . . . She did talk more with the kids [after the performance]. It shocked me. I was like, "Wow!"

The *Echoes from a Child's Soul* project was designed for children to have the power and control to choose methods to express their identity through the metaphor of unmasking. This aesthetic experience created a bridge toward personal transformation for children. As they participated, they were happy to be able to use the mask to become someone new, perhaps someone they always wanted to be. Ironically, in a sense they became aware of their "true self" (Merton, 1955) or who they want to become by showing others who they really are. The children expressed surprise after the *Echoes* project that their peers now perceived them in new ways. Bullies became friends, and social awareness through an increase in identity resulted in new relationships forming between children and teachers (Figure 5.12).

In light of the reciprocal *Seed of Unmasking,* the outcome of this transformation can be described as a guided exploration of whole-child learning, where multiple concepts (confidence, resiliency, voice, emotional imagination, and moral imagination) were engaged on multiple levels (spiritual, intellectual, social-emotional, and physical) both individually and as a compassionate collective community. Peeling away masks and unmasking created a sense of empowerment, heightened children's resiliency, and self-esteem grew (Clark, 2005, 2013). As a fifth grader proudly stated, "I'm more independent now. It felt nice that we gave our ideas and [the preservice teachers] took them."

Not only did these effects take place on a deeply personal level, but on a communal level as well. As one child revealed,

> Before when I never did the mask. . . everybody used to not show respect. . . when I did the mask everyone was nice to me, polite, and I think they were doing that because they got to see how I felt . . . It made me feel older inside.

Being able to show others who they really are also gave students a sense of power, freedom and confidence (Glasser, 2010). The exchange below demonstrates a form of unmasking as children revealed their voices in a real sense and felt a renewed freedom to become their true selves. The

FIGURE 5.12.   Fifth-grade Student *Echoes* Performers "Revealing the Real," 2011.

following two children express to each other in an interview conversation their sense of self as a result of participating in the *Echoes* (2011) project:

> Anthony: I learn that I can do anything I want. I'm free. I don't need to listen to people who judge me by my color. I felt open that I really don't care what other people say about me. It doesn't bother me. I know [who] I am. I know that I'm better than that.

> Marissa: Yeah. It gave me an opportunity for me to be more open to myself. They don't see you, but they see your mask . . . and it's like, when you put on your mask you feel free, open. You feel free to open yourself more and more open to the world. And they can see the real you.

Unmasking Within the KIVA

The beauty of the KIVA is that it immediately sets up a larger vision beyond the immediate for anyone who comes within its sphere. That is why we keep calling it a new paradigm. The knee-jerk, old technical testing rut of "Are we done yet?" doesn't even enter the picture. Even while teacher/ student compassionate artist teams may complete project components and the performance itself, everyone is left hungry and looking for more—candidates certainly, but often the children even more so (see Figure 5.13). As shown with the above comments, children are still truly enlightened and empowered. And our teacher candidates witness a "miracle"; that the one-way old paradigm, "I'm gonna use this place to become a teacher for me," becomes a multiway possibility paradigm, that with a spiritual-aesthetic core

FIGURE 5.13. Blowing away the cobwebs: Unmasked empowerment rap performance with teacher candidates and 5th-grade students, 2011.

FIGURE 5.14.   Teacher and Student Artists Together Following *Echoes* Performance, 2011.

goes, multidimensional, way beyond even a *two-way* service-learning reciprocity.

The poetry, raps, dance, songs, and community performance of *Echoes* were a testimony to the children's multiple talents and abilities, symbolizing the vast ocean of children that are at-promise (see Figure 5.14). A child's sense of themselves and the world is hidden in darkness, their true potential yet untapped by the educational system, held down by test-taking mandates. There is still hope for public education within future teachers that celebrate a child's imagination and create meaningful and adventurous experiences to release and honor a child's critical voice.

This is what the arts do for us; they bring us together, they inspire us, they make us think of a more compassionate world, they nurture our souls, unmask truth, and feed us with hope for the future. Artists hold the covenant of the world that has not yet come to be so that when corporate and environmental collapse happens it will be the artist once again who reinvents the world. Our imagination is our hope. Artist-teachers exercise the imagination so we can be reminded daily in our world that there is beauty and truth. When we are in our darkest hours, where do we go? We go into our imaginations. Or, in our paradigm, to the open KIVA that allows for the release of identity, like untapped lightning rods of revolutionary potential, that we might envision a new landscape for educational reform.

The next seed chapter explores *Inner Awareness* and the expansive aspects to sense of self that teacher candidates, once sleepwalkers and passive, are now awakened to possibility. We hope that everyone holding this book will try to unmask personal potential and touch the sacred imaginative realm within oneself.

REFERENCES

Adbusters. (2013). *Corporate flag.* Retrieved August 23, 2013, from https://www.adbusters.org/cultureshop/corporateflag.

Bridges, R. (1990). *Through my eyes.* New York: Scholastic Press.

Calkins, L., Ehrenworth, M., & Lehman, C. (2012). *Pathways to the common core: Accelerating achievement.* Portsmouth, NH: Heinemann.

Clark, B. (2005). *Moral imagination and art: Echoes from a child's soul* (Doctoral dissertation). University of Hartford, Connecticut. Retrieved May 10, 2012, from Dissertations & Theses: Full Text. (Publication No. AAT 315 7797).

Clark, B. (2009). Mustard seed: A personal search for "Ahimsa" (The truth of nonviolence). *Closing the Circle Exhibition.* B. Clark & M. Cipriano (Artists). New Britain, CT: New Britain Commission on the Arts.

Clark, B. (2013). Breaking the culture of silence in schools: Children's voices revealed through moral imagination. In D. G. Mulcahy (Ed.), *Transforming schools: Alternative perspectives on school reform* (pp. 87–106). Charlotte, NC: Information Age.

Clark, B., & French, J. (2012). ZEAL: An aesthetic revolution for education. *Critical Questions in Education, 3*(1), 12–22. Retrieved from http://education.missouristate.edu/assets/AcadEd/Zealfinal.pdf

Coles, R. (1990). *The spiritual life of children.* Boston, MA: Hougton Mifflin.

Csikszentmihalyi, M. (1996). *Creativity: Flow and the psychology of discovery and invention.* New York, NY: Harper Perennial.

Cullum, A. (1967). *Push back the desks.* New York, NY: Citation.

Eisner, E. W. (2002). *The arts and the creation of mind.* New Haven, CT: Yale University Press.

Elkind, D. (2007). *The power of play: Learning what comes naturally.* Cambridge, MA: Da Capo.

Fox, M. (2004). *Creativity: Where the divine and human meet.* New York, NY: Penguin.

French, J. (2005). *Culturally responsive pre-service teacher development: A case study of the impact of community and school fieldwork* (Doctoral dissertation). University of Connecticut, Storrs. Retrieved from Dissertations and Theses: Full Text database. (Publication No. AAI3167589).

French, J. (2012). Creating eco-social culturally responsive educators with community. *Green Theory and Praxis, 6*(1), 17–34.

French, J., & Clark, B. (2012). Revitalizing a spiritual compassionate commons in educational culture. *Religion & Education, 39,* 93–108.

Gardner, H. (1993). *Creating minds: An anatomy of creativity seen through the lives of Freud, Einstein, Picasso, Stravinsky, Eliot, Graham, and Gandhi.* New York, NY: Basic.

Gardner, H. (1994). *The arts and human development.* New York, NY: Basic. (Original work published 1973)

Gillum, J., & Bello, M. (2011, March 27). When standardized test scores soared in D.C., were the gains real? *USA Today.* Retrieved from http://www.usatoday.com/news/education/2011-03-28-1Aschooltesting28_CV_N.htm?sms_ ss=twitter&at_xt=4d8ff2dc3b0fe8d5,0

Glasser, W. (2010). *Choice theory: A new psychology of personal freedom.* New York, NY: HarperCollins.

Greene, M. (1998). *A light in dark times and the unfinished conversation.* New York, NY: Teachers College Press.

Greene, M. (2001). *Variations on a blue guitar: The Lincoln Center Institute lectures on aesthetic education.* New York, NY: Teachers College Press.

Highwater, J. (1982). *The primal mind: Vision and reality in Indian America.* New York, NY: Harper & Row.

Highwater, J. (Writer), Perlmutter, A. (Producer), & Lenzer, D. (Director). (1996). *Primal mind: Alternative perspectives on self, environment and the development of culture* [Documentary]. Primal Mind Foundation.

Jonsson, P. (2011). America's biggest teacher and principal cheating scandal unfolds in Atlanta. *Christian Science Monitor.* Retrieved from http://news.yahoo.com/americas-biggest-teacher-principal-cheating-scandal-unfolds-atlanta-213734183.html

Kelley, D. (2012). *How to build your creative confidence.* Retrieved from http://www.ted.com/talks/david_kelley_how_to_build_your_creative_confidence.html - 60333

Kohan, J. (2013). *Sacred art.* Retrieved from http://sacredpilgrim.com/

Lewis, H. (2006). *Excellence without a soul: How a great university forgot education.* New York, NY: Public Affairs.

McLain, P. (2011). *The paris wife.* New York, NY: Random House.

Merton, T. (1955). *No man is an island.* New York, NY: Harcourt Brace.

Pinchbeck, D. (2007). *2012: The return of Questzalcoatl.* New York, NY: Jeremy P. Tarcher/Penguin.

Ravitch, D. (2011). The death and life of the great American school system: How testing and choice are undermining education. New York, NY: Basic.

Shor, I. (1992). *Empowering education: Critical teaching for social change.* Chicago, IL: University of Chicago Press.

Tagore, R. (1913). *Gitanjali (Song offerings): A collection of prose translations made by the author from the original Bengali. Intro. by W. B. Yeats.* London, UK: Macmillan.

Yogananda, P. (1946). *Autobiography of a yogi.* Los Angeles, CA: Self-Realization Fellowship Press.

CHAPTER 6

THE SEED OF INNER AWARENESS

Seed of Inner Awareness Painting
(Clark, 2009)

A spiritual practitioner who has gained a certain degree of realization as a result of his or her long practice should not rest content. Instead, this practitioner should set out and attempt to communicate it to others, so that they too can share in the experience. Since the essence of all spiritual practice is the practice of love, compassion, and tolerance, once you have had a profound experience of these it is natural that you should share it with others.

—Dalai Lama XIV (1998)

Hearts and Minds Without Fear: Unmasking the Sacred in Teacher Preparation,
pages 149–174.
Copyright © 2014 by Information Age Publishing

Within us the sacred seed of inner awareness awaits to be sown. Meaning that once we accept and practice our imaginative abilities, we will find a limitless potential to love and create. This chapter will further explore the rich paradigm that the aesthetic presents as a means of revealing the sacred within all of us. Our divine nature and desire to create, in response to the world around us, guides us toward truth and rejects manipulation. When teacher candidates identify and express a sense of inner awareness, it is the result of experiencing freedom during the aesthetic experience rather than from the confinement of direct instruction. As inner awareness grows in teacher candidates and children, a love of self and empathy for others increases as self-doubt and fears are diminished. According to Clark (2005b), intrapersonal awareness increased when children

> completed the visualization process, internalized visual cues embedded in work of art and subsequently, as their personal symbolic language became more complex they developed imaginative reference points. An imaginative reference point can be defined as the schematic references that cue or stimulate the [children's] internalization of the symbolic realm. (p. 210)

While viewing Christina's World by Andrew Wyeth (1948), Clare, age 10, composed the following poem, titled "Through Christina's Eyes." She reveals an empathic voice for Christina, who is paralyzed and lying outstretched across an open field as depicted in the painting by Wyeth (Clark, 2005b, p. 155).

Through Christina's Eyes
Waiting helplessly in the field.
As afraid as a toddler all alone.
Needing help but no-one to help you.
Falling down and can't get up.
Nobody's support to make it through.
Through the world's eyes I know I can
but people doubt me because I'm different.
But really we are the same in a lot of ways.

Clare is a child labeled academically and socially at-risk by her teacher. For the purposes of this study (Clark, 2005b), Clare is perceived to be at-promise. She utilized metaphorical language after visually projecting herself into the shoes of Christina, the character in the painting. Perkins (1994) found that art and aesthetics provide instant sensory anchoring, personal engagement, wide-spectrum cognition, multiconnectedness, and a dispositional atmosphere to think deeply and broadly (pp. 82–86). According to Clark (2005b), children released empathic voices through their cognitive symbolic language and instantly realized that they were part of a larger community and possibly responsible for others. The arts do provide for us a wide spectrum of possibility to explore how we feel, what we believe, what is meaningful in our lives, and our relationships with others. As imagination grows, inner awareness grows.

Throughout the text, we have been weaving a tapestry of threads within our KIVA: the seeds of *Play*, *Voice*, *Hope*, *Change*, and *Unmasking* of the invisible emotional and imaginative realms. As reciprocal seeds are revealed, so too are aspects of our KIVA and who we might become as educators for children. In this seed chapter, we explore *Inner Awareness* from the perspective of being mindful of the heart and how our actions impact other lives. William Carlos Williams (1962), the renowned America poet and doctor, stated in his book, titled *The Doctor Stories*, "Outside myself there is a world" (p. x).

The aesthetic lifts the top off our narrow vision and egocentricity. The KIVA community members strive to be healthy both without and within to navigate the 21st century issues. This seed chapter will present how aesthetic education pedagogy has impacted preservice teachers' inner awareness, their sense of self as teachers, and beliefs about teaching children. Within, we will further propose a connection based on our collective experiences and research that the imaginative realm is in fact connected to and not separated from the spiritual realm where our inner voice abides.

While not readily understood by our own culture, this "soul force" within has been readily understood by multiple past cultures (see Celts in Chapter 4, "The Seed of Change," for instance). All true artists know how creativity evokes stirrings of the human spirit. When you take art out, it is antithetical to being human. Using imagination as a way to envision the possible and contradict the materialistic misnomer of "limited" knowledge allows for educators to have a greater sense of intrapersonal self-worth and voice their contributions. Once the sacred is unmasked, the imaginative inner voice dwelling within every individual awakens (Figure 6.1).

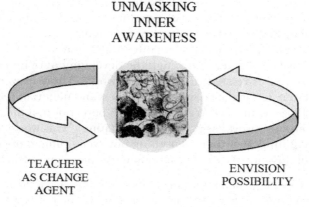

UNMASKING
INNER
AWARENESS

TEACHER
AS CHANGE
AGENT

ENVISION
POSSIBILITY

FIGURE 6.1.   Unmasking Inner Awareness Concept Map.

Inner awareness is achieved when a teacher believes in his or her students, aspires to new heights, knows the students, discovers the hidden potential of a child, and can envision possibility. The teacher has a very important obligation to be a change agent for the student, especially for children who have incarcerated parents, are homeless, underprivileged, or of a distinct oppressed minority. The teacher must be someone who can inspire and facilitate inner awareness for the child through the aesthetic. When the child releases his or her voice and inner thoughts and fears, the teacher acts as a mirror for the child to self-reflect. When teachers nurture an environment where all individuals can be mirrors for each other, inner awareness increases as understanding others impacts understanding oneself. As you meditate on the above seed painting (Clark, 2009) of inner awareness, multiple shadowed forms represent the interaction between compassionate community members, where listening, sharing, respect, possibility, and empathy grow (see Figure 6.1).

Letting Go

Our imaginative nature is revealed throughout all cultures and history on earth. Countless artists and spiritual aesthetic practitioners, who have realized their inner potential, have been our guides throughout the ages, from east to west. Artists and change-makers all have the common characteristic that they have high intrapersonal intelligence (Gardner, 1997). Daily reflection on who they are, what they do, and how their actions impact others is paramount for their personal growth, creativity, and spiritual awareness. "Perhaps the moral exemplar is most singular in the extent to which [s/he] sacrifices [s/he] personal goals for those of his family, the broader community, or even world society" (p. 132).

Through the creed of nonviolence based in Hinduism and the symbolic intergenerational skill actions of making his own clothing and salt, Mahatma Gandhi was able to shift mass consciousness and confound the entire British Indian Empire. Among the more recognized in the West, philosopher and poet Henry David Thoreau offered us natural world–inspired possibilities of civil disobedience through the development of inner awareness and sense of self as related to the natural world. Thoreau warned of our mindless slavery toward the day-to-day business and material/secular world. Thoreau (1992), cautioned Western society's perception of the artist as lazy versus the business world as productive by stating, "This world is a place of business . . . I think that there is nothing not even crime, more opposed to poetry, to philosophy, ay, to life itself, than this incessant business (p. 350).

> If a man walk in the woods for love of them half of each day, he is in danger of being regarded as a loafer; but if he spends his whole day as a spectator, shearing off those woods and making bald before her time, he is esteemed an

industrious and enterprising citizen. As if a town had no interest in its forest but to cut them down! (p. 351)

Inspired by Native American sand paintings as a healing process to restore one's innermost center, Jackson Pollack (1950) explored the deep recesses of the subconscious through drawing layers and layers, a dancing line on a massive canvas to evoke a cathedral-like feeling, asking the viewer to look toward higher human potential and have a spiritual experience (Frank, 1983). The abstract expressionists believed and were supported by Carl Jung, that artists express their voices and vision through their work. Like Pollack, Han Hoffman's painting abstractions were getting at the REAL. Martha Graham also explored the subconscious realm of human experience through dance, much like primal cultures did, where Native American ceremonial dances and Aboriginal vision quests sought other dimensions to pass into and dwell within (Highwater, 1982; Highwater, Perlmutter, & Lenzer, 1996).

In the scientific realm, quantum physicists like Alan Wolf have begun to unravel the material world, revealing these invisible understandings that ancient cultures have always known. That is, the true core energy of our selves and the universe is not of matter, but spiritual. Beyond the illusory material world of photons and atoms lies our imagination, where the "consciousness of God" or "realized compassion" moves faster than light (Wolf, 1999). As already asserted by early quantum physicists, consciousness has direct implications for the physical; for instance, depending on how they are perceived, photons are sometimes waves of energy and sometimes particles of mass (Asimov, 1988).

The claim that consciousness is purely a material world phenomenon of synapses and electromagnetic activity is challenged by research. In *Proof of Heaven* (Alexander, 2012), a neurosurgeon who personally underwent temporary brain death describes his profound experience of consciousness originating from another source than his corporeal form. Further popularized by the film and book *What the Bleep Do We Know!?* (Arntz, Chasse, & Vicente, 2007), is the idea that it may be consciousness that creates what we perceive as the material. Like the artists Pollack, Graham, and Hoffman, such "radical" scientists like Wolf and Alexander, "cutting-edge avant garde" film artists like Arntz, Chasse, and Vicente, and "beyond their time" science-writer-poets like Asimov or Bradbury ask us to use our imaginations to create spiritual possibilities and go beyond social or material illusion. But while imagination may move us in new directions, calling attention to such invisible-spiritual interdependence of events goes against our artificially prescribed material mindset. Even here, touching upon the ideas in the inner-most quantum or subconscious level where anything and everything can happen simultaneously may be surprising to us, but they are not to children.

In his 40 years of research with children all over the world, Coles (1991) found that children from all cultures spoke of a greater power, especially the children he worked with in a Boston hospital who were dying of polio. He found they were not afraid, because they knew their earthly body was not all that existed and that there was another level of experience for them after they passed.

Another example is when Coles (1991) visited Hopi children. One child stated a remarkable inner awareness of their relationship to the greater universe. Coles explains the indelible impression a little girl had on him as he reports the child saying,

> "Our people are here to wait until the time comes that no one hurts the land; then we will be told we've done our job, and we can leave." [Coles continues] . . . Again an upward tilt of her head, as I tried to make sense of the complex theology that had taken root in a girl barely a decade old, not especially well educated, and within her school not known by her teachers as "bright," as someone "good" for me to get to know—and yet, I would gratefully realize over a couple of years' time, a girl whose heart beat to Hopi rhythms and whose soul lay open to an entire landscape. (p. 27)

It is essential to protect and nurture children's imaginations, as they are so fragile and easily influenced by adult anger, bias, and negativity. Robert Coles learned to listen to children, and as he listened, he learned that the children would become his greatest teachers.

Spiritual educator and scientist Rudolph Steiner recognized the automatic tendency to falsely separate material from spiritual and strove to bring people to consider and practice unification in their daily life and learning. Heavily influenced by his own spiritual experiences and the work of Goethe (Steiner, 1950), Steiner and the heart of Waldorf educational philosophy ascribes to a comingling of spiritual and material worlds so that the twain should never be twixt. In his work, Steiner insisted that we not neglect the whole of who we are. But his creative genius was rejected by the mainstream public school education; and at the present, his ideas continue to be seen as outlandish and otherworldly precisely because of our "one-sided" focus on the material. Yet, ironically, it is to private Waldorf schools, founded by Steiner's philosophy, where top CEO's in California's Silicon Valley send their children to be immersed wholeheartedly in the arts and aesthetics (Richtel, 2011).

Savvy to the steadfast *status quo* perception of his work, Steiner empathetically reflected that from our particular dependent perspective and vantage point, many of us only permit ourselves a limited horizon (Stedall, 2012). As we transform ourselves to other levels—or metaphorically, by climbing the mountain—we discover that there are newer and further horizons than we could never have possibly imagined. Pinchbeck (2007) envisions that,

"From the current Earth, our evolutionary stream flows toward the Jupiter phase—identical, perhaps, with the Fifth World of the Hopi" (p. 179).

Pinchbeck (2007) goes on to illuminate Steiner's dream that "we will, eventually, become self-created entities of cosmic wisdom. . . [Steiner stated] 'Just as we have circulating blood, so have the Jupiter beings wisdom. It is their very nature'" (p. 179). Is it our very nature to capture like our ancient brothers and sisters a sense of cosmic inner awareness as Steiner presents? Having had our own experience within aesthetic education, Steiner's symbolic archetype wisdom rings true. Within our KIVA paradigm, inner awareness development has permitted ever-larger expanding horizons of spirituality, vision, and possibility for all involved.

Unfortunately, *en masse*, allowing our external culture to deny our inner awareness potential, we continue to play out a falsely perceived reality within our educational institutions, schools and classrooms. In blatant disregard and neglect, the emotional-spiritual and aesthetic curriculum has largely been dismissed and forgotten by public education teaching and learning practice. By confining ourselves within the droppings of numeracy and literacy standards, for example, any social emphasis is manipulated as a means to meet material ends rather than to enhance soulful compassion. Everyday messages reveal where our energy in education is placed: Newspapers report school districts' standardized test scores as towns' real estate prices shift accordingly; and bumper stickers brag, "My child is an honor student." Everywhere we see it is about *academic* curriculum excellence and not excellence in compassionate action, which is the prize for U.S. public schools and learning.

Higher education, which supplies our public schools with professionals, is also dedicated to conferring specialists and consultants who are experts in slanted corporal forms of curriculum. Rather than the subjective and aesthetic thinking processes, the rigor of memorization and expertise in content is demanded. Even school counselors and psychologists who may perhaps have more opportunity to engage in the spiritual domain, ultimately (due to the burden of administrative tasks) may not see that children are conforming to a dysfunctional system that accepts a teacher's static ends and means of delivering content. If counselors were abundant and given the freedom to work with teachers within the affective domain, then possibly the content material could emotionally enhance a child's well-being. Children, once naturally, spiritually, and creatively attuned, are thus systematically halted, stunted, manipulated, and silenced by schooling from their most important self-sustaining spiritual base, with an increasingly lopsided focus on the material.

Taking a cue from spiritual practitioner Thomas Merton (1955) and his observation of spiritual perspectives around the world, it may be our materialistic focus that prevents our children's and our own true inner spirits from flourishing. Or as Thoreau (1992) advised in *Walden*, to lose our true self to the material world and through the natural world expand our inner awareness of our vast capacity to understand the extent of our relationships with nature and with one another. Thoreau advised that with nature and a greater awareness of self, "we may be continually cheered by a like but more normal and natural society, that we are never alone" (p. 113). "I am no more lonely than the Mill Brook, or a weathercock, or the north star, or the south wind, or an April shower, or a January thaw, or the first spider in a new house" (p. 114). Both Merton and Thoreau, as many spiritual aesthetic practitioners before and after them, understood that the material world is an illusion and once we lose ego, we are able to transcend and truly create (French & Clark, 2012).

Yet this severe discordance or imbalance between the secular and spiritual world may be what ultimately fosters "burnout," where teachers, consistently self-denying access to their inherent life force sustaining energy, end up depleted in stark contrast to children's potential. So many educators have had to endure or, dare we say, suffer from, an overemphasis on literal and factual knowledge while allowing their spiritual core to wilt and withdraw from inexpression. Our country continues to allow schools that are "educating" our children to operate in this desert paradigm, which is void of the aesthetic, and to "educate" teachers to fill schools with a continued testing focus on content, curriculum, and method. Dishearteningly, we self-limit our own ability to accomplish and create everyday "miracles" in learning and teaching, and neglect passing on the spiritual torch of soul-force.

But what if the secular world were purposely used as a means of illuminating the spiritual, as Steiner proposed through his very accessible and vigorous "spiritual science" (Steiner, 1948) or *Eurythmy*. The expression of his aesthetic philosophy captures a sense of the Gestalt, the whole essence; akin to the beating of our hearts, the rhythm of our breath and the movement of our body through time and space in organic forms[1]. Or, as we have established in our aesthetic pedagogy, the *body of aesthetic* igniting the *soul of imagination* to nurture true creation and possibility.

What might our society become if aesthetic education were at the heart of our schooling experience for children? Is there still a chance? If we can foster an increased inner awareness through the aesthetic approach within teacher education, perhaps new teachers may view each and every child as a unique star in the sky, shining brightly with hope for their future dreams. As mentioned above through artists, spiritual practitioners, and change makers, teacher candidates have the opportunity to dissect, compare, and contrast ways in which the public domain is overwhelmingly steeped within a secular perspective. Once they know and can see what is divinely impor-

---

[1] See also http://www.rudolfsteinerweb.com/Rudolf_Steiner_and_Eurythmy.php

tant and even, perhaps, that teaching is *holy* work, then they can confidently believe that there is endless possibility for learning and teaching. From this newfound inner awareness, they would teach from this center as artistic and spiritual practitioners and child pedagogues. And, as the Dalai Lama implores above, if they then share these new heightened inner awareness perspectives, they just might create a new reality for their classrooms, schools, communities, and world.

In one case study, a teacher candidate reflected on her student teaching and how immersion in our KIVA over two semesters impacted her transfer of aesthetic education into her student teaching semester. Leann writes,

My experiences with the *Echoes from a Child's Soul* [see chapter 5, "The Seed of Unmasking"] and *Stepping Out of a Painting Project* [see chapters 8, "The Seed of Love" and 2, "The Seed of Hope"] were vital to my experiences at Central CT State University and were important for my path in becoming an elementary educator. With these experiences I saw first-hand the importance of adding arts into the classroom and allowing the students to have creative freedom. I, along with other CCSU students, would work with low readers and reluctant writers who were having trouble staying focused and staying on grade level with other members in their classroom community. In the classroom teachers were struggling to get these particular students to participate and get excited about their education but I saw each and every one of them flourish when given the opportunity to be a part of the creative writing process. One particular fourth grade student I worked with was shy to letting himself open up to others in the project but when he saw this community that was around him he felt supported enough to let himself try new things. When this young boy got the chance to write about the mask he created to portray himself it seemed as though he couldn't put the pen down. He wrote sentences upon sentences about how he made a lion mask because in school sometimes he had a voice as powerful and strong as a lion's roar. Having an opportunity in these projects and seeing how integrating the arts into a compassionate community allows students to exceed expectations and cherish their education influenced the way I went into my student teaching experience.

In student teaching I found it crucial to create a compassionate community with the nineteen first graders that were now my students. A community where students felt comfortable with sharing their hard work, questions and thoughts, all crucial and important aspects to a learning environment. We often had discussion based lessons during reading lessons where students led the discussions during interactive read loud, asking the students to think deeply about the text and ask other students questions. Doing these lessons and activities not only strengthened the community but also held the students accountable for their education.

I also integrated the arts often in my classroom and found that the students took their work with pride when they were allowed that creative freedom.

In student teaching we wrote a class fable, after studying the work of Leo Lionni, with an author's message to teach the reader, "You should be happy with yourself." Not only were students taking what they learned about finding an author's message while reading, which directly relates to Common Core State Standards, but also now they are using a high depth of knowledge to create their own fables to send that message and practice their writing craft. After the fable was created and published they used Leo Lionni as an inspiration to create their illustrations for the story using collage. Students had to illustrate their fables by using scraps of construction paper and other things together to make an illustration to go along with the writing.

Allowing students to connect to the lessons being taught because they are authentic for students and meaningful to their life is another important aspect of the classroom. In student teaching we read the book *Chrysanthemum* and asked text dependent questions to go along with the book club style discussion we were having. Knowing how to guide students questioning and scaffold learning in a meaningful way to make sure every individual child is getting the support needed from the teacher. In this lesson we asked an essential question of, how do our words and actions affect others around us? Students were allowed to connect to the story and sometimes connect it to other stories to truly comprehend and understand the story fully and deeply.

The *Echoes* project as well as the *Stepping Out of a Painting* project were both crucial to my success that I had in student teaching and the success I hope to have on future children in education.

Above, Leann explains how a 9-year-old boy, who is a reluctant writer and refuses to write for his teacher, is instantly inspired to work with Leann to create a lion mask that he will wear to become a lion. The little boy, as Leann described above, "couldn't put the pen down. He wrote sentences upon sentences about how he made a lion mask because in school sometimes he had a voice as powerful and strong as a lion's roar." As Dewey (1980) discussed, experiences with art directly connect to the senses and life of the learner. Art and morality are joined when the experience between the teacher and child is *real* and shouts into the child's soul in organic ways that content from a textbook could never reach.

Children have always gravitated to certain people, through who they are, their compassionate spirits, and because they see possibility and opportunity for greatness and love in learning and life. Parker Palmer stated from his extensive research in what constitutes a great educator that these are individuals who so closely self-identify with their content that they are one and the same (2007). In other words, any "student" within the proximity of such an individual cannot help but be enamored and inspired, not so much by the "content" but by the spirit medium through which it is born.

As any teacher who has experienced a "Zen" moment in a learning bonding experience that they and their students can never forget, faith and spirituality is about being in the moment, and really "seeing" the learner for the miraculous being they are, which is who we are simultaneously. Thomas Merton (1955), Anna Freud (1967), and Robert Coles (1991), who were all spiritual guides for education, saw this plainly because teaching to them was holy work—a witness to the sacred creative realm of each individual child.

So as we can probably count on one hand (or even two, if we were lucky enough) instances of such teachers from our own schooling experience, a great many present educators do have a spiritual gravity with people and children but are systematically told that this spiritual prowess is secondary to their material output. Those teachers who are particularly spiritually adamant with spunk are usually the ones who are very popular with children but are simultaneously often very unpopular with their colleagues, especially those who may have material gain at their demise, who may see them as annoying or "weak" or "troublemakers." They are called troublemakers by the status quo because these great educators by their inherent natural default are calling attention to hypocrisy, to what is important in learning, and advocating for a larger vision. And so, for the most part and to varying degrees, we may "face facts" and placate the secular domain in order to hold our jobs. Only a few spiritual practitioners simultaneously stick it out and stay in public teaching.

From our own experiences in public schools as teachers, as observers, and as parents, we are continually reinforced in our decision to teach future educators how to be spiritually compassionate practitioners and guides. That rekindling through the arts and aesthetic, and the compassionate inner awareness within, while simultaneously teaching how to nurture compassion within others, is supreme. The word compassion derives from the Latin *compati*: *com*, which means *together* and *pati*, which means *suffering*. In other words, compassion means suffering together, or in a Hebrew translation, "womb-like," for when one is compassionate, they are more than fully empathetic, they are sharing pain and experience with another, which is a hearkening to the ultimate closeness of mother and child (Joiner, 2012; Nielsen, 2012). The embodiment of compassion gives rise to lives led, for one example, by Mother Teresa. Mother Teresa described that she was

> more and more to realize that it is being unwanted that is the worst disease that any human being can ever experience. In these times of development, the whole world runs and is hurried. But there are some who fall down on the way and have not strength to go ahead. These are the ones we must care about. (as cited in Benenate, 1997, p. 14)

Mother Teresa continued to teach compassion within a community stating,

> Be kind in your actions. Do not think that you are the only one who can do efficient work, work worth showing. This makes you harsh in your judgment of others who may not have the same talents. Do your best and trust that others

do their best. And be faithful in small things because it is in them that your strength lies. (p. 15)

When we acknowledge that we share collective consciousness, when we have an inner awareness of our compassionate selves, we know that what we do unto another, we do unto ourselves. Understood in this way, compassion is the ultimate bridge to being present and sharing the suffering with others. The first step for our teacher candidates is to see below the surface of an angry, traumatized, or neglected child. We guide them to understand that the outer shell and façade of the child is not the whole expression of the child. Many teachers consciously or unconsciously reject children due to hidden bias from their backgrounds that has been triggered by myriad issues, the (dis)abilities, cultural characteristics, and personalities that all children have. However, a compassionate educator has a more developed inner awareness and sense of self, and so through spiritual formation and imaginative problem-solving skills, they believe ethically it is their responsibility to seek strategies in which to establish trust and deep personal connections with all children.

As detailed below, to develop the understanding of compassion, action, and a greater sense of self, our teacher candidates were mentored to change the way they think about homeless children and families, and how this impacts children's learning in schools. They shared a new vision with one another, based on developing a compassionate school community, expressing realness, genuineness, acceptance, empathy, and congruence. Utilizing effective and powerful communication through aesthetic expression, they treated their student audience with reverence and facilitated student social responsibility and feelings of self-worth. Those listening or watching were also, like our teacher candidates, given the opportunity to reimagine their relationship to homelessness, and through the aesthetic messages that were enacted on stage, hope surfaced throughout the school auditorium.

Where might this particular ripple effect instance of inner awareness have been carried? What if it were embraced in all of the schools where these future educators eventually obtained employment? When inner awareness grows, the teacher steps with their students into this invisible realm wherein realities not yet realized are revealed. The artist-educator begins to see the sacred both within themselves, the child, and their world (O'Reilley, 1998). And as the many sages and guides have already shown us, transforming the awareness of mass consciousness with truth will set us free.

The Need for Unlocking the Seed of Inner Awareness

Aesthetic education experiences impacted our preservice teachers' ideas in relation to human truths, self, children's lives, others, and our world (Clark & Ritzenhoff, 2008; Clark & French, 2012; French & Clark, 2012;

Greene, 1988). Significant to this research and future research, especially on teacher education's role in teacher training and in-service retention, was preservice teachers' emerging sense of identity as resilient teacher leaders for change. As one teacher candidate stated, "I know personally that I have gained more to my inner-being than ever. I have discovered things about myself, the type of person I am, and the type of person I want to be" (French & Clark, 2012, p. 102).

Having such a conviction of self-awareness and perception that new realities can be created is fundamentally powerful. If our future teachers can perceive themselves as change agents when engaged in aesthetic and authentic community contexts and issues, they become that change and can transfigure educational practice and reform (French, 2011, 2013). Unfortunately, solutions to everyday teaching problems (not to mention the macrosocial and ecological issues) are often left neglected because practitioners fail to critically examine and reflect upon their own perceptions and dispositions. In their attitudes toward teaching, practitioners need to be able to see multiple contextual solutions to problems rather than to be confined by their perceptions that there is one absolute, authoritative correct or incorrect answer (Ostorga, 2006). Thinking for substantial self-reflection or societal change must be an immersion of mind, body, and soul, facing divergent perspectives.

Dewey (1933) described attitudes that teachers must have to be effective reflective practitioners: "open-mindedness, responsibility and wholeheartedness" (as cited in Ostorga, 2006, p. 6). The highest order of reflective thought is the ability to engage in critical reflection (Merizow, 1991), "a learning process that results in the transformation of ways of knowing beliefs, attitudes, assumptions, and the perceptual and conceptual codes that form and limit the way we think and learn" (as cited in Ostorga, p. 10). In this light, educators must discern that truth is contextually bound. Given that we live in a multiverse, there are multiple truths and multiple forms of creative expression. Limited ideas of "right" and "wrong" become misnomers. In such a critical reflective spirit, teachers must be able to explore their own dispositions in balance with that of their students' by adopting multiple simultaneous perspectives and questioning the how and why of their thinking and actions.

Unfortunately, as was previously discussed in the seeds of Chapters 4, "The Seed of Change" and 5, "The Seed of Unmasking," amid the social and ecological turmoil of the world that demands such, we have seen little evidence in teacher education of peeling back layers of masks and nurturing such paramount characteristics of heightened inner awareness. In two studies specifically examining future teachers' reflective qualities, few possessed the "self-knowledge to identify their assumptions and evaluate how their assumptions influenced their teaching decisions" (Schussler, Stooksberry, & Bercaw, 2010, p. 350); and only one participant was observed as engaging in truly critically transformative reflection (Ostorga, 2006). The studies concluded that

> If teacher education programs are aimed at promoting educational reform, or aiming to prepare teachers who use sound effective teaching methods, then these programs have to include activities aimed at promoting such transformation. *This transformation needs to be situated at the very core of their being, at the affective level, where the values about practice are forged.* (Ostorga, 2006, p. 18; emphasis added)

> For candidates to use multiple perspectives to reflect on teaching situations and achieve parity in focusing on students and the self requires time and sequential scaffolding across a program. . . *To help candidates build an awareness of the self, such activities should include articulating desired ends, clarifying moral values, and understanding one's own cultural identity.* Candidates must then be guided to discern the contexts of different teaching situations so they can achieve their purposes . . . *Helping candidates achieve self-awareness must be purposeful and ongoing.* (Schussler et al., 2010, p. 361; emphasis added)

We agree that teacher education programs need an aesthetic imprint as to how they go about developing effective educators. We also have overwhelming evidence to support the means to do so. The conclusive statements above speak the path and place where we have put the energy of our activities: the inner-self, situating within our students "at the very core of their being, at the affective level, where the values about practice are forged" (Ostorga, 2006, p. 18). These studies' recommendations support our aesthetic paradigm.

How do we begin to *see* the child that is homeless, hurt, isolated, and marginalized? Teachers must nurture open hearts and open minds to see the children constantly in an ever-changing light, because what you *see* is not always what is (Cullum, 1971). Therefore, future educators during teacher preparation need to experience for themselves what they never thought possible while asking fundamental questions like *Who am I?; How do I perceive my sense of self?; What are my values and beliefs?*

Through an unmasking process series of aesthetic educational pedagogical practice scaffold course experiences (see Chapter 4, "The Seed of Change"), our future teachers' inner awareness beliefs have been "unlocked," leading to the revitalization of creative teaching skillsets supported by values and beliefs regarding teaching and learning that is transformative for both teachers and children. Ultimately, through the arts and aesthetic KIVA, we found that our preservice teachers were challenged to develop both intra- and interpersonal reflective dispositions for children and teaching, and a growing sense that they wanted to be urban teachers and leaders of change in education.

Through their self-development, our students began to see a larger purpose to education and what critical creative teaching and learning is or is not. Our class meetings became meaningful for preservice teachers to transform through the aesthetic experiences that were developed each semester, embracing the spirit of Albert Cullum, who said teacher education "should be four years of self-development, not how you are going to inject facts into people, how you have developed" (Gund & Sullivan, 2004).

Nurturing Inner Awareness Portal and Practice: Reimagining Homelessness

We have revealed here and in previous seed chapters that the aesthetic domain allows for all to come into a space of learning (KIVA) with who they are and what they bring. As elaborated upon in Chapter 2, "The Seed of Hope," people must be given, implicit in any issue presented, the sincere hope of being able to create and express a solution. We have said, each semester, that it really doesn't matter what particular social or ecological issue (like homelessness) we take up with our students and the children, what is important is the larger vision. Rather than a removed anthropological investigation or scientific experiment, children and adults are immersed together, engaging in a solution to an issue that genuinely concerns them all. We must always be able to have vision when tapping into building compassionate inner awareness. We are pointed toward the spiritual.

For example, our teacher candidates investigated the authentic issue of homelessness facing their university's surrounding local community in order to create curriculum in innovative ways to teach this social justice issue in schools. They explored their cultural biases and stereotypes, values, beliefs, identities, and sense of self as a teacher with invited community artists and activists leading myriad arts experiences. The artistic community forums contributed to a developing sense of the power of aesthetic education manifested in the creation and design of symbolic messages using masks, poetry, dance, music, and theater to address ending homelessness and breaking down stereotypes of poverty.

The purpose of the *Creating a Compassionate World Community* performance (Figures 6.2–6.5) was to create new perspectives and thoughts of what homelessness and compassion mean. Teachers had to figure out, symbolically, a new face on homelessness in order to then teach children to perceive homelessness and causes, breaking down stereotypes and bias against people in poverty. Symbolic ideas contained therein carried a compassionate message to build awareness, which was then integrated and shared within the community to empower transformative learning and societal contribution. When our students were able to reimagine their relationship with the idea of homelessness and with people who are homeless, they shared *a new vision* with one another and the school community.

FIGURE 6.2.   It Could Be Anyone: Preservice Teacher Performers From the *Creating a Compassionate World Community* Project, 2009.

Engaged in this process, our teacher candidates had developed a deepened awareness of homeless children in crisis. Their own understandings and beliefs on teaching and learning were expressed in such a way that truly conveyed that a deeply intrinsic impression had developed. The aesthetic had made its mark on their hearts and minds. They awakened, understanding what they did not have in their public school education and what they

FIGURE 6.3.   Expressions Of Joy, Compassion, and Calmness For and With Children. *Creating A Compassionate World Community* Project, 2009

FIGURE 6.4.   Bringing Home Messages Of Compassion and Justice: *Creating a Compassionate World Community* Project, 2009.

now wanted to provide for children in their elementary classrooms. They wrote,

> I have been truly blessed this semester with professors who understand what it truly means to teach. I have learned how to be the best I can be because you have let me explore who that truly is. This semester has taught me to be reflective, inquisitive, creative, and insane, to push back the desks. I have learned not to let [school policy] crush my spirit and to let my imagination shine through. I have learned that every student has the potential to be great, but you must be willing to find that touch of greatness. I have learned to practice compassion in and out of the classroom. I have learned to see all sides of a story. I have learned how to teach without fear and push boundaries. Most importantly, I have learned to be myself, whoever that is, without fear. I know that if I want to be the best teacher I can be I must continue learning that I am and what I believe in.

FIGURE 6.5.   The joy of being a part of something great: Children with teacher candidates and authors following performance: *Creating a Compassionate World Community* project, 2009.

This semester the biggest thing I learned was never to doubt what I believe in, because a person believes in something for a reason. I discovered what the reason for believing the things I do about teaching and education was this semester; I believe in these ideas because it is how students achieve greatness. I soared above the clouds with my learning this semester; I have never grown so much as a learner as I did this semester. I know if I bring these ideas and beliefs to my classroom my students will soar too and achieve absolute greatness. This semester I have learned that it is possible to assess students through authentic assessment. . . . tests are not needed 99% of the time. I have learned that learning can be a fun and joyful experience for everyone . . . It is impossible to put into words all I have learned this semester since all of what I have learned has been through and affected my heart.

The opportunity for these phenomena of a spiritual and creative community of learners to arise is because of an aesthetic education methodology that is enacted joyfully and spontaneously with children who become their greatest teachers. Utilizing effective and powerful communication through aesthetic expression, they treated the audience full of children with reverence. Through their skits, teacher candidates facilitated a sense of social responsibility for their community members facing homelessness, and feelings of self-worth that they could perhaps envision possibilities of lessening the effect of homelessness on children. Teacher candidates recreated their lived and educational reality and released moral and spiritual community values that were greater than they were (French & Clark, 2012).

Nurturing Inner Awareness Through the Aesthetic

Within the many studio paradigm community-based projects we have created, there has been significant increase in our teacher candidates' reflective dispositions to think deeply. The aesthetic allows a fluid transfer from the sacred within us, that which is lying dormant; an inner awareness that needs to be released and shared with others. In order to be fully realized, our humanness in the act of sharing is dignified; our sacred creative core that is shared in the community reciprocal action leads to new ideas, awareness, and hope. The aesthetic allows ego to be put aside so we are able to think about ourselves in relation to a child or about our identity as a teacher to a student. When we are able to do this, there is growth. When the focus is on a larger vision, by losing the self we gain a greater awareness of the whole and our place with others; permitting empathy, multiple perspectives, critical thinking, and transformational reflection.

With our students in our KIVA, we too are "border crossers" (Solomon, Manoukian, & Clarke, 2007) from the adult to child world, where we pay attention to what children know, not in a removed fashion, but through a holistic, aesthetic embrace. By working and playing with children, we provide a multifaceted aesthetic context in real time within real issues, wherein the moral inner core fiber qualities of reflection and disposition within our teachers are greatly enhanced. Through the aesthetic method and activity celebrating divergent thinking, we observe multiple instances of our students engaging in a transformative ways of knowing, in multiple contexts (course and fieldwork), with peers, children, teachers, community mentors, and through multiple modes of expression (scrapbook journaling, multimedia visuals, teaching philosophy and belief narratives, rap, poetry, dance, theatrical performance).

The components of these assignments are true to our own projects, except that rather than just imagining being a teacher, we bring our students together with the children in both school and community contexts to invent and implement innovative curriculum that bridges student core community identity and knowledge with that of schools. Thus, the successes of our "assignments" are also realized in real-time reality for our students. With a larger vision, the distancing of charity is eliminated and only compassion remains. And of course, when this happens, people feel genuinely happy. They feel great, empowered, unstoppable, and ready to embrace the next learning experience with motivation, excitement, and zeal.

We have seen this time and time again with our preservice teachers as well as with the children who are learning with them. As shown above with Leann, or previously told in Chapter 5, "The Seed of Unmasking," when one of our teacher candidates, John, embodied and applied his belief that people need to belong within the mask-making with children. Behind all the articulated structures of successful community-engagement programs, there is always a teacher or a teacher team who galvanizes the adults and children together. So it is with our aesthetic community program, except our "program" is purposely oriented toward opening and transforming within the KIVA, to creating teacher candidates who hold all the seeds of spiritual transformation.

Cullum also created an aesthetic dimension within his course content, avidly lighting up social imagination and learning through the arts. In interview (Gund & Sullivan, 2004) and his book (1967), Cullum speaks to the overwhelming assurance of the aesthetic domain:

> Sometimes adults do not sense the touch of greatness, or perhaps they feel threatened by it and reject such an atmosphere. But children are always eager to embrace greatness, not because they comprehend its depth, but simply because there is always an aura of excitement about greatness. There is always a mystery and a strength! (p. 69)

People always eventually seek spaces of greatness and moreover seek the people who create these spaces. Bill Strickland (2007), without naming it as such, created whole schools where the aesthetic was the critical ingredient that allowed for each student to be successful. The teachers, the curriculum, the infrastructure, right down to the purchased flowers to be placed by the entrance, all connoted to each person involved in the enterprise that they were worthy and that they were a part of something great. On site, in some of the most devastated inner-city slums, with no security or locked doors, his success has been astounding: He has founded many new national and international schools. Having been inspired by Mr. Strickland in person (2011), it is easy to see how his spiritual gravity is magnanimous. People believe and love him, and his ideas become and remain reality.

As has been told in Chapter 5, "The Seed of Unmasking," teachers need to remove the masks that are between understandings of their students and themselves. And, as described in Chapter 2, "The Seed of Hope," collaborative and reflective community-inclusive service learning led by culturally responsive facilitators showed the most promise in encouraging teachers to become transformative agents of change; teaching for social justice, diversity, and equality. Addressing the masked concerns of self, cultural funds of knowledge, and expectations, the literature is also emphatic that for teacher education programs to be successful, they must be very careful and deliberate about how they set up situations where people of divergent backgrounds and ways of knowing come together to learn (Sleeter, 2001).

Merely putting people together in a hodgepodge format to "learn" is unmasking in the wrong way. This can have disastrous results, such as internal metacognitive scars and/or a reinforcing of complex layers of masks reverberating between teacher-student connection and awareness. Indeed, instances of teacher education programs backfire among future teachers, and resultant reinforced current practice in school classrooms have been documented (Baldwin, Buchanan, & Rudisill, 2005; Davis, 1995; Whitehorse, 1996).

So what are the shapes and glue for the ultimate success of the multitude of activities, ideas, scaffolding, parallel course, and community fieldwork experiences that are successful in eliciting such powerful manifestations of participants' spirit and expression? We believe that beyond the placement within a community context, which is in and of itself a kaleidoscope of possibility (if given the practiced opportunity to see possibility within), the real core ingredient for community engagement successes, and our own program teacher candidates' success, was immersing them into this context through the aesthetic domain; the experiential learning through the arts.

Certainly any teacher program experience or educational project that has lasting impact must involve being mindful, forthright, careful, and deliberate, but when done within the aesthetic paradigm by a spiritual practitioner, then a space is created where everyone has an opportunity, rather than a hindrance, to learn. Providing teacher candidates multiple contexts within an emotional reflective portal and practice to consider, relate, and empathize (i.e., to share "suffering" together and to see from the perspective of another) is what may separate the failed community/school engagement experiences from those that are successful in promoting culturally responsive teaching practice in our future teachers. See also Chapters 2, "The Seed of Hope" and 7, "The Seed of Freedom" for further discussion and illustration (*Steppin' Out of a Painting* project) of this phenomenon.

In this book, "breaking all the rules" of which words, images, and diagrams can and cannot be used in academic research, we are attempting to directly describe, explain, and name this force at work. It is the spiritual aesthetic nature of encapsulating students in community-engaged projects that have a profound impact on their inner awareness success. It restructures the ways in which teacher candidates can see their roles as teachers, where the questioning of power enters the conversation naturally through the aesthetic and is not forced or intrusive but collaborative (Palmer, 1993).

Through the aesthetic paradigm, we are able to engage within a spiritual core, to create a space where collaborative and cooperative learning can happen successfully. Like lowering a diver into what could be perceived as shark-infested waters of the unknown, the aesthetic dispels the myth and false belief of "unknown, foreign, dangerous territory," allowing for the student to imagine all the possibilities and to be invited into the unknown. Through the *aesthetic*, our teacher candidates instead find themselves in a unique and special community that was never expected.

Inner Awareness Brings Freedom

The aesthetic domain is such that participants are compelled intrinsically to jump in. It is a warm, exciting embrace; a heartfelt, spiritual invitation that always finds an open portal of the mind. Within this paradigm, all knowledge is valued, and power is shared. As the arts are universal messages from all cultures, the aesthetic naturally invites all children who have been labeled in some way, shape, or form by the system to celebrate who they are, with dignity. The aesthetic develops inner awareness on so many levels, but most importantly, it empowers children to not accept marginalization, suffering in silence and despair from rejection (Delpit & Dowdy, 1995; Freire, 1997). Children who experience the arts and aesthetic while learning are no longer "at risk." When children encounter the arts, they "manifest an intuitive understanding of life experience," as the arts provide "a mirror to look inward, to see, to feel, and to think about what they know" (Clark, 2005a, pp. 429, 440).

The aesthetic permits instant empathy, the sharing of pain, perspective, suffering, or compassion in service to a larger vision. It allows us to experience a very spiritual conjecture that our experience is all one; that what pain we do unto others, we do onto ourselves; and that what joy we give, we receive. To serve within such a vast visionary paradigm, we suddenly realize the infinite well of compassion that each of us has as we are tapping not into a singular material body but into the collective spiritual cosmos, life force, or love that sustains us all (French & Clark, 2012). When we come home from a "long" "hard" day of true service and compassionate actions, we confront our long-held beliefs of traditional commonsense physics and find ourselves filled with more energy than when we had started. Experiencing this and remembering this, eventually, we can attain an inner awareness that can build and set us free.

For inner awareness to sustain itself, service and compassion must be practiced. Perhaps our students just have a taste of it when they take our courses, but it must be sustained for them, for us. In this very material-oriented and secularly construed world, we must remind ourselves of the truth in many ways, by surrounding ourselves with artists, innovators, change-makers, and spiritual practitioners of compassion and service. We are guides and maestros, possibilizing with individuals in our KIVA and re-alizing that our talents, when used, will never allow life to be stagnant. Once our teacher candidates realize their hidden talents, those talents will never be dormant again. Inner awareness has begun to grow with the aesthetic, continuing to act as a portal to connect their sense of self to the world.

Our students have consistently reported to us that although being im-mersed in the aesthetic is at first sometimes uncomfortable and even stress-ful, in the end, by growing very close to one another in this space, they look back to see that the process was essential and they wouldn't have wanted it any other way or with any other teacher guiding them through. In other words, the contrast of tension (or the unmasking process between their persona and their true self) was critical to building inner awareness epipha-nies. As one candidate reflected at the end of the semester,

> Today during class we created masks out of a papier-mâché substance. At the beginning of class I was not overly excited about the project. I felt like it was going to be a mess and that it was going to be more annoying than enjoyable. This lesson, however, truly taught me a lot. There had to be trust between my partner and me. I was allowing her to cover my mask with an unknown sub-stance at 8:00 in the morning. I had to trust that she wasn't going to hurt me. I had to trust her with my vision . . . .

> It was a partnership in building the mask. We helped each other create a masterpiece that symbolizes who we are as individuals. This activity opened me up and allowed me to get over the idea of getting dirty. I will become a teacher who is not afraid to pull up my sleeves and make a mess. I will create partnerships and a sense of trust within my community as well. I ended up learning more than I thought. This mask will symbolize the students that I encounter. It symbolizes the students that come in with a mask over their face and walls built up. I have to get my students to take their masks off and reveal themselves to me as we grow and learn together.

If our teachers haven't been exposed to the aesthetic since they were very young, or if they haven't had art since 9 or 10, by having them live and teach in the arts, they are being asked to reimagine everything that they grew to know and believe. We can't just say "teach this way to the students"; it first has to come from our students so that they can then teach it. We create, borrowing a metaphor from Shakespeare, "a stage upon a stage" (1992). When you are in the play, you can then create the play. Or in our particular context, a school within a school. It is a feedback cycle, reciprocal, aesthetic immersion into a family of creativity, where everything we know is collapsed into shared epistemological beginnings. Beyond "metacognitive development," our students are immersed heart and soul within the KIVA. In our view, this is the core purpose for their teacher education experience, otherwise they won't know how to use the power of the aesthetic with children.

For both of us to continue teaching this way, the motivation is to know that perhaps one of our teacher candidates will understand what children really need to thrive and that the arts, dance, painting, and such are natural for children to play with. Our teacher candidates will also perceive their true selves, true potential, and continue to explore the possibility that as a teacher they may be the hope for a child. And at this crucial time in public schools where there is malnutrition of the imaginative spirit, there is no better time than now.

Chapter 7, "The Seed of Freedom," explores the potential, if given the chance, that humans have to be

> creative, imaginative, thoughtful, resourceful, patient, persistent, and ever-changing beings. Placing our compassion in one another and ourselves, we find an ever-loving voice within us . . . which tells us that we do not need to be constrained, that we have choice, that we have calm within, and that . . . is our true selves. (French & Clark, 2012, p. 107)

When the heart is moved, the imaginative core is no longer separated from the spiritual core. The truest sense of self may be when we are in love with what we are doing. And having had this experience, our students can then embody and then transfer to the children they will teach.

REFERENCES

Alexander, E. (2012). *Proof of heaven: A neurosurgeon's journey into the afterlife.* South Yarra, Australia: Macmillan Australia.

Arntz, W., Chasse, B., & Vicente, M. (2007). *What the bleep do we know: Discovering the endless possibilities for altering your everyday reality.* Deerfield Beach, FL: Health Communications.

Asimov, I. (1988). *Understanding physics.* New York, NY: Hippocrene.

Baldwin, S., Buchanan, A., & Rudisill, M. (2005). What teacher candidates learned about diversity, social justice, and themselves from service-learning experiences. *Journal of Teacher Education, 56*(5), 315–327.

Benenate, B. (1997). *In the heart of the world: Thoughts, prayers, & stories, Mother Teresa.* New York, NY: Barnes & Noble.

Clark, B. (2005a). Moral imagination and art: Echoes from a child's soul. *Forum on Public Policy: Issue Child Psychology, 1*(4), 428–446.

Clark, B. (2005b). *Moral imagination and art: Echoes from a child's soul* (Doctoral dissertation). University of Hartford, Connecticut. Retrieved May 10, 2012, from Dissertations & Theses: Full Text. (Publication No. AAT 315 7797).

Clark, B. (2009). Mustard seed: A personal search for "Ahimsa" (The truth of nonviolence). *Closing the Circle Exhibition.* B. Clark & M. Cipriano (Artists). New Britain, CT: New Britain Commission on the Arts.

Clark, B., & French, J. (2012). ZEAL: An aesthetic revolution for education. *Critical Questions in Education, 3*(1), 12–22. Retrieved from http://education.missouristate.edu/assets/AcadEd/Zealfinal.pdf

Clark, B., & Ritzenhoff, K. (2008). UMC New Britain collaborative on the cutting edge: University museum community collaboration. *The International Journal of the Inclusive Museum, 1*(2), 63–78.

Coles, R. (1991). *The spiritual life of children.* Boston, MA.: Houghton Mifflin.

Cullum, A. (1967). *Push back the desks.* New York, NY: Citation.

Cullum, A. (1971). *The geranium on the windowsill just died, but teacher you went right on.* New York, NY: Harlin Quist.

Dalai Lama. (1998). *The good heart: A Buddhist perspective on the teachings of Jesus.* (G. Jinpa, Trans.). Somerville, MA: Wisdom.

Davis, K. (1995). Multicultural classrooms and cultural communities of teachers. *Teaching and Teacher Education, 11*(6), 553–563.

Delpit, L., & Dowdy, J. (Eds.). (2002). *The skin that we speak: Thoughts on language and culture in the classroom.* New York, NY. New Press.

Dewey, J. (1933). *How we think: A restatement of the relation of reflective thinking to the educative process.* New York, NY: D.C. Heath.

Dewey, J. (1980). *Art and experience.* New York, NY: Macmillan.

Frank, E. (1983). *Jackon Pollack.* New York, NY. Abbeville.

Freire, P. (1997). *Pedagogy of the heart.* New York, NY: Continuum.

French, J. (2011). Revitalizing community based language arts curriculum practice through ecojustice education. *New England Reading Association (NERJA), 47*(1), 43–50.

French, J. (2013). Methods & mindsets for creating eco-social community educators. In D. G. Mulcahy (Ed.), *Transforming schools: Alternative perspectives on school reform* (pp. 37–66). Charlotte, NC: Information Age.

French, J., & Clark, B. (2012). Revitalizing a spiritual compassionate commons in educational culture. *Religion & Education, 39,* 93–108.

Freud, A. (1967). *Psychoanalysis for teachers and parents* (B. Low Trans.). New York, NY: Emerson. (Original work published 1935)

Gardner, H. (1997). *Extraordinary minds. Portraits of 4 exceptional individuals and an examination of our own extraordinariness.* New York, NY: Harper Collins.

Greene, M. (1988). *The dialectic of freedom.* New York, NY: Teachers College Press.

Gund, C. (Producer), & Sullivan, L. (Director). (2004). *A touch of greatness* [Motion picture]. First Run Features.

Highwater, J. (1982). *The primal mind: Vision and reality in indian america.* New York, NY: Harper & Row.

Highwater, J. (Writer), Perlmutter, A. (Producer), & Lenzer, D. (Director). (1996). *Primal mind: Alternative perspectives on self, environment and the development of culture* [Documentary]. Primal Mind Foundation.

Joiner, M. (2012, November). *Service is the soul's work: A Veterans Day reflection.* Sermon presented to the Universalist Church of West Hartford, West Hartford, CT. Retrieved from http://www.westhartforduu.org/WorshipFellowship/SermonsOnline/ServiceistheSoulsWork/tabid/335/Default.aspx

Merton, T. (1955). *No man is an island.* New York, NY: Harcourt Brace.

Mezirow, J. (1991). *Transformative dimensions of adult learning.* San Francisco: Jossey-Bass.

Nielsen, J. (2012, April). *Heartstones and heavy lifting: A sermon for Easter Sunday.* Sermon presented to the Universalist Church of West Hartford, West Hartford, CT. Retrieved from http://www.westhartforduu.org/WorshipFellowship/SermonsOnline/HeartstonesandHeavyLifting/tabid/217/Default.aspx

O'Reilley, M. R. (1998). *Radical presence: Teaching as contemplative practice.* Portsmouth, NH: Boynton/Cook.

Ostorga, A. (2006). Developing teachers who are reflective practitioners: A complex process. *Issues In Teacher Education, 15*(2), 5–20.

Palmer, P. (1993). *The violence of our knowledge: Toward a spirituality of higher education.* Paper presented at the the Michael Keenan Memorial Lecture, the 7th Lecture, Berea College, KY. Retrieved from http://www.kairos2.com/palmer_1999.htm

Palmer, P. (2007). *The courage to teach: Exploring the inner landscape of a teacher's life.* San Franciso, CA: Jossey-Bass.

Perkins, D. (1994). *The intelligent eye: Learning to think by looking at art.* Santa Monica, CA: Getty Center for Education in the Arts.

Pinchbeck, D. (2007). *2012: The return of Questzalcoatl.* New York, NY: Jeremy P. Tarcher/Penguin.

Richtel, M. (2011, October 22). A Silicon Valley school that doesn't compute. *New York Times.* Retrieved from http://www.nytimes.com/2011/10/23/technology/at-waldorf-school-in-silicon-valley-technology-can-wait.html?pagewanted=all&_r=0

Schussler, D. L., Stooksberry, L. M., & Bercaw, L. A. (2010). Understanding teacher candidate dispositions: Reflecting to build self-awareness. *Journal of Teacher Education, 61*(4), 350–363.

Shakespeare, W. (1992). *Hamlet: Prince of Denmark* (4th ed.). New York, NY: Harper Collins.

Sleeter, C. E. (2001). Preparing teachers for culturally diverse schools: Research and the overwhelming presence of whiteness. *Journal of Teacher Education, 52*(2), 94–106.

Solomon, R. P., Manoukian, R. K., & Clarke, J. (2007). Pre-service teachers as border crossers: Linking urban schools and communities through service learning. In R. P. Solomon & D. N. R. Sekayi (Eds.), *Urban teacher education and teach-*

ing: Innovative practices for diversity and social justice (pp. 67–87). Mahwah, NY: Erlbaum/Routledge.

Stedall, J. (Producer), & Stedall, J. (Director), (2012). *The challenge of Rodolf Steiner* [Motion Picture]. Cupola Productions.

Steiner, R. (1948). *Spiritual science and medicine.* London, UK: R. Steiner.

Steiner, R. (1950). *Goethe the scientist.* New York, NY: Anthroposophic.

Strickland, B. (2007). *Make the impossible possible: One man's crusade to inspire others to dream bigger and achieve the extraordinary.* New York, NY: Random House.

Strickland, B. (2011). *Make the impossible possible.* Paper presented at the Examining Educational Disparity And Minority Youth, Quinnipiac University, Hamden, CT.

Thoreau, H. D. (1992). *Walden and other writings.* New York, NY: Barnes & Noble. (Original work published 1854)

Whitehorse, D. (1996). New directions in teacher thinking: Linking theory to practice. In F. A. Rios (Ed.), *Teacher thinking in social contexts* (pp. 325–341). Albany: State University of New York Press.

Williams, W. C. (1962). *The doctor stories.* New York, NY: New Directions.

Wolf, F. A. (1999). The quantum physical communication between the self and the soul. *Noetic Journal, 2*(2), 149–158.

CHAPTER 7

THE SEED OF FREEDOM

Seed of Freedom Painting
(Clark, 2009b)

Freedom creates change
Change takes courage and skill
Courage is faith in action
Action requires inquiry, meaning and forgiveness
Forgiveness is a force of love
Love and truth unite
Freedom is peace and harmony of possibility.
Oh smallest seed, oh greatest of possibilities,
break down the fears of teaching
and open my mind
so that I might seethe soul force of my imagination.
—Barbara Clark (1998/2013)

Caged birds accept each other but flight is what they long for.
—Tennessee Williams (1966)

Hearts and Minds Without Fear: Unmasking the Sacred in Teacher Preparation,
pages 175–196.
Copyright © 2014 by Information Age Publishing
All rights of reproduction in any form reserved.

To begin our conversation on freedom, a short story by Lao Tzu is necessary: "Lao Tzu asked one of his disciples, 'Who are all those people you have brought with you?' The disciple whirled around to look. Nobody there. Panic! Lao Tzu said, 'Don't you understand?'" (Merton, 1965, p. 129).

Lao Tzu is teaching his disciple that he is not alone when presenting himself. The disciple is in panic because he cannot see anyone around him. The "short-sighted" or "no-sighted" disciple is ignorant that as we evolve and walk through this life, many who walked before us are now walking beside us and are carried in our hearts and minds at all times. The disciple does not understand that he is connected to millions of people and all matter that has gone before him. He is connected to people now and he is responsible to many others in the bigger picture. He doesn't see that he is not just responsible to himself.

Over the past several decades, our own societal increase in *narcissism* is quite evident, especially in the gap between the rich and the poor, and is made manifest among our schools in wealthy areas and schools in poor areas. A mindset thrives that the poor are "less than." It is the absolute epitome of narcissism: The poor will function in our assembly lines and fast food industry, but the rich deserve better because they are rich. Like the disciple, we too easily forget that we are not alone. It is a mindset that besets the stage where poor children must be taught through test-scripted curriculum in a Dickensian classroom and where wealthy children require rich, experiential environments in order to thrive and grow.

The American view that "rich is good" and "poor is bad" has indeed led us to reduce the freedoms in education that children and teachers have working in poor school districts. As Kozal (1991) first pointed out through his classic research, *Savage Inequalities: Children in American Schools*, this lack of freedom for children to thrive within equitable classroom and school environments is America's greatest failing. In one local example of the school community inequity surrounding our campus, teacher candidates who work in schools northeast of the campus will be in classrooms of 16 to 22 children, but if they stay in the local school system, they will work in classrooms of 28 to 32 children.

This chapter further investigates how the reciprocal relationships and integration of the previous harmonic seeds of aesthetic education ultimately reveal our deepest potential toward the freedom to possiblize new ideas. Freedom, in this respect, is the space to perceive and envision possibility while looking both inwardly and outwardly to others. In education, it is a rare occurrence to hear teachers speak of freedom as a natural goal in the transformation of their classroom environment for children. Rather, discourse pervades of "how do we manage children to do what we want them to do?" Applied practice instances of self-direction and choice for children are increasingly rare commodities in public education today.

Our book has presented concepts as seed paradigms that guide children toward the freedom to discover their vast depths of potential that we all hold as humans. But it is even more critical to cultivate awareness of future teacher candidates to recognize the ocean of potential within the children that they teach, guide, and mentor. For instance, as teacher candidates cultivate and recognize the importance of the *Seed of Play* (see Chapter 1), the *Seed of Freedom* is connected, for one must be *free* to *play*: "A teacher in search of his/her own freedom may be the only kind of teacher who can arouse young persons to go in search of their own" (Greene, 1988, p. 14).

If love is important, then teachers must be *free* to *love* their children. As humans, we know the complexity of our nature; what makes us happy and satisfied, fulfilled and inspired, curious and playful, and saddened and loved. We must be free to express ourselves to think together, create together, and explore together. But we must also be free to turn inward and retreat to contemplate and reflect in silence.

Our Bill of Rights in the United States guarantees freedoms that if lost would drastically change our country. Yet in our schools, we have already built our cells: Over the past 15 years consecutively, teachers have lost their freedom to teach and implement the arts and aesthetic experiences that make curriculum authentic in their classrooms. The public education system is a top-down management that restricts a professional's choice of implementation of methods and practices for the ways children learn best. As previously presented in this book, we have eyewitnessed in schools at-large the painful and frustrating losses of freedom for children in America's classrooms.

The lack of freedom for teachers to express what they know is best for children has ultimately contributed to children's plummeting test scores, their frustration resulting in anger and sometimes violent behavior, and an increase in bullying and dropouts. To address the well-being of children, *Compassionate Schools: The Heart of Learning and Teaching* (2009) is an online handbook filled with strategies to guide teachers in how to work with children experiencing trauma in their lives (Walpow, Johnson, Hertel, & Kinkaid, 2009). Elias (2013) explains the dire statistics of those children placed in the pipeline (see below) when a child's well-being is sacrificed rather than implementing educational strategies that are compassionate and kind.

Ultimately, less freedom of choice means less learning, especially for children facing trauma. Sadly, we adults will not admit that the well-being of our children has been compromised in our schools and perhaps even worse, our children are at risk of a failing future, as already evidenced by the increasing amount of children in the pipeline (see *School to Prison Pipeline*)[1].

---

[1] See http://www.tolerance.org/magazine/number-43-spring-2013/school-to-prison

Students from two groups—racial minorities and children with disabilities—are disproportionately represented in the school-to-prison pipeline. African-American students, for instance, are 3.5 times more likely than their white classmates to be suspended or expelled, according to a nationwide study by the U.S. Department of Education Office for Civil Rights. Black children constitute 18 percent of students, but they account for 46 percent of those suspended more than once.

For students with disabilities, the numbers are equally troubling. One report found that while 8.6 percent of public school children have been identified as having disabilities that affect their ability to learn, these students make up 32 percent of youth in juvenile detention centers.

The racial disparities are even starker for students with disabilities. About 1 in 4 black children with disabilities were suspended at least once, versus 1 in 11 white students, according to an analysis of the government report by Daniel J. Losen, director of the Center for Civil Rights Remedies of the Civil Rights Project at UCLA. (Elias, 2013, pp. 39–40)

Many children who face marginalization or have been unjustly labeled at-risk by the school's system, need mindful guidance from teachers and administrators in order to trust that it is safe to share their inner voice and personal experiences (MacDonald & Shirley, 2009). Children who have suffered from trauma or rejection will not immediately trust. To make an analogy of the bridge children must cross in order to begin to trust another adult, we present Victor Frankel's description of his feelings (emotional imagination) when finally freed from a concentration camp. Frankel (1984) states,

We wanted to see the camp's surroundings for the first time with the eyes of free men. "Freedom"—we repeated to ourselves, and yet we could not grasp it. We had said this word so often during all the years we dreamed about it, that it had lost its meaning. Its reality did not penetrate into our consciousness; we could not grasp the fact that freedom was ours.

We came to meadows full of flowers. We saw and realized that they were there, but we had no feelings about them. The first spark of joy came when we saw a rooster with a tail of multicolored feathers. But it remained only a spark; we did not yet belong to this world. (p. 109)

In 1939, escaping Hitler's invasion of Vienna, Anna Freud arrived in London. She worked at the the Hampstead War Nursery with children (young war victims) who had survived the concentration camps and were sent to England (Coles, 1992, pp. 22–23). For many months she observed the children as silent and withdrawn. Freud explains her work with the young victims of war:

They did not need pity from us, or want pity from us. They did not need us crying for their awful experiences. They needed us to take the measure of their lives, so far, and then to try to earn from them some trust—and that was a big, big thing to earn from them. When I sat down to write about those children, I felt waves of sadness come over me; but I also realized how tough they were—and I don't mean "callous" or "hard-hearted." All children—all grown people!—can be "tough" at certain moments, with certain people. Those children were not sweet and kindly—victims we could regard as angels! They had developed certain strengths, and they also had significant "deficits" in their "personalities.". . . They had learned to survive against the worst odds in the world, and now they had to learn to survive with us—and so we had to stop and think not only what was "wrong" with them, but what we thought was the "right" way to behave with them . . . . They themselves didn't know [whom] to cry for—they had lost their parents at such an early age. . . They were united with one another against the future—the dangers they feared (to be) around the corner. (Freud, as cited in Coles, 1992, p. 22)

Before the war, Freud worked in the Children's Hort School with Viennese teachers and children of working parents (1927), a type of kindergarten after-school program (Coles, 1992). Freud (1967) was very concerned with the growing neglect of children (p. 15). The Children's Hort School provided freedom for the children from school and society, but also safety, mentorship, and guidance from isolation and loneliness while parents were at work. Coles had extensive conversations with Anna Freud, who was a pioneer for teachers (especially American teachers) to understand children. Coles explained Freud's position, stating,

A child may fall toward a teacher right off: an earned, seemingly gratuitous emotional disposition that can be a powerful determinant in a child's educational life . . . [Freud explained] children often "bring with them a preconceived attitude of mind, and may approach the teacher with the suspicion, defiance, or feeling of having to be on guard which they have acquired through their personal experience of other adults. (p. 37)

Freud shared with Coles, "That the best teachers, actually, persuade their children to take the initiative in 'leading out' themselves" (as cited in Coles, 1992, p. 32). At first our teacher candidates may not grasp the concept of freedom of expression that the aesthetic encounter provides for children. Both preservice and in-service teachers must understand that when working with children to be expressive and creative it may take a variety of experiences, as trust grows in the relationship, to "spark" their ideas. The more the child feels they can trust their mentor, the more they will slowly release their voice (Clark, 2005a). For this very reason, the arts and aesthetics as we have explained throughout this book provide multiple interpretations, a landscape of ideas and is highlighted as potential theme venues as a stepping-off point for children. The arts immediately make connections to the child's life in very deep and personal ways.

One specific example of teaching preservice teachers the concept of the "*masks* children and teachers wear to hide trauma" was titled *Aesthetic Education and Masked Emotions: A Model for Emancipation Teacher Preparation* (Clark, 2009a). This model was designed with the New Britain Museum of American Art in New Britain, Connecticut. The museum became the environment for our studio paradigm. Below, Clark (2009b) describes the museum model and underlying psychology for teacher candidates' development of values, beliefs, and sense of self.

Masked Emotions Revealed

As preservice teachers viewed the 9/11 mural (Figure 7.1), visual data was collected and recorded based on their personal histories, beliefs, emotions, and perceptions in relationship to the 9/11 mural images and Erikson's (1963) psychosocial theory of development. The aesthetic experience activated the preservice teachers' imaginations in an authentic fashion, thereby connecting Erikson's theory to the current events and challenges faced in the educational arena. Preservice teachers' discussions and reflections portrayed how trauma impacts the development of a child. One preservice teacher stated, "I recognize the fact that I will be in a position to influence (I hope it will be a positive influence) students during times of emotional stress" (focus group notes, September 18, 2007). When confronted with the mural's symbolic imagery and in conjunction with children's development as related to cultural memories and life experiences, another preservice teacher revealed,

FIGURE 7.1.   *The Cycle of Terror and Tragedy* by Graydon Parrish (2001–2006). Oil on canvas, 214′ x 78′, New Britain Museum of American Art, Permanent Collection (http://www.nbmaa.org).

This has affected me in a way that I didn't think it would. When 9/11 first happened, I was a sophomore in high school and didn't know anyone that lived or worked in New York, so I didn't really feel as though I was directly affected. I never really talked about it with my family or friends because they really didn't seem to be affected by it either. All I remember is my dad talking about how he disliked foreigners. Then when looking at the painting that expressed so much emotion of those who were directly affected that opened my eyes to all of the others out there. It was then that I started to think about the effect that it had on not only the people directly related but also the children and the questions they would have about it. (focus group notes, September 18, 2007)

The children blindfolded in the mural painting, *The Cycle of Terror and Tragedy*, appear innocently juxtaposed within the adults' vision of horror, devastation, and destruction, impacted one preservice teacher's moral imagination. She wrote,

> A world that moves . . .
> From law and structure to flower of mourning.
> From innocent children to broken adults.
> From a world of blind children to adults who can SEE.
> (as cited in Clark, 2009a, p. 46)

The museum environment provided an aesthetic landscape to freely explore the mural and share with others thoughts, feelings, reactions, personal voices, and experiences. This model provided for many preservice teachers a firsthand experience with freedom of expression as related to the traumas children face in their lives. The teacher candidates were deeply touched and impressed with the societal pressures and events that are a real and significant aspect of a school community. They knew that they must be prepared to face trauma with children in their classrooms and in local and global communities. The freedom to examine tragedy of the magnitude of 9/11 in our country through an aesthetic entry point led to a deeper understanding of freedom of voice for teachers and for children in expressing their emotions (Clark, 2009a). Greene (1988) explains how freedom to create within a community comes into being:

> Freedom shows itself or comes into being when individuals come together in a particular way, when they are authentically present to one another (without masks, pretenses, badges of office), when they have a project they can mutually pursue. When people lack attachments, when there is no possibility of coming together in a plurality or a community, when they have not tapped their imaginations, they may think of breaking free, but they will be unlikely to think of breaking through the structures of their world and creating something new. (pp. 17–18)

We propose a new paradigm for preparing teachers and saving our children. One that is based on the freedom to experience, to love, to examine one's beliefs, to play, to change, to create, and to be mindful. In our Western culture, this concept is indeed hard to grasp as we live mentally in a *uni*verse rather than a *multi*verse of possibility.

In a multiverse, all things and ideas are possible. Thus, to attain and create freedom in learning and teaching, teacher candidates need to first have the freedom to *perceive* possibility. The vast interconnectedness of the universe must be realized in order to be open to creating change. Harkening to the quantum discussion in chapter 6, "The Seed of Inner Awareness," David Bolm (1980), professor of theoretical physics, describes the implications of our physical reality and interconnectedness:

> As sometimes particles, sometimes waves, sometimes mass, sometimes energy, all interconnected and constantly in motion. Once we see this fundamentally open quality of the universe, it immediately opens us to the potential for change; we see that the future is not fixed, and we shift from resignation to a sense of possibility. We are creating the future every moment. (as cited in Jaworksi, 1998, p. 183)

In order to be truly free, we must be able to see what *is*, to see the truth as a guide to living. Zajonc (2006), a research scientist in quantum physics, believed that seeing was the first step toward the development of consciousness. Zajonc stated,

> As contemplative educators, I believe that we are all engaged in an important project, one with a long tradition. The project of ancient philosophy was to live a right life, to embody virtue not only legislate it, to engender creativity and the capacities for insight, not only memorize formulae. (p. 13)

Our preservice teachers, in order to understand freedom and possibility, need to expand their consciousness and knowingly believe that they are creating the future in every moment they are working with children. To be free, we must perceive ourselves first in the eyes of others and our place in our community. Freedom to perceive possibility for children is sacred work that impacts their hearts, minds, and souls. Educators must *see* that at this critical level our work with children is the future.

Szabo (2005) presents collected poems by Thomas Merton from 1967. Merton was a significant spiritual leader and teacher in America, internationally renowned and revered for his writings for peace during the Vietnam War of the 1960s. Szabo explains Merton's poetic and divine inspiration for his poem titled, *In Silence*:

> Merton experienced mystic's profound understanding that silence is language of its own with as much influence and power as works (his study and

practice of Zen was of great importance to this revelation). His poetics "danc-es in the water of life," in which sound and silence create their own music and art . . . He embraces his search, he courageously and prophetically spoke out against all threats to peace and safety for his American compatriots, while at the same time he persistently sought unity with all humanity. (p. xxxi)

In Silence
Be Still
Listen to the stones of the wall
Be silent, they try
To speak your
Name.
To the living walls.
Who are you?
Who
Are you? Whose
Silence are you?
(Merton, 1957, p. 90)

Thomas Merton presents a metaphysical question in his poem. The question is, "Whose silence are you?" Do preservice teachers know whom they are teaching and do they know who they are? Do preservice teachers know that they must know who they are, and do they know their children? The silence, created due to not knowing the freedom they hold to get to know their children, is deafening and alarming. Not knowing the potential that your children hold within is so wasteful and may in fact prohibit the child from ever knowing themselves. Merton (1955) states,

> Our choices must be really free—that is to say they must perfect us in our own being. We must make the choices that enable us to fulfill the deepest capacities of our *real* selves. From this flows the second difficulty: We too easily assume that *we are* our real selves, and that our choices are really the ones we want to make when . . . Our choices are too often dictated by our false selves. (p. 25)

Preservice teachers need to understand that only through the freedom of possibility will they have the courage to develop their children's potential and sense of "real self." Throughout our methods courses, in order to understand the power of potential that freedom unleashes, our preservice teachers must recognize who they are and what they believe in. We attempt to stop their fall into the "bucket of crabs," certification mandates, increasingly inhibiting teacher education curricula, whereby no freedom is possible (Highwater, 1982; Highwater, Perlmutter, & Lenzer, 1996). Preservice teachers must be given the freedom to develop their sense of self and beliefs (see Chapter 5, "The Seed of Unmasking").

How do we have a sense of the wings needed to fly the freedom path? A child's mind must be viewed as a multiverse of possibility. Teachers may need the courage of an aviator like Lindbergh for example, to pursue freedom so that children's hearts and minds can soar to new heights, leaving the ground of mediocrity and worksheets. Berg (1998), in his biography on Charles Lindbergh, captures the miraculous power of Lindbergh's transatlantic flight. We are all presented at some point in our lives, choices and opportunities to ascend mountains that might appear unachievable, but with courage beside us (that others have inspired) and the sense of freedom of spirit and adventure planted within us, we, like Lindbergh, can do what we once thought we could not do. Berg writes,

> Is he alone at whose right side rides Courage, with skill within the cockpit and Faith upon the left? Does Solitude surround the brave when adventure leads the way and ambition reads the dials? Is there no company with him for who the air is cleft by Daring and the darkness is made light by Emprise?

> True, the fragile bodies of his fellows do not weigh down his plane, true, the fretful minds of weaker men are lacking from his crowded cabin; but his airship keeps the course he holds communion with those rarer spirits that inspire to intrepidity and by sustaining potency give strength to arm, resource to mind, content to soul. (p. 249)

Can teacher candidates keep the course and endure the status quo they face in field experiences? Aesthetic education methods are utilized within an arts-based workshop to motivate the preservice teachers to aspire toward freedom against the paradigm of mediocrity and status quo. Like Lindbergh, our preservice teachers are guided to soar to great heights and dare to course the uncharted territory of possibility, imagination, and innovation.

Freedom Possibilizing Compassion

In our methods courses, each class begins with a mustard seed, one singular tiny seed, to represent the infinite possibilities a preservice teacher holds within. Greene (1988) states that freedom in the classroom provides the "room for human action and interaction" (p. 120). Preservice teachers are asked to question, to explore truth, to examine the world on many levels, to be knowledgeable of cultures, and articulate actively in discussion about critical concepts, changes, discoveries, and to be willing to take risks. Greene (1993) explains the critical nature of the aesthetic that opens our eyes to see in new ways:

> I believe they can open new perspectives on what is assumed to be "reality," that they can defamiliarize what has become so familiar it has stopped us from asking questions or protesting or taking action to repair. Consider the

advancing invisibility of the homeless or how accustomed we have become to burnt-out buildings or to the contrasts between a holiday-decked Fifth Avenue and a desolate "uptown." It may be that some of Beckett's work (Waiting for Godot, perhaps, or Endgame) might defamiliarize our visions of the lost, the disinherited. It may be that time spent with Edward Hopper's rendering of lonely city streets, of luncheonettes on Sunday mornings, might move us into seeing once again. (p. 214)

Preservice teachers expressed a sense of freedom that comes as a result of participating in the aesthetic methods, creative learning, and possibility within the KIVA (see Chapter 4, "The Seed of Change"). Each class meeting was designed as a creative arts studio so that preservice teachers could explore aesthetic teaching methods and address innovative social/ecojustice themes in the world community. The preservice teachers revealed that the overwhelming sense of freedom they felt and the personal control of learning they experienced unlocked new voices and new products of the aesthetic imagination to perceive learning and teaching beliefs through sounds, movement, masks, and poetry. As Botstein (1998) remarks,

> What the products of the aesthetic imagination do is create realities in our social experience about which we ultimately have to talk. And they create, in a way, diversionary experiences that open up the range of how we talk to one another. What the arts do is create something that does not already exist, that is not predictable or entirely rational, which forces us to talk to ourselves and to other people in new ways. So in a classroom full of racial, gender, class, ideological, and economic strife, hostility, suspicion, and everything else, the arts create something that forces some conversation that cannot be totally reduced into preexisting labels and categories of expected discourse. It's irrelevant whether the art under discussion is good or bad in some kind of museum sense. Its existence demands response in a way that circumvents the habitual, destructive ways in which we now converse. (p. 67)

Botstein presents the arts as the universal medium used to break through cultural divides and social norms, for teacher candidates to share, discuss, and experiment with social and ecological issues, as illustrated within our KIVA paradigm, where aesthetic methodology is utilized through mixed methods.

For instance, after viewing the documentary titled *The Cove*, teacher candidates were collectively outraged by the dolphin hunting and slaughter for profit in Taiji, Japan. Teacher candidates created a marine aquarium simulation of trained dolphins, demonstrating the significant trauma that dolphins encounter in captivity. This performance captures the freedom of the teacher candidates to confidently become dolphins, to portray a symbolic message for children in an authentic way that critically questions this ecological justice issue. Teacher candidates decided as a result of this program to stop paying for entertainment that supported the cruel abuse against dolphins. Teacher candidates revealed that they became teachers of change and that curriculum must be authentic and problem-based.

Emily Dickinson unites the heart and mind within the creative act to capture an immediate emotional and intuitive portrait of her experiential feelings. Dickinson's (1960) poetic voice envelops us with a feeling that portrays the cautious steps teacher candidates take as they venture out of the box and experience aesthetic methods that will be utilized to inspire children (p. 875).

> I stepped from plank to plank
> So slow and cautiously;
> The stars about my head I felt,
> About my feet the sea.
> I knew not but the next
> Would be my final inch—
> This gave me that precarious gait
> Some call experience.

With the sense of freedom to create and take action, the preservice teachers perceived their beliefs and realities becoming collectively "unmasked," and in turn realized the vast potential for children to free their voices and ideas. Where stereotypes, prejudices, false judgments, and accusations once existed, the freedom of unmasking ideas opened space in a learning community and opened new vibrant possibilities for social and ecological community action. The *Seed of Freedom* concept map (Figure 7.2) below illustrates the reciprocal relationship between aesthetic methods within the KIVA and the resulting empowerment by children and teacher candidates after participating in the community experiences.

An art-based aesthetic methodology supports and opens a door for preservice teachers to be leaders and change-makers, to have a sense of freedom

UNMASKING
FREEDOM

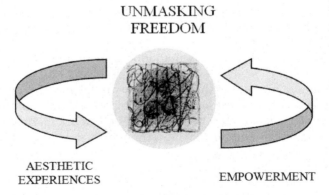

AESTHETIC
EXPERIENCES   EMPOWERMENT

FIGURE 7.2.   Unmasking Freedom Concept Map.

and control in designing aesthetic curriculum and community programs that will impact children. They see that creative and innovative action can change children's lives. While meditating on the painting (Clark, 2009b) of the seed of *Freedom,* reflect on the vertical lines in front of shadowed faces much like the two friends below (Figure 7.3). If we are to be truly free, we must step outside of ourselves and seize the experience with open minds and open hearts.

The children (Figure 7.3) were at first reluctant to write when they first met the preservice teachers. Their fear of not knowing the teacher candidates prevented them from feeling free in order to release their voice. A variety of aesthetic educational strategies presented within a creative studio format for preservice teachers was based on multiple methods that included reflective dispositions (Perkins, 1994), visual thinking (Arnheim, 1996), aesthetic education (Gardner, 1993; Greene, 2001), mixed-media thinking activities (Clark, 2009a; Eisner, 2002) and community mentorship (Bowers, 2006; French, 2013). With teachers, community members, artists, and educators as guides and mentors, teacher candidates and children side by side, freely explored aesthetic methods in a studio classroom so that an infinite variety of answers to one problem could take shape symbolically and expressively.

When teacher candidates have the freedom to work with children in this manner, described here using masks, poetry, and movement, there is an increased emergence of their beliefs when they see children change. The following rap was created by children and teacher candidates and performed on stage in the *Echoes* project.

My Class
Everyone is different.
No two the same.
Gotta keep the peace.

FIGURE 7.3. Two Friends Preparing For the *Echoes* Community Performance: *Freedom Revealed,* 2011.

Make the world sane.
Just because they're different.
Don't make them less.
This is our rap.
We're ready to confess.

Children in the *Echoes* project expressed their personal voice after completing their masks. A sense of freedom was depicted in the trusting community created whereby children released their ideas and took risks. The following quotes are by 10-year-old children in a local urban school.[2]

STUDENTS' RESPONSE TO "MAKING THE MASK" AFTER THE ECHOES PROJECT

when I put [on] my mask I felt extraordinary because I'm proud of my mask and I am proud of the way I formed it.

My mask makes me feel extraordinary and every time I put it on I'm proud of myself. I am proud of my mask and I'm proud of what I do.

I feel happy when I wear my mask. Sometimes I am mad but my mask is happy. I get mad because I have to go to school.

Sometimes I feel like I'm embarrassed about some things I do. If I could wish for something I would wish for not to be embarrassed about anything.

If I could wish for something it would be making no mistakes.

If I could change one thing in my life it would be to have a better life.

In these examples listed above, the children were learning through modeling by teacher candidates, freedom of choice, options, and alternatives, and through pathways to confront and soothe anger and frustration. This method provided an aesthetic portrayal of freedom from anger for the child labeled a "bully" by the school. Children were transformed after the community performance. Through the aesthetic experience within the community setting, they had an opportunity to perceive themselves and others in new ways. The concept, compassion, modeled authentically in the skit, was a pathway to freedom for the child and an escape from the anger he carried each day to school. Greene (1993) agrees with Dewey (1934) that the arts "overcome the anesthetic in experiences" and "help us break with the mechanical and routine" (p. 214).

---

[2] To view Echoes Project video, visit www.compassionateteaching.com and click on *Our Book* tab on home page, then click on *Unmasking* tab.

Steppin' Out: Freedom Found in Aesthetic Methods

Stepping Out of a Painting: Releasing a Child's Voice was a project partnership between Teacher Education, Art Education Departments, and a local urban middle school, primarily of African American and West Indies immigrant children. The project was designed to target 6th-grade children's visual literacy and language arts skills. Many of the 6th-grade children were reluctant writers yet were extremely expressive and talented in the arts. The teacher candidates were White, stepping into a primarily Black school. This school was specifically chosen so that our teacher candidates would understand how segregated our schools have become since the 1996 *Sheff v. O'Neil* Connecticut Supreme Court desegregation case.[3]

The *Steppin' Out* project provided teacher candidates the opportunity to learn how to become aesthetically and culturally responsive to children's backgrounds and identities other than their own. In collaboration, children and teacher candidates freely expanded and illuminated purposes and possibilities of education for teacher identity, underlining the importance of nurturing and reinforcing community interconnection with local and international artists (Clark & French, 2012; French, 2011). Teacher candidates began to understand how aesthetic methods honored, celebrated, and dignified individual children's voices and their cultures. Released to a greater vision of community strength through the aesthetic, *school* became a shared social imagination experience (Greene, 1993).

Children teamed with teacher candidates to create symbolic aesthetic messages inspired by murals and works of art by African American artists. The arts-based workshop activities were designed in order to introduce aesthetic methods uniting curriculum from both visual and language literacies. The methods utilized ensured the freedom for each individual child to learn and express unique ideas and perceptions from their daily lives in relation to the artwork presented. This project encompassed cutting-edge aesthetic methodology that celebrated children's imagination and creativity, and provided authentic methods through the arts for children to visualize their feelings, express their voice, increase self-esteem and resiliency, and share their work with the community.

One child named Latoya was inspired after looking at a variety of artwork and wrote the following poem entitled *Individuality*:

Individuality
People and kids,
We are all
flowers of the same tree.
Music to dancing,

---

[3] http://www.courant.com/news/education/hc-sheff-oneill-timeline-flash,0,105112.flash.

Colors to Abstract,
Nature to rainbow,
Sky to sun,
Day to night,
Individuality!

Latoya saw firsthand how her friends worked together on a mural uniting all shapes, textures, and images into a larger idea. She understood that the mural represented their individuality and celebrated their cultures. Another child, Deseree, expressed a sense of freedom of voice as she reflected on her life and how creativity and art played a part of it. Deseree composed the following poem, *No Light No Sun*:

No Light No Sun
No light no sun
Keeps our creativity in a box,
Does not like us to be who we are.
Life is not perfect,
Be who you are.
You can't enjoy life without a lil' bit of creativity,
To be able to open the box you have to believe-
add magic to it.
Don't be afraid of taking chances,
Rules make you play safe,
Think outside the box,
Be creative,
Let your feet off the ground
and fly
on your own for once.
Don't have no regrets into what you believe.
Don't just sit there and do nothin'
Go explore the world,
Don't let the world force you to smile

Even though Deseree is in sixth grade, we can see by her poem that she has already experienced what it feels like to not be free to express one's self and how important it is to be true to who you are and to take risks. As she states, "Don't just sit there and do nothin' . . . Go and explore the world." She ends her poem with a powerful reminder that no one can force you to be what you are not. This reminds us of how many children choose not to learn when they feel their culture, family, and self is oppressed in school (Kohl, 1994).

Images from Romare Bearden's (1967) painting, titled *Summertime*, were used for motivational and visual data for children to explore African American art.

FIGURE 7.4. *Summertime* by Romare Bearden, 1967 (http://images.easyart.com/i/prints/lg/2/5/25043.jpg).

While viewing the Bearden's painting, *Summertime* (Figure 7.4), 6th-grade children explored relationships between characters and their daily lives (Clark, 2005b). Children were especially focused on the character in the painting dressed in black, sitting on the chair, and placed by Bearden on the sidewalk in front of a building. Poetry by Langston Hughes (1994) was integrated and juxtaposed with the painting. Children explored poetic voices for inspiration.

My Soul
Empty as the silence,
Empty with a vague,
Aching emptiness
Desiring,
Needing someone
Something . . .

The children and the teacher candidates examined together several examples of African American painters and poets like the poem above by Hughes (as cited in Rampersad, 2002, p. 104). Reflective intelligence and the disposition to think broadly, deeply, and adventurously are active when looking and thinking about art (Perkins, 1994). Children related to the various characters and images depicted in the paintings and poetry. The cognitive scaffolding and reflective thinking process revealed ideas that were recorded in journals and shaped by the children into poems, stories, and mural paintings with mentorship from their teacher candidates.

Aesthetic education pedagogy provides a continuum of possibilities to practice metacognition, realities for children to make real-world connections to what they know and what they will learn, by expressing their thinking in both visual and written forms. The following rap poem was composed by a group of 6th-grade girls. They shared their writing and then synthesized the shared ideas. Here they express the adolescent desires, dreams, and frustrations they face in middle school and leave the reader with a message stating, "But you don't want to get us mad—cuz deep inside we can get really bad."

Girl Rap

We may be pretty girls
But we aren't wearing pearls
Supposed to be in the kitchen cooking dinner
All star on the field, court, ring we are winners
Not supposed to be out makin' bacon
But we're out and it's the real money that we're making
Maybe you're not familiar with a girl like me
I'm independent ain't no Barbie
I don't need the pink car I don't need the Ken
I'm going somewhere that you ain't never been
Keep dreamin' if you think you can hold me back
We're rising to the top on the fast track
We might look girlie with our hair all curly
But when we go in the spot we hit the top
We go up and down with the beat and the sound
But when we hit the floor we bring it some more
We dance so cool you want our moves
We so fly we hit the sky
Yellow, orange, dark blue, red, all the colors
Of the rainbow instead
First people thought we were really sweet
But they are wrong; we are girls
Just because we're girls we like flowers
But look at us we got a lot of power
I'm beautiful without make up
So forget the cover-girl
And the poofy dress
Cause we ain't going to twirl
You may think we're just pretty girls
But you don't want to get us mad
'cuz deep inside we can get really bad

The 6th-grade girls want the reader to *see* them, to *hear* them shout, "*look at us we got a lot of power.*" Yes they do have power, however diminished by the public school system and mandates the teachers must follow. The following poem by Langston Hughes captures the concept of the "genius child," which causes us to wonder that perhaps some of our children may feel isolated, voiceless, and/or a nonlearner for myriad reasons. This poem represents the potential in all children. *Nobody Loves a Genius Child* revealed Langston Hughes' identity with race and childhood difficulties. As Palmer (1993) and Kozal (1991) would warn us, we are indeed waging a violent war in schools against a child's freedom. The following poem by Hughes (1930) captures the tragedy of potential lost in our public schools.

Nobody Loves a Genius Child

This is a song for the genius child.
Sing it softly, for the song is wild.
Sing it softly as ever you can—
Lest the song get out of hand.
Nobody loves a genius child.
Can you love an eagle,
Tame or wild?
Wild or tame,
Can you love a monster
Of frightening name?
Nobody loves a genius child.
Kill him—and let his soul run wild

Aesthetic education methodology within a creative community whereby children are given mentors and guides, may be the vehicle for children to realize the freedom to perceive themselves as learners, writers, artists, inventors, scientists, and compassionate friends to each other. This innovative aesthetic creative community project promoted freedom, the transformative power of releasing children's feelings and voices, especially children who may be below grade level for reading and writing. The arts impacted the imaginative realm wherein children had instant access to discriminate what they see, feel, and think about the characters in the works of art in relationship with their own lives (Clark, 2005a).

Our teacher candidates realized the meaning and importance of nurturing a community-centered interdependent and inspirational learning space for their future students (French, 2013). Reciprocally, the children became our teacher candidates' greatest teachers and revealed how much their public schooling in various suburban schools had actually limited their knowledge and understanding of other cultures and realities. They knew now that reports and bias toward this community and test scores were not a truthful depiction or portrait of the beauty the children embodied. They had clear eyes to understand how dangerous our segregated schools are and how much freedom of expression is lost due to ignorance and closed minds. They wondered why the children were reluctant writers who tested low in the writing strands when their work through this activity was so powerfully descriptive and insightful.

The next seed chapter of *Love* presents the absolute right of a child to feel dignified and loved by their teacher every day they go to school. This is their right. The absence of love causes great pain in a child, resulting in their withdrawal from learning and from participating in their own life.

REFERENCES

Arnheim, R. (1996). *The split and the structure*. Berkeley, CA: University of California Press.

Berg, S. (1998). *Lindbergh*. New York, NY: Berkley.

Botstein, L. (1998). What role for the arts? In W. Ayers & J. Miller (Eds.), *A light in the dark times: Maxine Greene and the unfinished conversation*. New York, NY: Teachers College Press.

Bowers, C. A. (2006). *Revitalizing the commons: Cultural and educational sites of resistance and affirmation*. New York, NY: Lexington.

Clark, B. (2005a). Moral imagination and art: Echoes from a child's soul. *Forum on Public Policy: Issue Child Psychology, 1*(4), 428–446.

Clark, B. (2005b). Moral imagination and art: Echoes from a child's soul (Doctoral dissertation). University of Hartford, Connecticut. Retrieved May 10, 2012, from Dissertations & Theses: Full Text. (Publication No. AAT 315 7797).

Clark, B. (2009a). Aesthetic education and masked emotions: A model for emancipatory teacher preparation. *Critical Questions in Education, 1*(1), 40–50. Retrieved from http://education.missouristate.edu/AcadEd/75534.htm

Clark, B. (2009b). Mustard seed: A personal search for "Ahimsa" (The truth of nonviolence). *Closing the Circle Exhibition*. B. Clark & M. Cipriano (Artists). New Britain, CT: New Britain Commission on the Arts.

Clark, B. (2013). *Forgiveness*. Original Poem.

Clark, B., & French, J. (2012). ZEAL: A revolution for education, unmasking teacher identity through aesthetic education, imagination and transformational practice. *Critical Questions in Education, 3*(1), 12–22.

Coles, R. (1992). *Anna Freud: The dream of psychoanalysis*. Reading, MA: Addison-Wesley.

Dewey, J. (1934). *Art as experience*. New York, NY: G.P. Putman's Sons.

Dickenson, E. (1960). *The complete poems of Emily Dickenson*. (T. H. Johnson, Ed.). Boston, MA: Little, Brown

Eisner, E. W. (2002). *The arts and the creation of mind*. New Haven, CT: Yale University Press.

Elias, M. (2013). The school to prison pipeline. *Teaching Tolerance Magazine, 43*, 39–40. Retrieved from http://www.tolerance.org/magazine/number-43-spring-2013/school-to-prison

Erikson, E. H. (1963). *Childhood and society*. New York, NY: Norton.

Frankel, V. (1984). *Man's search for meaning*. New York, NY: Pocket Books.

French, J. (2011). Revitalizing community based language arts curriculum practice through ecojustice education. *New England Reading Association (NERJA), 47*(1), 43–50.

French, J. (2013). Methods & mindsets for creating eco-social community educators. In D. G. Mulcahy (Ed.), *Transforming schools: Alternative perspectives on school reform* (pp. 37–66). Charlotte, NC: Information Age.

Freud, A. (1967). *Psychoanalysis for teachers and parents.* (B. Low, Trans.). New York, NY: Emerson. (Original work published 1935)

Gardner, H. (1993). *Creating minds: An anatomy of creativity seen through the lives of Freud, Einstein, Picasso, Stravinsky, Eliot, Graham, and Gandhi.* New York, NY: Basic.

Greene, M. (1988). *The dialectic of freedom.* New York, NY: Teachers College Press.

Greene, M. (1993). Diversity and inclusion: Toward a curriculum for human beings. *Teachers College Record, 95*(2), 213–221.

Greene, M. (2001). *Variations on a blue guitar: The Lincoln Center Institute lectures on aesthetic education.* New York, NY: Teachers College Press.

Highwater, J. (1982). *The primal mind: Vision and reality in Indian America.* New York, NY: Harper & Row.

Highwater, J. (Writer), Perlmutter, A. (Producer), & Lenzer, D. (Director). (1996). *Primal mind: Alternative perspectives on self, environment and the development of culture* [Documentary]. Primal Mind Foundation.

Hughes, L. (1994). *The collected poems of Langston Hughes* (A. Rampersad, Eds.). New York, NY: Random House. (Original work published 1902-1967)

Jaworksi, J. (1998). *Synchronicity: The inner path of leadership.* San Francisco, CA: Berrettt-Koehler.

Kohl, H. (1994). *"I won't learn from you" and other thoughts on creative maladjustment.* New York, NY: New Press.

Kozal, J. (1991). *Savage inequalities: Children in America's schools.* New York, NY: Harper Collins.

MacDonald, E., & Shirley, D. (2009). *The mindful teacher.* New York, NY; London, UK: Teacher College Press.

Merton, T. (1955). *No man is an island.* New York, NY: Harcourt Brace.

Merton, T. (1957). *The strange islands.* New York, NY: New Directions.

Merton, T. (1965). *The way of Chuang Tzu.* New York, NY: New Directions.

Palmer, P. (1993). *The violence of our knowledge: Toward a spirituality of higher education.* Paper presented at the Michael Keenan Memorial Lecture, the 7th Lecture, Berea College, KY. Retrieved from http://www.kairos2.com/palmer_1999.htm

Perkins, D. (1994). *The intelligent eye: Learning to think by looking at art.* Santa Monica, CA: Getty Center for Education in the Arts.

Rampersad, R. (2002). *The life of Langston Hughes: Vol 1: 1902–1941, I, too, sing America.* New York, NY: Oxford University Press.

Szabo, L. (2005). *The dark before dawn: New selected poems of Thomas Merton.* Toronto, Canada: Penguin.

Walpow, R., Johnson, M., Hertel, R., & Kinkaid, S. (2009). Compassionate schools: Compassion, resiliency, and academic success. Compassionate schools: The heart of learning and teaching. *State of Washington, Office of Superintendent of Public Instruction.* Retrieved May, 2013, from http://www.k12.wa.us/compassionateschools/heartoflearning.aspx

Williams, T. (2008). *Camino Real.* New York, NY: New Directions.

Zajonc, A. (2006). *Love and knowledge: Recovering the heart of learning through contemplation.* Retrieved from http://www.arthurzajonc.org/uploads/zajonc- love-and-knowledge.pdf

CHAPTER 8

THE SEED OF LOVE

Seed of Love Painting
(Clark, 2009b)

You can't cross the sea merely by standing and staring at the water . . . Love's gift cannot be given, it waits to be accepted.

—Rabindranath Tagore

Let us love what we love, let us be ourselves.

—Vincent van Gogh (1881)

All, everything that I understand, I understand only because I love.

—Leo Tolstoy

Hearts and Minds Without Fear: Unmasking the Sacred in Teacher Preparation,
pages 197–216.
Copyright © 2014 by Information Age Publishing
All rights of reproduction in any form reserved.

LOVE AND HIGHER EDUCATION:
PREPARING TEACHERS FOR THE 21ST CENTURY

A great tragedy in public education has been the moral neglect of loving the children we teach. The child, to a great degree in the latter part of the 20th century and beginning of the 21st century, has been viewed as an inconvenience. What is worse in many cases are children who have been terminated, rejected, thrown away, and abused. What type of society would treat their future in such a careless and violent manner? What factors led to the inner-armament against children (Dalai Lama, 2011, 2013)?

In the chapter of *Love*, the seeds of compassion unite within the KIVA celebrating human wholeness and creativity. Creativity and compassion unmask the divine within us as teachers of children wherein the learner is filled with a sense of love for the experiences shared and knowledge gained with one another. The teacher celebrates the independent voice of the child that is released into the KIVA and community, lifting up the souls of others in the shared experience and thus revealing the sacred. In this learning paradigm, all involved become richer from the love of one's experience in relation to one's deepest conscious motivations to feel loved, inspired, and connected to a greater good of all. Palmer (1993) presents the concept of "soul-making" in education, whereby "every epistemology becomes an ethic . . . the shaping of the lives of human beings."

An intuitive sense of love grows within the soul of the teacher and child as the *Seeds of Play, Hope, Voice, Change, Unmasking, Inner Awareness,* and *Freedom* unite, grow, and flourish within the heart and mind. Thus, the KIVA members sense a deep belonging and moral affinity toward one another as intrapersonal awareness unites with interpersonal understanding. Empathy and compassion are now made visible in the creative and sacred actions by all. This is the ultimate expression of love between teacher and learner, a shared bond and trust to learn; to continue to experience and question life and all the mysteries that living holds.

Maria Montessori (1901) declared the 20th century to be the *Century of the Child*. She wanted the world to focus on children, their needs, joys, imaginative dreams, and personalities (Standing, 1962). Children are misunderstood. Adults, mass media, and marketing provoke children into skipping over childhood to enter adulthood before it is developmentally appropriate.

Fried (2001) stressed the need for a passionate teacher who with practice knows how to engage the child's imagination, because such a teacher is "in love with a field of knowledge, deeply stirred by issues and ideas that challenge our world, drawn to the dilemmas and potentials of the young people who come into class each day—or captivated by all of these" (p. 1). Such a teacher is in love with the art of teaching, the art of learning, and inspires the art of creative thinking to impact the world. Yet competency indicators for evaluating beginning teachers in the field does not have love for teaching and for children as critical criteria. To love teaching and to love one's students is not a part of the Elementary Education certification preparation mandates and curricula covered. Zajonc (2006b) stated, "The curricula offered by our institutions of higher education have largely neglected this central, if profoundly difficult task of learning to love, which is also the task of learning to live in true peace and harmony with others and with nature" (p. 1). Palmer (1993) writes,

> We do violence in much more subtle ways. My operating definition of violence is that violence always involves violating the integrity of the other. We do violence whenever we violate the integrity or the nature of the other, whether the other is the earth, or another human being, or another culture. I want to suggest that in our institutions of higher education we are deeply devoted to a mode of knowing that often issues in violence, thus understood.

Are we doing violence toward children's hearts, minds, and souls in schools each day when teaching in a classroom void of love or any shred of compassion or caring? We found it imperative to present the concept of love for children and one another within our methods courses. Love is ever-present when struggling with the "perfect" lesson plan to celebrate curiosity, creative and divergent thinking whereby children experience myriad authentic pathways. Love for each child is critical so that teachers can plan activities that will inspire a child's hunger to learn, activities that are unique to their individual culture and style of learning, and that build upon their realities and wonderings of life. For without love for one's children that we see and teach each day, our endeavors become empty, meaningless, and machine-like, not human-like.

What is the meaning of our actions in education? Is teaching only work or is teaching an act of love? The following excerpt from *On Work* by Kahlil Gibran (1994) presents our teacher candidates with the question: *Can all children feel loved in your classroom and can you love both your work and your children?*

> When you work you are a flute
> through whose heart the whispering
> of the hours turns to music.
> Which of you would be a reed, dumb and silent,
> when all else sings together in unison?
> But I say to you that when you work
> you fulfill a part of earth's furthest dream,
> assigned to you when that dream was born,
> And in keeping yourself with labour you are in truth loving life,
> And to love life through labour is to be intimate with life's inmost secret.
>
> And what is it to work with love?
> It is to weave the cloth with threads drawn from your heart,
> even as if your beloved were to wear that cloth.

It is to build a house with affection,
even as if your beloved were to dwell in that house.
It is to sow seeds with tenderness and reap the harvest with joy,
even as if your beloved were to eat the fruit.
It is to charge all things you fashion with a breath of your own spirit,
And to know that all the blessed dead
are standing about you and watching.

Work is love made visible.
And if you cannot work with love but only with distaste, it is better that you
should leave your work and sit at the gate of the temple and take alms of those
who work with joy.

For if you bake bread with indifference, you bake a bitter bread that feeds
but half man's hunger.

And if you grudge the crushing of the grapes, your grudge distils a poison in
the wine.
And if you sing though as angels, and love not the singing, you muffle man's
ears to the voices of the day and the voices of the night.

We decided to go back to the initial question, asking ourselves, What is
education for? What do we want for our children when they graduate? Do
we hope our children will fully participate as citizens in a democratic society? For teachers, if they are educating children to thrive in a democratic
society, then they must design a learning community that is based on beliefs such as tolerance, patience, empathy, compassion, and love. With love
comes acceptance, celebration, and interest in diversity and celebration of
cultural identity.

We have found it critical to immerse our teacher candidates in a variety
of experiences in order to begin to understand children and their need to
feel love from their teachers. As described in previous chapters, we work
with our teacher candidates so that they will embrace the critical belief in
loving the children they teach. This is an ongoing process that uses aesthetic methods to reveal love in trusting relationships. However, our teacher
candidates at the university level can oftentimes confuse a loving compassionate professor as being "weak," and perhaps one that they do not feel is
preparing them for the "real" world of public education.

Zajonc (2006a) found it difficult to speak about knowledge and love in
the academic world of higher education. He stated, "I would like to add
another element, one that is extremely difficult to speak of within the academy, yet which I feel is central to its work, namely the relationship between
knowledge (which we excel at) and love (which we neglect)" (p. 1). The
curricula offered by our institutions of higher education have largely neglected this central, if profoundly difficult task. We have embraced the task

to unmask love in learning and the sacred in relationships; however, this is a very daunting experience as not all of our colleagues are not modeling this critical relationship as Zajonc describes for our teacher candidates. One teacher candidate alarmingly shared what a professor had suggested to her in another course to "not be creative or innovative at least in the first 3 or 4 years of teaching."

We know that the intensive sequencing system to achieve certification pushed many teacher candidates into a form of narcissistic thinking such as "how do I get this and that course done so I can student teach and graduate on time?" This attitude however may not really be the students' fault, but rather an outcome of our society's pressure to get ahead, placing the individual's interest ahead of the community's needs. For us, the absence of compassion, kindness, care, and love for others was rather alarming as students pushed forth to graduate. We could easily see that many teacher candidates were in fact in competition with one another and would consciously or unconsciously undermine each other's sense of achievement (Palmer, 1993; Zajonc, 2006a).

Zajonc (2006a) proposes an epistemology of love for higher education curricula, a greater vision of what knowing and living are really all about. He questioned why in the academy [and in teacher preparation] the concept of loving work, loving teaching, and loving one another is a seemingly foreign language. When is the concept of love presented as a topic of investigation and an overall goal integrated within teacher candidates' beliefs (p. 2)? It seems that as a human being and a teacher of young children, to love what one does and to love the children one teaches is an inherently natural phenomenon to develop. Zajonc (2006b) presented Rilke's poetic thoughts on the importance of emphasizing the concept of love in education:

> To take love seriously and to bear and to learn it like a task, this is what [young] people need. . . . For one human being to love another, that is perhaps the most difficult of all our tasks, the ultimate, the last test and proof, the work for which all other work is but a preparation. For this reason young people, who are beginners in everything, cannot yet know love, they have to learn it. With their whole being, with all their forces, gathered close about their lonely, timid, upward-beating heart, they must learn to love. (p. 1)

How do we teach teacher candidates to "learn to love" as Rilke (1975) presents? Is that a moral obligation of higher education in preparing teachers before they step into the classroom? Would not every parent feel satisfied, to a high degree, if they knew that their child was indeed loved by their teacher? The question before us as professors was how do we address the importance of love for others to our teacher candidates within our curriculum studies? Fromm (1989) believed that love must be practiced, and one must have faith in order to practice love. "Love is an act of faith, and whoever is of little faith is also of little love" (p. 115). We knew that our teacher candidates had to witness our faith in their potential, a belief that they could reach beyond what they perceived impossible.

As explained throughout the various seed chapters, we decided to enact curriculum that would create an environment to unmask the concept of love whereby students would learn to work with one another, and for others who have less and need more. How would this impact their teacher beliefs while engaged in an authentic apprenticeship modeled by professors; one that was focused on love and compassion at its core? How do we confront a love that is critical in our world when so many individuals and children are feeling unloved and unworthy? Our aesthetic projects were designed to promote love in action in order to investigate the impact on the teacher candidates' beliefs and philosophy of teaching.

Love in action is especially vibrant when teacher candidates explored compassionate action for homelessness and their sense of social responsibility for homeless children and families in our surrounding university community. The seed of love grows within the teacher candidates' beliefs through the dynamic and imaginative interplay of the other seven seeds (see KIVA map in Chapter 1, "The Seed of Play"). Each seed symbolizes the unmasking of the sacred imaginative realm within each one of us so that in turn we might envision a new landscape of learning. How do teachers enact their love for learning and model for children by contributing to the community? Our research revealed that over 400 children within the city of our university were designated homeless. How do we teach future teachers to have empathy and compassion for children who are struggling with issues such as homelessness, lack of healthy food, or suitable clothing for school?

One specific example of introducing homelessness to children utilized symbolic messages that were presented through the voices of familiar storybook characters (see also *Michelle's Story* in Chapter 1, "The Seed of Play"). Children were drawn to the imaginative characters and invited into a discussion of the endless possibilities of revealing love in action as modeled by the characters. Messages of love are embodied in the storybook characters selected by the teacher candidates to depict a new face of homelessness. Various skits were designed by teacher candidates as part of the final school community performance for 300 children, titled *Creating a Compassionate Community to End Homelessness*.

The teacher candidates stated that their message to the children in the school audience promoted the modeling of acts of love by creating a chain of compassion within a school community. In their performance, the teacher candidates represent a busy world, not noticing or stopping to help homeless people, running in mindless patterns. The teacher candidates represent this through a pattern of clapping until the whistle blows and time stops. A moment of time is then captured as if in a still life; the scene freezes in *A Silent Demonstration.*[1]

The skit starts with a busy cacophony on the street representing a moment in time that focuses our eyes on one individual homeless person. Suddenly, a whistle blows, signaling all of the people to lower to the ground and freeze. Slowly the world stops spinning and the audience is directed to reflect on the life of this homeless person as the world passes them by. As teacher candidates and children investigated the emotional impact on homeless children and families, they were surprised to find that an overwhelming amount of homeless individuals expressed their frustration that people ignored them and passed them by as if they didn't exist. This symbolic representation exhibits how these loving acts of kindness may ultimately impact the larger world community. Our research revealed,

Pre-service teachers realized ZEAL for children and teaching, challenging pre-service teachers to develop intra and interpersonal reflective dispositions, and a growing sense that they wanted to be urban teachers and leaders of change in education. . . As one pre-service teacher wrote: "*our ideas and imagination were the driving force of the class.*" Another pre-service teacher stated, "*I have learned so much about myself this semester, not only about teaching, but also about myself as a person. I learned that I could be a performer on a stage, or even in a classroom, with an audience full of my students. I've learned that I have the potential to become a great storyteller with puppets as my props. I've also learned that I am capable of much more than I thought, and with this knowledge I would like to make myself a promise: I promise to become a transformative teacher, to create a welcoming, caring, and compassionate community, where students feel empowered and safe, and strive to become life-long learners. I promise.*" (Clark & French, 2012, p. 15)

Preservice teachers' exposure to critical aesthetic educational pedagogy, enacted through community engagement, increased their citizenship opportunities to unite socially, empathically, cognitively, and spiritually for the greater good of their immediate and local community partners (French & Clark, 2012). Vincent van Gogh (1880) strove throughout his life as an artist to create a community of artists. During his struggle and need for love within a community, he expressed his thoughts on love in a letter to his brother:

One cannot always tell what it is that keeps us shut in, confines us, seems to bury us, but, however, one feels certain barriers, certain gates, certain walls. Is all this imaginative fantasy? I do not think so. And then one asks: "My God! Is it long, is it forever, is it for eternity?" Do you know what frees one from this captivity? It is every deep serious affection. Being friends, being brothers, love, that is what opens the prison by supreme power, by some magic force.

---

[1] To view Compassion: A Silent Demonstration video, visit www.compassionateteaching.com and click on Our Book tab on home page, then click on Love tab.

UNMASKING
LOVE

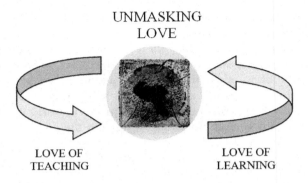

LOVE OF
TEACHING

LOVE OF
LEARNING

FIGURE 8.1. Unmasking Love Concept Map.

Like van Gogh, teacher candidates need a sense of community throughout their development to feel like they belong to a greater good as they
pursue understanding the art of teaching innocent hearts and minds. Our
teacher candidates participated in an aesthetic education partnership between the arts and community members that invited the inclusion and participation of diverse learners, including those with special needs. Teachers
who have a vision of their classes as compassionate communities are more
likely to promote social justice and build upon their students' strengths to
facilitate empathic cognition and an increased sense of love for others in
their thinking.

The seed of love concept map above (Figure 8.1) illustrates the reciprocal nature of teachers who love their work, love to teach, and the transformative power it has on the child who loves to learn. Meditate at the very
heart of the *Seed of Love* painting (Clark, 2009b) to reflect on ways in which
love is perceived and experienced in your life.

> Ultimately, the reason why love and compassion bring the greatest happiness
> is simply that our nature cherishes them above all else. The need for love lies
> at the very foundation of human existence. It results from the profound inter-
> dependence we all share with one another. (Dalai Lama, 2013)

Love and Efficacy: Development of Preservice Teachers' Sense of Self

The imaginative realm, when ignited by the aesthetic, naturally unites
art and morality (Dewey, 1980), whereby moral imagination is revealed
and we are lifted to a higher consciousness to perceive who we really are
and possibly begin to love one another. The arts activate our moral feeling, moral seeing, and moral thinking systems, so that our emotional and

moral imagination increases to think outside ourselves to build empathic understandings and concern for others (Clark, 2013, p. 91). As emotional and moral imagination is awakened within individuals and shared within a learning community, social imagination expands (see Conceptual Framework Spiral Maps 1 and 2 in Chapter 4, "The Seed of Change").

We walk toward the light, hand in hand, to what might be a better place for all. Seemingly, the universe and all consciousness has become one, a collective consciousness. Within a collective consciousness, there is an infinite amount of possibilities. The power of the aesthetic is a vehicle to pass on skills, archetypes, and patterns (done so well by primal minds) with one another. Through this, new realities that have otherwise been unseen lift us toward a sense of hope in one another. Our teacher candidates found themselves creating a space for love to see possibility within one another, which ultimately for some teacher candidates became the critical core of their beliefs on teaching and learning. One teacher candidate, Yesenia, stated, "I want to keep my transformation with me always!!! I am going to practice the seeds in my life as a teacher. I felt like my colleagues were my brothers and sisters—they are like my family . . . and I love them."

Demonstrating the love of her work with children and peers, Yesenia composed lyrics to the tune of a popular song to sing during the *Make a Wave* performance that addressed the dolphin slaughter for profit (see also Chapter 4, "The Seed of Change").

The following lyrics were sung to the song by Alicia Keyes (2009), titled *Unthinkable.*

The Cove Gives Me a Feeling
Moment of truth you'll see
Someone's gotta take a stand today
And that's you and me
Let's go save the dolphins at The Cove in Taiji
If you have some way to help
You should do it right now
(**ECHO:** You should do it right now)
BRIDGE:
The Cove gives me a feeling that I've never felt before
And I don't like it, we need to change this
It's becoming something that's impossible to ignore
Please save the dolphins
(**ECHO:** Please save the dolphins)
CHORUS:
So I ask that you would please
Just listen
To the cries of the dolphins saying please set us free
So I ask you are you ready
Now I ask you will you help me

VERSE 2:
Why put them in captivity
We should not support any of these type of facilities
Let's go green and spread the news to all who will join our cause
Release them from our possession
Let's just do it right now
(**ECHO:** Let's just do it right now)
BRIDGE:
The Cove gives me a feeling that I've never felt before
And I don't like it, we need to change this
It's becoming something that's impossible to ignore
Please save the dolphins
(ECHO: Please save the dolphins)

Yesenia worked tirelessly on her song, having the freedom and courage to teach her peers the song so that they could model and join in singing to motivate and inspire the 1,000 fifth-grade children attending the community performance. The children were all in unison singing the song as they knew the music of Alicia Keyes and could easily adapt the lyrics while focusing on the intent of the words. A 5th-grade child stated after the performance in a writing reflection,

> One thing I learned from the amazing performance. And it was that people kill 23,000 dolphins a year. I kind of was depressed when I saw that. The feelings that were evoked by watching is terrifying to me. Because it is horrible to see dolphins endangered in the zoo, in places to entertain, or anything. It is like cause and effect. The cause is people use dolphins for bad reasons. The effect is they get killed and they get extinct.

Other teacher candidates during the *Make a Wave* project had opportunities to show their love of learning and creative commitment to the task of teaching children about the dolphin slaughter in Taiji, Japan. Kelsey was so moved after viewing *The Cove* that she decided to contact Richard O'Barry, the leading activist in the documentary. She describes her motivation stating,

> The extent of my involvement in the Make a Wave project surprised me. After viewing The Cove documentary in class, I was really moved and wanted to really jump-in to bringing awareness to this issue. I wrote letters reaching out to local media outlets, as well as public figures such as Richard O'Barry, Bob Barker and Oprah inviting them to attend our performance on May 14 as well as asked them for any assistance they could provide us with raising awareness. I was able to get a written letter to read during the performance from Ric O'Barry, and spoke back and forth with one of his colleagues (Mark Berman) at the Earth Island Institute to get materials to distribute to the different local schools' libraries. I was able to also get in contact with Bob Barker's organiza-

tion (via Kathleen McGibbon), the Sea Shepherd Conservation Society, and received more materials to distribute.

Kelsey was in her second sequence of the Elementary Education Program and is currently teaching in Connecticut. She continued to share what an impact her participation in the *Make a Wave* project had, as it focused on the love of nature and our relationship with the natural world. Kelsey's sense of efficacy to love her work for ecological change was demonstrated in her speech to 1,000 children. Kelsey reflected on the experience:

> Overall I am very thankful that I was able to be a part of such an amazing experience. As a result of the *Make a Wave* project, I was able to develop more confidence in the classroom. I feel this project allowed me to find my voice and make me believe more in myself as an individual and as a teacher. This project impacted me in a way that made me feel like I can conquer any adversity I face inside or outside of the classroom and I truly can "be the change." The preparation for the *Make a Wave* project also contributed to my sense of self. I found it beneficial to be able to collaborate with other pre-service teachers about the different elements of the performance. I learned through my collaboration with them to take the ideas of others into careful and respectful consideration and that everyone's voice needs to be heard.

Another example of a teacher candidate demonstrating love in action is Donnie and his experience with the *Compassionate Community to End Homelessness* school play (Figure 8.2). Donnie worked for a week in his garage painting scenery for his compassion scene. The cardboard scenery was

FIGURE 8.2.   Love in Action: Our Teacher Candidate Getting the Stage Ready For *Compassionate Community To End Homelessness* School Play, 2009.

lit up with golden lights; his love for his peers and his work was revealed through his remarkable contributions. His peers were amazed that he spent so much time on his project. He is currently teaching at a local city public school. Donnie shared that now he "*has two compassionate teachers*" for inspirations.

Aesthetic education practices, when embedded in a compassionate community setting, reveal the spiritual in education. A very deep personal connection to the other, that when united, we can share in the good and the bad, we can celebrate, pray, hope, dream, we are not alone in the lifelong quest to perhaps make our community better (Eisner, 2002; Greene, 2001).

> As children grow older and enter school, their need for support must be met by their teachers. If a teacher not only imparts academic education but also assumes responsibility for preparing students for life, his or her pupils will feel trust and respect and what has been taught will leave an indelible impression on their minds. On the other hand, subjects taught by a teacher who does not show true concern for his or her students' overall well-being will be regarded as temporary and not retained for long. (Dalai Lama, 2013)

The Dalai Lama, one of the world's greatest teachers across cultures, expresses the critical facet of our teacher preparation work with young teacher candidates. They must be immersed in community programs that they design for children in order to fully understand the reciprocal nature of planting seeds of love. A sense of love was revealed as interpersonal relationships were deepened and shared during the compassionate community performances with parents, children, and local community partners.

As a result of participating in an artistic and critical civic engagement curriculum (Boyte, 2012; French, 2013), preservice teachers expressed their self-identity as teachers for change. Our teacher candidates realized that the aesthetic education partnership between the children and the teacher, wherein the arts are an intrinsic aspect of learning, form an exemplary teaching model (Clark, 2009a; Clark & French, 2012). "Thus, the arts should not be at the fringes of education but should exist as a discipline that promotes significant overall cognitive results and develops the moral imagination which leads to a greater understanding of one's self, others and the world" (Clark, 2005, p. 443).

The teacher candidates ultimately embraced a sense of love for the work and relationships they continue to build with children (see Figure 8.3). As the teacher candidates get to know the children, they begin to perceive a much deeper sense of the complexity of the child's worldviews, life experiences, and thinking. The aesthetic experience with the children opened the eyes of the teacher candidates so that now they "see" the child with compassionate eyes. Zukav and Francis (2003) explain the connection of the mind to the soul:

FIGURE 8.3. Unmasking Love: Teacher Candidate and Fifth Grade Student From *Echoes* Project, 2011.

Compassion brings you out of your self-created isolation and into the larger world of joy and pain that is the human experience. When you see only personalities, compassion is harder because you focus on differences that frighten you, and you judge what you fear—such as skin color, body shape, sex, culture, religion, hair style, and anything else that is different . . . Appearances always differ, but when you see the essence beneath appearances, your judgments disappear and you create a world in which harm is not possible because your relationships become soul-to-soul. (p. 177)

In order to build upon Zukav and Francis's (2003) mind/soul connections to develop compassionate action in our teacher candidates when working with children (especially with those suffering trauma), we knew our teacher candidates needed cutting-edge firsthand experiences so that they could identify and draw upon their own inherent abilities to love, to be patient, to listen, to be kind, and compassionate (Yeo, 1997). We embodied Zajonc's (2006a) testimony reflecting on his university course experience, which stated,

We learned from experience to start with the knowledge pole of the course. Discussions concerning love require trust as well as sophistication, both of which take time to engender in a class. We adopted a slower, more reflective pace for the course (p. 7) . . . In this manner, as it turns out, the task first put to us by Rilke, learning to love, is also the task of learning to know in its fullest sense. (p. 13)

We witnessed our teacher candidates *Unmask the Sacred* through their work, their contributions to children, their community, and their peers while realizing a greater sense of themselves as teachers. Despite institutional barriers, governmental and societal reform measures, there still exist creative and hopeful young people who want to become teachers who nurture the heart, mind, and soul of a child. They respect and revere a child's imagination and love children. They ultimately evolve through their aesthetic experiences with us, and their stories authentically capture the essence of how the reciprocal interplay of the eight seeds within the KIVA unmask their beliefs to love the children they teach.

Unmasking the Sacred in Teacher Preparation

It is of great importance to continue to unmask the compassionate *Seed of Love* and release creativity within all future teachers for our children and for their future. Creativity is a powerful force that can do great good or great evil as seen throughout history. Fox (2004) presents the poet Denise Levertov, who warns us "that man's capacity for evil, then, is less a positive capacity, for all its horrendous activity, than a failure to develop man's most human function, the imagination, to its fullness, and consequently a failure to develop compassion" (p. 37).

Levertov's warning is expressed in *The Zoo Keeper's Wife* by Diane Ackerman (2007). This book tells the story of Henryk Goldszmit (pen name Janusz Korczak), the ultimate teacher, who was an example of love and sacrifice for children while facing the horror of Hitler's extermination of the Jews in the Warsaw Ghetto. Janusz Korczak ran a progressive orphanage in Warsaw that was captured and moved to the Ghetto in 1940. Korczak would not allow the underground to help him escape because he would not abandon the children. He stayed and taught the children how to shape a functioning republic in the Ghetto: a just community of forgiveness.

Janusz Korczak was a child pedagogue, pediatrician, and psychologist that harvested hope through the arts and aesthetics because he loved, understood, and cared for children. He invented games and plays for children, and staged *The Post Office* by Rabindranath Tagore, India's spiritual poet (see *Mind Without Fear* in Chapter 5, "The Seed of Unmasking"). Korczak utilized the arts to fill the children's imagination, instilling within the children moral strength and imaginative fortitude to rise above the fears and to "accept death serenely" (Ackerman, 2007, pp. 182–187).

Can we prepare teacher candidates to have the qualities of Janusz Korczak? Teaching becomes a symbol of love, giving what is best and good for children by feeding their minds, hearts, and souls with uplifting stories, literature, plays, games, sensory experiences, a love for numbers and letters, debates, and experiments. We envision an elementary education preparation program wherein teacher candidates have within them the seeds of moral strength and imaginative fortitude to share with children.

If we can truly unmask our fears in public education and realize the potential that all children have, we may begin to perceive teachers as ambassadors of hope who enable children's inner light, creativity, and compassion to shine through in all that they do for one another and for their community. Our children deserve teachers who love to teach and love the children they teach each and every day. Our children should not suffer doubt, ridicule, or fear of learning in their classrooms. Their hearts and minds must be without fear, with heads held high and spirits of creativity and compassion lifted and released for all to see.

The masks we hide behind that blind us from love may very well be as Merton (1979) states, "like a shadow over the soul." However, we wait as "God must move and reveal Himself and shake the world within the soul and rise from His sleep like a giant" (p. 318). Merton presents the following poem, *Living Flame of Love*, by Saint John of the Cross (1991) describing the "awakening of the soul," which is the final unmasking to reveal the purest seed of love humankind may achieve.

1. O living flame of love
That tenderly wounds my soul
In its deepest center! Since
Now you are not oppressive,
Now consummate! if it be your will:
Tear through the veil of this sweet encounter!

2. O sweet cautery,
O delightful wound!
O gentle hand! O delicate touch
That tastes of eternal life
And pays every debt!
In killing you changed death to life.

3. O lamps of fire!
in whose splendors
The deep caverns of feeling,
Once obscure and blind,
Now give forth, so rarely, so exquisitely,
Both warmth and light to their Beloved.

4. How gently and lovingly
You wake in my heart,
Where in secret you dwell alone;
And in your sweet breathing,
Filled with good and glory,
How tenderly You swell my heart with love.

Saint John's poem is a divinely inspired and creative tribute to the *Holy Spirit*, inspiring from within a "soul force" of love for others, or what Gandhi (1957) called *Satyagraha*, where truth and firmness unite as a powerful love force. Many teachers like Janusz Korczak, who loved children, were willing to sacrifice their lives. As a child pedagogue, Korczak understood that a child's soul by nature thirsts to be loved and to give love. According to Ackerman (2007), Joshua Perle witnessed 200 children leave the Ghetto for deportation to the concentration camp Treblinka. Perle states,

> A miracle occurred, two hundred pure souls, condemned to death, did not weep. Not one of them ran away. None tried to hide. Like stricken swallows they clung to their teacher and mentor, to their father and brother, Janusz Korczak. (p. 186)

The absence of the love of teaching and for children in our public schools has developed into a present dark time. Children are chained to the dreary habits of daily test assessments. Too many teachers and administrators wear masks of indifference and become the gatekeepers of testing reforms, which is a violent oppression of a child's imagination and a teacher's compassion. *Dag Hammarskjöld* (1964) urges us to love and in that loving action "realize [our] individuality by becoming a bridge for others, a stone in the temple of righteousness" (p. 53). *He* stresses the importance of expressing our light to one another, "to take the Way" to be fruitful through our life journey (p. 53).

Echoing silence
Darkness lit up by beams
Light
Seeking its counterpart
In melody
Stillness
Striving for liberation
In a word
Life
In dust
In shadow
How seldom growth and blossom
How seldom fruit
(p. 51)

We must provide experiences for children so that they express their truth; "we must reach to live, that everything is and we [are] just in it" (p. 51).

Ashley, a teacher candidate, expresses the profound impact of her experiences within the KIVA paradigm and shares the following story. She explains how she transferred aesthetic methodology into her student teaching classroom. Her love in action inspired trusting relationships.

KIVA Unmasks Love and Transfers to Student Teacher's Classroom

Ashley's Story

Throughout my education courses, I had the wonderful opportunity to be a part of two authentic learning and teaching experiences. The program that I was involved in titled, *Steppin' Out of a Painting,* along with the *Echoes* project taught me a great deal about children and how they learn best. These experiences also shaped my beliefs about teaching.

During these experiences my classmates and I worked with reluctant learners; some were shy, some had little to no confidence in themselves, and some students were in a place where they felt as if they just weren't capable of learning. Through these experiences I learned that students could truly benefit from expressing themselves through the exploration of dance. By the end of the experience the students who did not say much or participate often in the beginning, broke out of their shells and confidently performed a dance in front of a packed audience and smiled from ear to ear.

I also learned that reluctant writers benefited from getting their thoughts and ideas down through drawing, painting pictures, and orally expressing their thoughts. Their confidence skyrocketed as they realized their thoughts mattered; they realized they were capable of doing the work because the main focus was initially on their ideas instead of their raw ability to spell or write. Through these experiences I have learned that there is no "one right way" to teach or learn. Students learn through a variety of ways, and movement and art are just two ways in which students can demonstrate understanding.

Throughout my student teaching these experiences were in the back of my mind as I created lesson plans. For example, I created a performance task for a fairy tale unit in which students had to create their own fairytale. For the planning process, I gave students the option of creating a storyboard for their fairytale with pictures instead of writing it in words. The students drew the plot and then orally explained what was happening to me. Finally, students put their drawings and thoughts down on paper in the form of a story. I noticed a great deal of improvement in my students' writing; especially with those who often had trouble thinking of ideas and putting their ideas into the form of a cohesive story. Because students had the chance to get their thoughts and ideas down in a way that made sense to them, it then made the entire writing process more enjoyable and less stressful.

Last but not least, these experiences have taught me that there is more to teaching than teaching content. Before any content can be taught and learned, students and their teacher must have a connection. I had the wonderful chance to establish relationships with students and I saw firsthand the positive affect our relationship had on their ability to demonstrate learning.

I have learned that once the teacher and the student establish trust, then true learning and teaching take place. When you watch a child come in on the first day with no smile and no desire to do work, and then you see them leave on the last day with smiles and work to show off that they are truly proud of, you know as a teacher that you have made a difference in the life of a child. Through the combination of art, movement, and creating trusting relationships, I have learned that anything is possible.

Love must be presented as a cornerstone in our mission for the public education of children. Today more than ever, teachers must be prepared to be ambassadors of hope and peace with their heads held high to confront the lethal problems the 21st century is facing. As guardians of the Earth and all its creation, we have selfishly consumed at such a rapid pace that the very nature we come from is disappearing before our eyes. Teachers must know how to be social- and ecojustice advocates that teach children love and respect so that they are truly peacemakers as they move throughout their lives.

If we are brave enough to unmask our fears as teacher educators in preparing the next generation of teachers, we will do everything in our power to help teacher candidates to love children; love to teach; and know how to teach peace, compassion, and hope. This will ensure that the final seed of love is an everyday phenomenon in our children's lives in school. When we plant the seed of love we are truth seekers; we become transformed through love as love reveals truth, and in a reciprocal fashion, when we "dance" with one another as we learn, we complete a unified and empathic understanding for a greater good. The mask of fear has melted away from our soul and love reveals itself to be the truest form of wisdom for all humankind.

REFERENCES

Ackerman, D. (2007) *The zoo keeper's wife.* New York, NY: W.W. Norton.

Boyte, H. (2012, September 27). *Hope and higher education: The powers of public narratives* [Weblog post]. Retrieved from http://www.huffingtonpost.com/harry-boyte/college-community partnerships_b_1917951.html

Clark, B. (2005). Moral imagination and art: Echoes from a child's soul. *Forum on Public Policy: Issue Child Psychology, 1*(4), 428–446.

Clark, B. (2009a). Aesthetic education and masked emotions: A model for emancipatory teacher preparation. *Critical Questions in Education, 1*(1), 40–50. Retrieved from http://education.missouristate.edu/AcadEd/75534.htm

Clark, B. (2009b). Mustard seed: A personal search for "Ahimsa" (The truth of nonviolence). *Closing the Circle Exhibition.* B. Clark & M. Cipriano (Artists). New Britain, CT: New Britain Commission on the Arts.

Clark, B. (2013). Breaking the culture of silence in schools: Children's voices revealed through moral imagination. In D. G. Mulcahy (Ed.), *Transforming schools: Alternative perspectives on school reform.* Charlotte, NC: Information Age.

Clark, B., & French, J. (2012). ZEAL: An aesthetic revolution for education. *Critical Questions in Education, 3*(1), 12–22. Retrieved from http://education.missouristate.edu/assets/AcadEd/Zealfinal.pdf

Dalai Lama. (2011). 11 year old talks with the Dalai Lama. *YouTube.* Retrieved from http://www.youtube.com/watch?v=vXS-PIKLoSU&feature=related

Dalai Lama. (2013). *Compassion and the individual.* Retrieved from http://www.dalailama.com/messages/compassion

Dewey, J. (1980). *Art as experience.* New York, NY: G. P. Putman/Perigee. (Original work published 1934)

Eisner, E. (2002). *The arts and the creation of mind.* New Haven, CT: Yale University Press.

Fox, M. (2004). *Creativity: Where the divine and human meet.* New York, NY: Penguin.

French, J. (2013). Methods & mindsets for creating eco-social community educators. In D. G. Mulcahy (Ed.), *Transforming schools: Alternative perspectives on school reform* (pp. 37–66). Charlotte, NC: Information Age.

French, J., & Clark, B. (2012). Revitalizing a spiritual compassionate commons in educational culture. *Religion & Education, 39,* 93–108.

Fried, R. (2001). *The passionate teacher: A practical guide.* Boston, MA: Beacon. (Original work published 1995)

Fromm, E. (1989). *The art of loving.* New York, NY: Harper & Row. (Original work published 1956)

Gandhi, M. (1957). *Autobiography: The story of my experiments with truth.* Boston, MA: Beacon.

Gibran, K. (1994). *On work.* Retrieved June 25, 2013, from http://phys.lsu.edu/~gokhale/theprophet.html#Work (Original work published 1923)

Greene, M. (2001). *Variations on a blue guitar: The Lincoln Center Institute lectures on aesthetic education.* New York, NY: Teachers College Press.

Hammarskjöld, D. (1964). *Markings.* (L. Sjöberg & W. H. Auden, Trans.). New York, NY: Knopf.

Keyes, A. (2009). Unthinkable. *The Element of Freedom.* Long Island, NY: J. Records.

Merton, T. (1979). *The ascent to truth.* San Diego, CA: Harcourt Brace. (Original work published 1951)

Palmer, B. (1993). *The violence of our knowledge: Toward a spirituality of higher education.* The Michael Keenan Memorial Lecture, the 7th Lecture, Berea College, KY. Retrieved from http://www.kairos2.com/palmer_1999.htm

Rilke, R. M. (1975). *Love and other difficulties.* (J. J. L., Mood, Trans.). New York, NY: W. W. Norton. (Original work published 1904–1925)

Standing, E. M. (1962). *Maria Montessori: Her life and work.* New York, NY: New American Library. (Original work published 1957)

St. John of the Cross (1991). The living flame of love (K. Kavanaugh & O. Rodriguez, Trans.). In *The collected works of St. John of the Cross.* Washington DC: ICS. Retrieved from http://www.ourgardenofcarmel.org/livingflame.html (Original work published 1542–1591)

Tagore, R. (2007). *The English writings of Rabindranath Tagore: Volume two Poems.* New Delhi: Atlantic Publisher.

Tolstoy, L. (1869). *War and Peace.* Retrieved from www.fullbooks.com/War-and-Peace28.html

van Gogh, V. (1880, July). Letter to Theo van Gogh (J.van Gogh, Trans.). In R. Harrison (Ed.), *WebExhibits* (No. 133). Retrieved from http://www.webexhibits.org/vangogh/letter/8/133.htm

van Gogh, V. (1881, November 23). Letter to Anthon van Rappard (J. van Gogh-Bonger, Trans.). In Robert Harrison (Ed.), *WebExhibits* (No. R06). Retrieved from http://webexhibits.org/vangogh/letter/10/R06.htm

Yeo, F. (1997). *Inner-city schools multiculturalism and teacher education: A professional journey.* New York, NY: Garland.

Zajonc, A. (2006a). Love and knowledge: Recovering the heart of learning through contemplation. *Teacher College Record, 108*(9), 1742–1759. Retrieved from http://www.arthurzajonc.org/Teaching.php

Zajonc, A. (2006b). Cognitive-affective connections in teaching and learning: The relationship between love and knowledge. *Journal of Cognitive Affective Learning, 3*(1), 1–9. Retrieved from http://www.arthurzajonc.org/Teaching.php

Zukav, G., & Francis, L. (2003). *The mind of the soul: Responsible choice.* New York, NY: Simon & Schuster.

AUTHOR/EDITOR BIOGRAPHIES

Barbara Clark, EdD is Associate Professor of Teacher Education at Central Connecticut State University (CCSU) in New Britain, Connecticut. Her research on the moral imagination of children and aesthetic education has contributed to the CCSU University, Museum, Community Collaborative, and numerous compassionate community engagement events codesigned with Dr. Joss French. These unique compassionate community events uniting the university, community, and schools addressed the homeless initiative in the city of New Britain, the dolphin slaughter for profit in Taiji, Japan, the local park watershed pollution, and children of incarcerated parents. Dr. Clark brings her education classes to the surrounding community schools to coteach with children. An aesthetic lens such as dance, masks, visual art, and theater focuses on specific social and ecological issues the children face in their community. Dr. Clark's work in the New Britain public schools was recognized by the Board of Education and has received over the past 3 years awards for Contribution to the Fine Arts Programs, Service to Youth, and Friend of the Schools. Dr. Clark is a working artist and has exhibited her work at many galleries and museums both local and national, including the Wadsworth Atheneum in Hartford, Connecticut, and Slater Museum in Norwalk, Connecticut.

Hearts and Minds Without Fear: Unmasking the Sacred in Teacher Preparation,
pages 217–218.

James Joss French, PhD is Associate Professor of Teacher Education at Central Connecticut State University (CCSU) in New Britain, Connecticut. In educators, he sees opportunity for social and community action, and aims to foster educators' aspiring and enduring commitments to serve as change agents for their students. His research in ecosocial justice education examines teachers' cultural competence and their ability to collaboratively address critical issues in communities and schools. Coteaching with Dr. Barbara Clark, school staff and children, Dr. French's course events have addressed critical global and local issues, including the homeless initiative in the city of New Britain, the dolphin slaughter for profit in Taiji, Japan, social identity exploration with children of incarcerated parents, and sustainable mindset development through indigenous and intergenerational knowledge exploration. His teaching has been recognized by multiple consecutive Excellence in Teaching Honors at CCSU and New Britain District's Board of Education. Dr. French is also a father of two (Ariana and Lucas), musician, puppeteer, and actor and brings these varied and multidimensional ways of perceiving the world into his teaching and scholarship.